Binge Watching

This book is part of the Peter Lang Media and Communication list.
Every volume is peer reviewed and meets
the highest quality standards for content and production.

PETER LANG
New York • Bern • Berlin
Brussels • Vienna • Oxford • Warsaw

Bridget Rubenking and
Cheryl Campanella Bracken

Binge Watching

Motivations and Implications of Our Changing Viewing Behaviors

PETER LANG
New York • Bern • Berlin
Brussels • Vienna • Oxford • Warsaw

Library of Congress Cataloging-in-Publication Data

Names: Rubenking, Bridget, author. | Bracken, Cheryl Campanella, author.
Title: Binge watching: motivations and implications of our changing
viewing behaviors / Bridget Rubenking and Cheryl Campanella Bracken.
Description: 1 Edition. | New York: Peter Lang, 2020.
Includes bibliographical references and index.
Identifiers: LCCN 2019059967 (print) | LCCN 2019059968 (ebook)
ISBN 978-1-4331-6190-2 (hardback) | ISBN 978-1-4331-6191-9 (paperback)
ISBN 978-1-4331-6192-6 (ebook pdf)
ISBN 978-1-4331-6193-3 (epub) | ISBN 978-1-4331-6194-0 (mobi)
Subjects: Binge watching (Television) | Television viewers. | Human behavior.
Classification: LCC HE8700.65 .R83 2020 (print) | LCC HE8700.65 (ebook) |
DDC 302.23/45—dc23
LC record available at https://lccn.loc.gov/2019059967
LC ebook record available at https://lccn.loc.gov/2019059968
DOI 10.3726/b14726

Bibliographic information published by **Die Deutsche Nationalbibliothek.**
Die Deutsche Nationalbibliothek lists this publication in the "Deutsche
Nationalbibliografie"; detailed bibliographic data are available
on the Internet at http://dnb.d-nb.de/.

© 2020 Peter Lang Publishing, Inc., New York
29 Broadway, 18th floor, New York, NY 10006
www.peterlang.com

All rights reserved.
Reprint or reproduction, even partially, in all forms such as microfilm,
xerography, microfiche, microcard, and offset strictly prohibited.

Table of Contents

List of Tables	vii
Chapter One: Introduction: A Look at Binge Watching	1
Chapter Two: A Historical Perspective: The Evolution of Television Viewing and Audience Research	21
Chapter Three: An Industry Perspective: Changing Competitors, Content, and Content Curation	43
Chapter Four: A Social Perspective: Family Viewing, Co-Viewing, and Social TV	77
Chapter Five: Motivations to Binge Watch	113
Chapter Six: Implications of Binge Watching	137
Chapter Seven: Conclusion: Where Do We Go From Here?	171
Index	191

List of Tables

Table 2.1: Evolution of Television Technology — 31
Table 5.1: Sub-dimensions of Automaticity and the Active Audience — 130

CHAPTER ONE

Introduction: A Look at Binge Watching

The term "binge watching" is used casually among television viewers, interested industry parties, and academics to denote longer viewing sessions of sequential television episodes, often via streaming services. A simple google search for "best shows to binge watch" yields dozens, if not hundreds, of articles and listicles of suggestions of what to binge watch this weekend depending on your mood, the season, or the genre and streaming service of one's choosing. Beyond being a buzz word in popular culture, binge watching and related new viewing patterns are quickly replacing traditional appointment viewing and cutting into basic time-shifted television viewing. Industry reports and empirical academic articles present a clear picture: A convincing majority of television viewers *are* binge watchers. In 2013, over 60% of Netflix subscribers reported regularly binge watching, per Netflix (West, 2014). This was before Netflix became available in over 200 additional countries by 2016. Netflix currently has 125 million worldwide subscribers, 56.7 million of which are based in the United States (Richter, 2018). For many, Netflix is nearly synonymous with binge watching (Fiegerman, 2017; Matrix, 2014), and the impact of Netflix and other streaming services cannot be underscored in the role they play in enabling these new viewing behaviors.

A worldwide report by Ericsson Consumer Labs (2015) reveals approximately three-quarters of individuals with access to any streaming service or video on-demand report binge watching. And across the world, numbers of subscribers to streaming services are only increasing. A Harris Interactive poll of U.S. adults reported that 43% regularly watch streaming TV, while 23% report that streaming content is the way they most often watch TV (Harris Polls, 2014). These numbers increased among millennials (18–36-year-olds) from 2012 to 2014; jumping to 67% of millennials regularly streaming TV content and 47% reporting that streaming is the most common way they watch TV. In 2017, the number of household broadband subscriptions surpassed cable subscriptions for the first time; In 2019, the number of streaming service subscriptions surpassed cable subscriptions (Roettgers, 2019). Some reports show that viewers are spending more time binge watching than they are engaging in typical appointment viewing of television (Hallinan & Striphas, 2016).

Research on age and binge watching indicates there are some differences, but they are not as stark as one may imagine. Americans aged 18– 39 are more likely to binge watch than Americans aged 40 or older (Shannon-Missal, 2013). About 89% of millennials engage in binge watching, whereas only 67% of individuals over the age of 55 engage in binge watching. However, more "moderate" binge watching (2–3 episodes per session) is quite common across all age groups, with those aged 18–24 binging only slightly more (West, 2014). Binge watching is also not exclusively occurring in college dorms and apartments. While younger audiences are binge watching more frequently, 60% of all audiences *regularly* binge watch television (Harris Interactive Poll, 2014). Binge watchers also feel good about their binge watching: 73% view binge watching positively, 76% of those who subscribe to a streaming service watch several episodes in one sitting as a "welcome refuge from the busy world we live in," and many say they view in part because there is so much good content to watch. A full 79% of streamers say binging content makes the show itself better (West, 2014).

These increases in viewing television content via streaming services and large percentage gains over several years are an even more critical data point when one considers that many of these numbers from industry reports – and academic research studies – are *already several years old*. "Binge watching" awarded Collins Dictionary's "word of the year" in 2015 is already proving to be more than a passing fad, or a way of viewing that can be attributed to only smaller subsets of a television viewing public.

Watching a television series in long, continuous stretches is a fundamentally different experience than what television viewing has meant to audiences for decades. It is an experience that we argue has far-reaching implications for industry and particularly for the academic study of individuals and new media. A fundamental change in *how* individuals view television likely also impacts processing of content, motives to view, and effects of viewing, which presents a development that media entertainment scholars cannot ignore.

The earliest academic investigations of binge watching – which are still heavily cited in the subsequent literature – include a fair amount of largely descriptive investigations of who is binge watching and their possible motives (Petersen, 2016; Pittman & Sheehan, 2015). Some take a critical-cultural approach (Jenner, 2014; Matrix, 2014); some received media attention with headlines that were mismatched with the data analyzed (Sung, Kang, & Lee, 2015); and many were thesis/dissertation work, or conference papers and proceedings (Karmaker, Kruger, Elahi, & Kramer, 2015; Pena, 2015; Sung, et al., 2015; Wheeler, 2015). Following this early work by media scholars, research coming out of health disciplines began studying binge watching as a health issue of concern or addiction (Exelmans & Van den Bulck, 2017; Walton-Pattison, Dombrowski, & Presseau, 2016). We (the authors of the current text) were also working on exploratory research on binge watching at this time. In fact, the state of the available research encouraged us to propose a book on this topic. We are convinced that binge watching is a critical game-changer for media processing and effects *and* that this new norm of viewing will play a tremendous role in industry and technology changes to come. Selfishly perhaps, we were concerned that the media processing and effects research tradition of which we are a part of was not taking this shift in how we spend the majority of our media entertainment time (Madrigal, 2018), as seriously as we deemed it to our shared assumptions and methodological tools. Based on this concern, we proposed this text in 2017.

Then, 2018 saw a flurry of well-done, theoretically driven pieces on binge watching, including Riddle, Pebles, Davis, Xu, and Shroeder (2018); Tefertiller and Maxwell (2018); Tukachinsky and Eyal (2018); Walton-Pattison, Dombrowski, and Presseau (2018), among several others. The advancement in the theoretical rigor applied to studies of binge watching in just the past few years has been extremely beneficial to our goal of synthesizing what we already know about binge watching. Our goal is to continue these efforts and identify areas of study related to binge watching that will carry both applied and theoretical implications in the future. Clarifying the concept of binge watching and placing it in the context of other new media behaviors, synthesizing what is known, and identifying impactful areas of study for the future are critical contributions to the field.

This introductory chapter attempts to briefly lay out a proof of concept about binge watching: Discriminating the main phenomenon of interest from other modes of viewing is the first order of business, as is presenting clear evidence from industry and academic texts that this is a widespread, qualitatively distinct way of viewing television. We then introduce the three basic arguments of this text as a whole, prior to summarizing each chapter which follows in demonstrating evidence for the major three tenets introduced.

Proof of Concept: A Complete Conceptualization of Binge Watching

What's in a name? A lot. Too many things, in the case of the term "binge watching," and not enough consistency among those studying it in industry or the academy. The Collins Dictionary's word-of-the-year definition of binge watching is as follows:

> to watch a large number of television programmes (especially all the shows from one series) in succession. (Collins Dictionary, 2015)

Much of the industry data and preliminary academic research utilizes a variation of this definition. This is a helpful start, but clearly a more thorough and complete conceptualization would be ideal for industry insiders and academics alike. The term "binge watching" caught on quickly. One writer observed the term "binge watch" first used in an online forum of *X-Files* fans by a user who reported "massive binge watching" of videotapes in the early 1990s (Zimmer, 2013). The term became part of our everyday lexicon amid Netflix's frequent use of the term in 2013, when two of their early successful and critically acclaimed originals (*House of Cards* and *Orange is the New Black*) premiered. Netflix also conducted and released research findings on binge watching on its own platform. They defined binge watching as "watching between 2–6 episodes of the same TV show in one sitting" (West, 2014). In 2013, they actively used the term "binge watching" in releasing survey results of subscribers, which revealed that most Netflix subscribers were "binge watching" (where 2–3 episodes in one sitting was average), and they felt positive about the binge-watching experience (West, 2014). By 2017, Netflix had moved onto the term "binge racer," to denote viewers who view an entire new season within 24 hours of its release (Netflix, 2017). The top binge raced shows at the time were *Gilmore Girls: A Year in the Life*, *Fuller House*, and *Marvel's The Defenders*. While Netflix says that binge racing is a fast-growing trend – increasing 20 times over between 2013 and 2017 – the term has not become as widely used as the original. Netflix went out of their way to normalize binge racing, pointing out that users everywhere were binge racing different content:

> And before you assume that racers are just basement-dwelling couch potatoes, know that for these super fans, the speed of watching is an achievement to be proud of and brag about ... TV is their passion and Binge Racing is their sport. (Netflix, 2017)

The peak of Netflix using the term may have been the press release the preceding quote appeared in. D'Souza (2019) notes that following this press release, Netflix has started shying away from use of the term "binge" in all contexts.

Normalizing binge watching was a major goal of Netflix since the beginning of its streaming service option. Netflix has every reason for binge watching to be discussed as a tongue-in-cheek "guilty pleasure" of sorts. When there are listicles of recommended shows to binge, it is better for business, as opposed to growing concern about the negative impacts of binge watching on mental and physical health.

Indeed, using a concept that is already widely known, or a metaphor, has its advantages and disadvantages in academic applications. We should be studying a phenomenon that is prevalent enough to enjoy widespread popular discussion about it: It is a sign of practical relevance of the topic of study. Shoemaker et al. (2004) outline the positives and negatives of using metaphor and analogy in theory building. They use Merriam-Webster's dictionary definition of metaphor: "a figure of speech in which a word or phrase literally denoting one kind of object or idea is used in place of another to suggest a likeness or analogy between them." Metaphors can help crystallize a vague notion, generate ideas or hypotheses, and provide coherence to a theory (Shoemaker et al., 2004). They also can help people remember the theory or concept and make it easier to understand. However, Shoemaker et al. note some drawbacks to using metaphors, including the possibility that metaphors are misleading; believing that metaphor alone is enough when explicit and testable clarifications are needed; metaphors may be chosen for their catchiness rather than accuracy; and metaphors can oversimplify matters. Despite these drawbacks, metaphor and analogy influenced concepts are commonly used in mass media research: agenda-setting, boomerang effects, hypodermic needle, gatekeeping, framing, sleeper effect, and the list goes on. As mentioned in other places in this text, some researchers use alternative terms for binge watching, including "marathoning" (Perks, 2015, 2018; Tukachinsky & Eyal, 2018). We've elected to embrace and refine the term here, largely due to its widespread use and the advantages stated above.

The viewing of multiple sequential episodes is generally accepted as part of the definition of binge watching. However, a number of questions about what constitutes a binge remain. Is it binge watching when college students put on old episodes of *Friends* on Netflix and then proceed to do homework, clean up around the house, and talk to others – a somewhat surprisingly frequent media behavior uncovered in our own focus groups on binge watching? Is it binge watching only when someone feels compelled to play another episode, stay up a little later than planned – in other words, is the compulsion to view part of the experience? Can binge watching be intentional, or done with the company of others, or is it purely a singular activity? Is it binge watching when a fan watches the 1 p.m. and the 4 p.m. American football games on a Sunday, or watches a marathon of two or more *Harry Potter* films programmed on cable television on a Saturday?

A key factor in conceptualizing and measuring binge watching is distinguishing it from just watching *more* TV. "Heavy viewers" have been a term since the onset of cultivation theory came into prominence in the early 1970s (Gerbner, 1969). Binge watching, a phenomenon that necessarily touches on habitual and dependent viewing, needs to be conceptualized as a distinct mode of viewing as compared to general heavy television viewing. Over the past decade, the average amount of television viewing has begun to slowly decrease from an all-time high of 8 hours and 55 minutes daily in 2009 (Madrigal, 2018). If the total amount of viewing is (slowly) decreasing, yet the number of binge watchers and time spent binge watching are increasing, it is clear these are different phenomena. We argue throughout this text that binge watching can be differentiated from general heavy viewing in a number of ways.

After our own review of previous binge watching research and several data collections, we offer the following definition of binge watching:

> *Long periods of focused, deliberate viewing of sequential television content that is generally narrative, suspenseful, and dramatic in nature. Binge watching may be a planned, purposeful activity, or unintentional.* (Rubenking & Bracken, 2018)

This is a slightly modified definition of what was proposed in Rubenking, Bracken, Sandoval, and Rister (2018). We have modified this definition to omit any mention of time. Previous definitions had suggested four hours or more, based on both focus group and survey data of binge-watching college students (Rubenking et al., 2018; Rubenking & Bracken, 2018). First and foremost, binge watching focuses on the viewing of sequential programs in the same series. Largely afforded by streaming services (and discussed in Chapter 3 in great length), viewing entire seasons of a series over a few days of binge watching, or even one long day or night of binge watching, provides a different viewing experience than simply watching different types of content, from different sources, throughout a day of television viewing.

Second, binge watching is fundamentally characterized by a focused mode of viewing. Despite "focused viewing" existing along on a continuum rather than a dichotomy, this generalized distinction is crucial. When individuals are involved in binge watching, they are generally engaged and focused on the content, that is, leaving *Friends* episodes running continuously on a screen while one's primary task is *not* viewing that screen is *not* binge watching, given the current definition. Setting one's phone to silent and watching four episodes of *The Handmaid's Tale* prior to new episodes being released, for example, is binge watching. Focus and engagement with television content amid media multitasking or "second screening" options is a growing cross-disciplinary area of research, and also critical to mass media processing and effects scholars. While maintaining that binge watching is a *focused and engaging mode of television viewing*, it is important to note that these concepts exist on a continuum and viewers live in a viewing world with numerous mediated distractions which shape what television viewing looks like today. This is explored in more detail in Chapters 4 and 7.

Also critical to this definition is the qualification of content being *narrative*.

Participants in Rubenking and Bracken (2018) spoke almost exclusively about binge watching *narrative* content. While preferences for specific genres were as varied as typical television viewing preferences, the frequency and enthusiasm of responses laid out a clear association between wanting to see what was going to happen next in (often suspense-driven) dramatic narratives. Participants in these focus groups often said they would watch sitcoms or sports programming for hours; they failed to naturally distinguish this type of viewing as binge viewing. Individuals binge watch *stories*. The exclusion of non-narrative content is not universally employed among those who have published academically, nor the industry entities that have surveyed viewers about basic binge-watching behaviors. Although, in studies where binge watching is experimentally operationalized, narrative dramatic content has been exclusively utilized.

Lastly, binge watching may be unintentional or intentional. It may be driven by a habit gone awry, *or* it may be purposeful and planned in advance of viewing. Focus group research reveals many individuals talk about a planned night in, binge watching a television show as a reward for completing some larger task, or as a planned activity ahead of a series' new season premier date. However, participants also talk about tuning in for an episode or maybe two, and then unintentionally staying up later than expected, watching episode after episode. Characteristics of the delivery platform (e.g., Netflix's automatic start of a next episode after 15 seconds or less for Netflix produced programs) as well as the content itself (e.g., cliffhangers) were discussed as reasons to continue viewing longer than intended. How over-the-top, or OTT, services manage audience flow to maximize length of viewing is addressed in Chapter 3.

The social aspects of television viewing have long been present and not adequately addressed in related research. This remains true in the study of binge watching, though a reading between the lines would indicate that binging is more often experienced alone. One practical issue that likely influences this is time: It takes a considerable amount of time to binge watch, and non-cohabitating family, friends, or partners may not be able to schedule as many binge viewing sessions as one could alone. In our focus group studies, most people cited examples of binge watching alone – some even complained about others interrupting them by asking questions about the show or talking about something else. Although, watching with others in planned circumstances was also discussed.

Binge watching alone and without distraction may have gotten easier for 305 college students, with the help of "The HBO Box." A 2019 HBO promotion introduced a large cardboard box complete with holes for airflow, cutouts for legs at one end, and a shelf to put your viewing device on, marketed to college students trying to escape an annoying roommate and binge watch in bed. Contrary to the dozens of comments on the video introducing the promotion on HBO's YouTube channel, the November 2019 promotion was not an ill-timed April Fool's joke (HBO, 2019; Kooser, 2019). It was a real promotion: A giant cardboard box giveaway to college students so they can watch HBO without distraction.

Qualifying the difference between binge watching and other types of viewing is crucial to the academic study of this phenomenon. We explored the differences between binge watching and appointment viewing of television via a survey of university students and adults representative of U.S. demographic characteristics. The results demonstrate completely unique predictors, or antecedents, of binge watching and appointment viewing frequency across both samples: Binge-watching frequency was predicted by being younger, increased use of viewing to regulate one's emotions, to seek out and feel suspense and anticipation, and in large part by viewing habits already established. Appointment viewing, on the other hand, was driven by being older and viewing self-efficacy (Rubenking & Bracken, 2018). Binge watching appears to be associated with emotionally satisfying experiences that include suspense and engagement with a compelling narrative. Previous entertainment research would suggest that this type of experience is deeply satisfying (Bartsch, 2012), so it is not alarming that it has quickly become a habit for users. Indeed, habit was the largest predictor of binge-watching frequency, which reveals how entrenched this mode of viewing already is in the lives of college students and adults alike.

Binge watching is related to other changes and ways of television viewing and media consumption. Starting with the VCR and the timeshifting ability it afforded (as discussed in Chapter 2), viewers have seized opportunities which give them more control and agency over their viewing experience. Changes in distribution strategies and the technologies available to us have allowed for a host of different *patterns of viewing:* There is a middle ground between traditional appointment viewing and binge watching. Indeed, some effects studies explore "marathon" viewing sessions, which is characterized as working one's way through a series or season over a period of time, such as a week (Perks, 2015, 2018; Tukachinsky & Eyal, 2018). When entire series are available for viewing at once, many viewers choose to watch a season over several consecutive nights, in a serialized or sequential type of viewing, for example. One would imagine that this is more common than self-pacing an entirely available season of content to one episode, watched once a week, as the traditional appointment viewing model of watching narratives would have dictated. Watching shows in this middle-ground way is also sure to play a role in several outcome variables of interest to those in industry and academia.

So, to answer the questions posed just a few pages prior on the basic conceptualization of binge watching: Binge watching can feel compulsory *and/or* also be planned activity; binge watching can be done alone, or with others. We're defining binge watching as including narrative content, so while there are obvious narrative features of a sports event, sports programming is not generally considered narrative content. With continued blurring of lines between television series, miniseries, and films in the industry, we'll use the language of television, but acknowledge that narrative films also fit into this model.

First Things First: But Is Binging All Bad?

The inclination to find negative consequences of binge watching is inherent to the term "binge watching." *Binging* on anything denotes behavior in excess. The dangers of binge drinking and binge eating have been well documented, as have other pathological behaviors, such as gambling and online gaming. Binging is about overindulgence. Instead of individuals watching one episode of a new series in an evening, it is now commonplace, indeed, *more likely* for them to settle in and watch multiple episodes of a new series or season of an anticipated television program.

Media "addictions" (discussed in more depth in Chapter 6) have been defined as an "involuntary and out of control habit that individuals experience in regard to a specific medium" (Brunsdon, 2010, p. 65). Indeed, long before binge watching was coined as a term, researchers have studied addiction and dependency on television. The occasional (and nearly always correlational) study linking negative mental or physical health conditions with binge watching receives headlines in the popular press. These research articles represent a range of strength in methodology, and the more damning the headline for binge watching, the more likely that the original research article has not yet undergone the more rigorous peer review associated with journal publication (Karmakar et al., 2015; Sung, Kang, & Lee, 2015). Still others present well-designed research inquiries into the relationships between binge watching and various health outcomes, such as sleep disorders (Exelmans et al., 2017; Walton-Pattison et al., 2016) and addiction-based theoretical approaches. The results are mixed for binge-watching individuals. The linking of binge watching and negative health outcomes is not universal, though the research (reviewed in-depth in Chapter 6) consistently finds that heavy television viewing is related to a more sedentary, unhealthy lifestyle. Several more studies fail to find links directly between binge watching and measures or themes of addiction, and examinations of other negative outcomes have mixed results (Flayelle et al., 2017).

Despite the negative connotations of "binging," some have framed binge watching as a thoroughly immersive and enjoyable consumption mode, which often hinges upon viewing suspenseful, engaging narrative content (Giuffre, 2013; Rubenking et al., 2018). A host of generally more positive outcomes have also been studied alongside binge watching, including media entertainment, enjoyment, cognitive involvement, identification with characters, parasocial interaction, and as a healthy coping mechanism. Perks (2015, 2019) has offered the term "media marathoning" to capture the mindful engagement inherent to the behavior. From a user perspective, binge watching appears to be associated with emotionally satisfying experiences that include suspense and engagement with a compelling narrative (Rubenking et al., 2018). Clearly, there is something quite rewarding about binge watching, or people wouldn't do it. In short, more empirical data is wanted; as are consistent theoretical approaches to studying binge watching as a media behavior that likely has both negative and positive outcomes.

The Central Arguments of This Text

Binge watching is pervasive among television viewers and can be distinguished from other viewing behaviors. We propose three basic arguments in this text. These are based on empirical research by others and ourselves in industry and academia on the topic, as well as our own understanding and expertise with the larger body of research exploring psychological-level processing and effects of new media and the underlying assumptions and paradigms which shape such research.

1. *Binge watching, a new norm in television viewing, presents a critical and consequential difference in viewing from the currently accepted assumptions under the existing methodological and theoretical framework employed in the academic study of media effects.*

It can be characterized by extended viewing time, content and platform characteristics, and a focused, deliberate mode of viewing. This fundamental difference in how individuals interact with and consume television should call into serious question the current paradigm of mass media effects. This paradigm includes the nature of television viewing, the assumptions of the field, the questions central to the study of the field, as well as the methodologies employed to investigate them.

2. *Binge watching is a human-centered phenomenon.*

Binge watching is not purely a result of technological determinism or merely an "effect" of new(er) television technologies. It has benefited greatly from changes in industry distribution platform choices, content quality and quantity options, and more viewer-centered (personal and customizable) business models. However, the practice of "binging" on media entertainment did not start with *Netflix's* streaming service: Engaging in dramatic narrative entertainment content for excessive periods of time has existed since the novel. There is currently a medium which requires less cognitive effort than reading *and* that has a plethora of narrative content, *and* that content is easily accessible anywhere with an Internet connection at affordable subscription rates.

3. *Binge watching research can and should move beyond exploratory, descriptive studies and into more theoretically and operationally rigorous areas.*

The study of binge watching has emerged into a predictable pattern of areas of inquiry to those familiar with the social scientific research on any new widely accepted media technology or behavior. Individuals are fundamentally watching television in a different way than they were before: It is a logical first step to ask them, "why?" However, by now, we have a decent idea of motives and basic effects. *It is time to become more rigorous in the operationalization of binge watching and the design of studies as well as to make directional predictions regarding motives, effects, and relationships with related variables that are based in theory.*

Taken together, these arguments posit that binge watching is a unique, distinct new norm in entertainment "television" viewing that is human-driven and demands a reevaluation of the current paradigm studying how individuals make media choices, process content, and are influenced by exposure to that content.

In light of assertion number one, this text comes together at an interesting time for the concept of binge watching. It has received some basic empirical inquiry from those in the industry hoping to make user-driven changes based on the most up-to-date available information about *how* people are viewing. No unifying theoretical or methodological approach has emerged as dominant in the field. However, the theoretical approaches of media entertainment and media addiction have emerged as possibilities. In the academic literature, binge watching hangs in the balance of being taken seriously as a new media behavior and incorporated into theoretically and methodically rigorous research programs or being relegated to the pop culture lexicon. It is our argument that binge watching is a *qualitatively* different way of experiencing television content, and thus has a myriad of different implications on everything that television influences (learning, entertainment, attitude and behavior change, advertising spending, subscription revenue, distribution styles, content creation, etc.) Research is presented throughout the text to support this argument, most notably in the chapters documenting what theory and previous research have contributed to our knowledge base on binge-watching motives, habits, and outcomes in Chapters 5 and 6.

The argument that binge watching presents an obstacle to the dominant mass media effects academic tradition is by far the boldest argument presented. Binge watching joins media multitasking, second screening, coviewing, Social TV, and others as meaningful, new variables relevant to how audiences now engage with older mediums and messages. More attention among media entertainment scholars should be paid to how this new norm of television viewing influences a number of processing and effects issues. If we study television media effects such as learning from news stories, attitude change based on a pro-social entertainment-education storyline, or multidimensional media enjoyment and entertainment in studies designed with a single-exposure in a methodological way that no longer vaguely resembles how individuals watch television, when does that start to concern scholars? The mass media effects paradigm has for too long relied on one-shot effects-driven studies, and simply put, binge watching is the nail in the coffin of the external validity of such research. Certainly, one-shot effects studies have been criticized for a number of methodological concerns before (Lang, 2013; Weber, Mathiak, & Sherry, 2008). However, the disconnect between what *actual* television viewing looks like across the United States, and world, and how researchers who study the effects of television advertisements, PSAs, and news and entertainment programming has *never been so disparate*. Demonstrating the importance of binge watching and new viewing behaviors on all the variables scholars explore in this realm is also a central goal of the current text.

Postulate 2 may seem overly academic, or overly basic. It is neither. Academic mass media effects research has too often ignored the more macro-level decisions which affect viewer choices and behavior. Academic research often focuses so much on *message* characteristics, while media *platform, structure*, and *form* variables have often gone understudied. The changes in how we access television content and the content choices available have never been more diverse. These changes have occurred at a breakneck speed. Evidence exploring industry and society-level impact on television viewing over time (Chapter 2) and on present binge-watching practices is explored primarily in Chapters 3 and 4.

Our third and final argument is asking for a lot. In order to move forward, we need to have a shared understanding of the term "binge watching." This necessitates agreement on conditions of the term and transparency in its measurement. The Netflix 2013 data that first triumphed "binge watching" was based on survey data where binge watching was defined for participants as anywhere between 2 to 6 episodes. A person could watch two half-hour episodes and be done with a "binge" in less than an hour. Consideration of time spent, content being viewed, and involvement in the viewing task must be a part of defining binge watching

Researchers in media effects and other disciplines have characterized stages in the development of an area of inquiry, and some have used the term "generations" of research. Dobrow (1990), for example, discusses the first generation of research on VCR use as research done to quantify and characterize users and uses. A second generation of research explored patterns of use and gratifications observed. The third generation is the first to place a new media behavior in a larger context. She states,

> It is possible that this is the pattern of research that has followed the introduction of every new communication technology: Numbers and demographic pattern studies precede those studies about patterns of use, uses and gratifications, and other effects studies. Only after a technology has been established and penetrated a substantial percentage of the households in a given country, are researchers able to step back and try to assess the technology's place within a social and/ or cultural context. (Dubrow, p. 2)

This is an excellent and still accurate description of the state of the field, as we see evidence of it in early studies on home computers, the Internet, social media, and connected mobile devices. As already cited in this chapter, we know large percentages of those who subscribe to a streaming service binge watch, although we need to clarify our definition of "binge watching." As Chapter 5 documents, there are studies which explore the uses and gratifications of binge watching. Chapter 7 concludes the text with a review of evidence in support of these arguments, a summary of knowledge in the field generated by the research synthesized here, and proposes forward-facing approaches to move into subsequent generations of research.

In This Text: A Review of What Follows

The goal of the current text is to place binge watching in the larger, situated context of television viewing history and today's media landscape realities, to examine and synthesize what current empirical and theoretically driven research tells us about this phenomenon at the industry, society, and individual levels, and to pave a way forward for binge-watching research. This text is grounded in an empirical, social scientific approach to human and media interaction. Research in media studies, cultural studies, and Internet and digital media studies have explored related phenomenon in a distinctly separate, parallel fashion over time. Indeed, the ongoing discourse on the false dichotomy of "old media" vs. "new media" among such scholars as Chun (2008); Manovich (2001); Natale (2016) and Peters (2009), among others, is worth noting here. This text is interested in the present state of television viewing, afforded both by changes in technology and distribution practices, but is also reliant on an inherent human quality: storytelling. It is beyond the scope of this book to present the work of these separate disciplines, although we do not conceptualize that approach as at odds with the current social scientific one outlined here. Chun's (2008) observation that "to call something new is to ensure that it will one day be old" (p. 148) is an important reminder that as we document the present in hopes of predicting some small part of the future, it is important to qualify and quantify the interactions and behaviors we are interested in beyond a "new" label. Please note that this text was written before the COVID-19 pandemic and we anticipate that people's media behaviors may be impacted due to the disruption in our work, home, and social lives.

Chapter 2: A Historical Perspective: The Evolution of Television Viewing and Audience Research

Chapter 2 offers a historical overview of entertainment-based television messages and audience reception that has paved the way for binge watching and other new viewing behaviors. Early television ownership and audiences are explored to trace how the role of television in society has evolved. Watching television quickly became a favorite leisure activity and continues to be one of the most common leisure activities among Americans (U.S. Bureau of Labor, 2017). This chapter explores the history of media processing and effects research and how evolving television technologies impacted audiences. The growing number of programming options afforded by cable, as well as the ability to time-shift television viewing started by the introduction of VCR recording in the 1980s are explored. Timeshifting continues to allow television audiences more program options and has freed audiences from restraints of the television schedule. Timeshifting and the increasingly individual-curated television experiences offered through new television technologies are examined.

Chapter 3: An Industry Perspective: Changing Competitors, Content, and Content Curation

The goal of this chapter is to break down the relevant *industry competitors, content characteristics,* and *content curation strategies* that afford binge watching in today's media landscape. Specifically, this chapter examines changes in television distribution, content, and audience flow strategies. It does so by examining the role of a "network," and reviews recent mergers and new players in the streaming wars.

Following is a discussion of what types of content make for good "binging" as we know it – and what types of content viewers (surprisingly) spend the most time viewing. Several series are discussed, and characteristics of narratives that may encourage binge watching are identified. Lastly, this chapter discusses old and new strategies to manage audience flow. Current over-the-top (OTT) services rely on big data and new technology features to curate content for numerous niche audiences. How viewing suggestions and platforms may evolve to entice viewers to view old favorites and carefully selected new content is discussed.

Chapter 4: A Social Perspective: Family Viewing, Co-Viewing, and Social TV

Chapter 4 provides an examination of the changes in viewing practices over the past several decades and how these behaviors may influence binge-watching practices. Special attention is paid to the role of coviewing over time and how group dynamics impact viewing choices. Situational determinants, such as media environment, audience availability, and group viewing influence viewing behaviors by impacting when and what audience members watch on television. While audiences have always engaged in viewing programming with others, who those others are, and where they are physically located, however, is changing. Communication technologies are also impacting our viewing behaviors and now allow us to engage in second screening and multitasking. Coviewing via social media and messaging apps, with known and unknown others, is another viewing behavior on the rise. The implications for content choices and social viewing and binging on content are discussed at length.

Chapter 5: Motivations of Binge Watching

New ways of experiencing ever-expanding media technologies never fail to elicit researchers' examinations of *why* individuals have adopted this experience or behavior, and *how* it differs from previous media experiences and behaviors. This chapter explores the most-often used theoretical approaches to this question concerning binge watching: uses and gratifications and media habituation. It then synthesizes the current literature to establish the degree to which individuals consciously seek out binge watching to meet certain needs and do so again and again as a part of quickly learned, and automatic, habit. The review of current literature on why people binge watch suggests more theoretical rigor is needed, including at least the specification of motives/ gratifications to binge watch made a priori. Empirical data from both theoretical approaches is explored, revealing unique contributions of each.

Chapter 6: Implications of Binge Watching

This chapter looks at the downstream outcomes of binge watching on individuals and industry. Although we see binge-watching motives and outcomes as related, over-time occurrences, this chapter examines the current literature on what comes after the binge. Binge watching is as explored as a strategy to: find enjoyment and meaning; achieve need satisfaction and well-being goals; aid in meeting therapeutic or coping needs; feel close to mediated others via parasocial relationships; and manage one's ideal cognitive involvement. Next, the potential negatives are reviewed: theories of addiction and media technology–related models of addiction and etiologies, followed by research on the potential health and emotional well-being costs associated with television viewing and binge watching. Lastly, a review of cord-cutting and changes in subscription-based options, as well as the potential impact on traditional television advertising, are discussed considering the adoption of binge watching and other new viewing behaviors.

Chapter 7: A Conclusion: Where We Go from Here

This chapter is organized into three sections: The first section presents further evidence of the three central arguments of the text, laid out above in this chapter: Binge watching is a fundamental change in television viewing; it is a human-centered phenomenon; and the field of research can now move beyond exploratory, descriptive studies. The second section summarizes our other major findings: Binge watching is entertaining and enjoyable; it is not an "addiction"; and while Netflix has been great for binge watching, it is not synonymous with it. We conclude with identifying areas large and small worthy of study. We discuss possible future research topics such as how binge watching may influence content and platform subscription decisions, how it may displace other entertainment activities, and its role in interpersonal relationships and across cultures. Overall, we suggest the early research on binge watching reaffirms its prevalence and the entertainment value of binge watching – the future for the study of binge watching within the media processing and effects tradition looks bright.

References

Bartsch, A. (2012). Emotional gratification in entertainment experience. Why viewers of movies and television series find it rewarding to experience emotions. *Media Psychology, 15*(3), 267–302. doi: 10.1080/15213269.2012.693811

Binge watching. (n.d.). In *Collins Dictionary online*. Retrieved from https://www.collinsdictionary.com/word-lovers-blog/new/top-10-collins-words-of-the-year,259,HCB.html

Brunsdon, C. (2010). Bingeing on box-sets: The national and the digital in television crime drama. In J. Gripsrud (Ed.) *Relocating Television* (pp. 63–75). London: Routledge.

Chun, W. H. K. (2008). The enduring ephemeral, or the future is a memory. *Critical Inquiry, 35*(1), 148–171. Doi: 10.1086/595632

Dobrow, J. R. (1990). *Social and cultural aspects of VCR use.* Hillsdale, NJ: Lawrence Erlbaum.

D'Souza, D. (2019, May). Netflix doesn't want to talk about binge watching. *Investopedia.* Retrieved from: https://www.investopedia.com/tech/netflix-obsessed-binge-watching-and-its-problem/

Ericsson Consumer Lab (2015), 'TV & Media 2015: The empowered TV & media consumer's influence', Ericsson Consumer Lab. Retrieved from http://www.ericsson.com/res/docs/2015/consumerlab/ericsson-consumerlab-tv-media-2015-presentation.pdf. Accessed 21 June 2017.

Exelmans, L., & Van den Bulck, J. (2017). Binge viewing, sleep, and the role of pre-sleep arousal. *Journal of clinical sleep medicine: JCSM: official publication of the American Academy of Sleep Medicine, 13*(8), 1001–1008. doi: 10.5664/jcsm.6704

Fiegerman, S. (2017, April 17). Netflix nears 100 million subscribers. *CNN.* Retrieved from http://money.cnn.com/2017/04/17/technology/netflix-subscribers/index.html

Flayelle, M., Maurage, P., & Billieux, J. (2017). Toward a qualitative understanding of binge-watching behaviors: A focus group approach. *Journal of Behavioral Addictions, 6*(4), 457–471. doi: 10.1556/2006.6.2017.060

Gerbner, G. (1969). Toward "cultural indicators:" The analysis of mass mediated message systems. *AV Communication Review, 17,* 137–148.

Giuffre, L. I. Z. (2013). The development of binge watching. *Metro,* 178, 101–102.

Hallinan, B., & Striphas, T. (2016). Recommended for you: The Netflix prize and the production of algorithmic culture. *New Media & Society, 18*(1), 117–137. doi: 10.1177/1461444814538646

Harris Interactive Poll. (2014, April 8). Americans taking advantage of ability to watch TV on their own schedules. *Harris Interactive Poll.* Retrieved from http://www.harrisinteractive.com/NewsRoom/HarrisPolls/tabid/447/ctl/ReadCustom%20Default/mid/1508/ArticleId/1176/Default.aspx

HBO. (2019, November). HBO Introducing the HBO Box. Retrieved from: https://youtu.be/QDAixIPcoqU

Jenner, M. (2016). Is this TVIV? On Netflix, TVIII and binge-watching. *New Media & Society, 18*(2), 257–273. doi: 10.1177/1461444814541523

Karmakar, M., Kruger, J. S., Elhai, J., & Kramer, A. (2015, November). *Viewing patterns and addiction to television among adults who self-identify as binge-watchers.* Paper presented for the American Public Health Association, Chicago, IL.

Kooser, A. (2019, November). HBO made a giant cardboard box where you can hide and watch TV, alone. *CNet.* Retrieved from: https://www.cnet.com/news/hbo-made-a-giant-cardboard-box-where-you-can-hide-and-watch-tv alone/?fbclid=IwAR3T00rhXvRFXAZ-dUeHOoHVF8N28q6QpqMe5G3PHFh3R1lQQG2Vu0w-AxXc

Lang, A. (2013). Discipline in crisis? The shifting paradigm of mass communication research. *Communication Theory, 23*(1), 10–24. doi: 10.1111/comt.12000

Madrigal, A. C. (May, 2018). When did TV watching peak? *The Atlantic*. Retrieved from: https://www.theatlantic.com/technology/archive/2018/05/when-did-tv-watching-peak/561464/

Manovich, L. (2001). *The language of new media*. Cambridge, MA: MIT Press.

Matrix, S. (2014). The Netflix effect: Teens, binge watching, and on-demand digital media trends. *Jeunesse*, 6(1), 119–138. doi: 10.1353/jeu.2014.0002

Natale, S. (2016). There are no old media. *Journal of Communication*, 66(4), 585–603. doi: 10.1111/jcom.12235

Netflix. (2017), October. Ready, set, binge: More than 8 million viewers "binge race" their favorite series. Retrieved from: https://media.netflix.com/en/press-releases/ready-set-binge-more-than-8-million-viewers-binge-race-their-favorite-series

Pena, L. L. (2015). *Breaking binge: Exploring the effects of binge watching on television viewer reception*. Doctoral dissertation, Syracuse University.

Perks, L. G. (2015). *Media marathoning: Immersions in morality*. Lanham, MD: Lexington Books.

Perks, L. G. (2018). Media marathoning through health struggles: Filling a social reservoir. *Journal of Communication Inquiry*, 313–332. doi: 10.1177/0196859918814826

Peters, B. (2009). And lead us not into thinking the new is new: A bibliographic case for new media history. *New Media & Society*, 11(1–2), 13–30. doi: 10.1177/1461444808099572

Petersen, T. G. (2016). To binge or not to binge: A qualitative analysis of college students' binge watching habits. *Florida Communication Journal*, 44(1), 77–88.

Pittman, M., & Sheehan, K. (2015). Sprinting a media marathon: Uses and gratifications of binge-watching television through Netflix. *First Monday*, 20, doi: 10.1207/S15327825MCS0301_02

Richter, F. (2018, April). *Netflix hits 15million subscribers*. *Statista*. Retrieved from https://www.statista.com/chart/10311/netflix-subscriptions-usa-international/

Riddle, K., Peebles, A., Davis, C., Xu, F., & Schroeder, E. (2018). The addictive potential of television binge watching: Comparing intentional and unintentional binges. *Psychology of Popular Media Culture*, 7(4), 589–604. doi: 10.1037/ppm0000167

Roettgers, J. (2019, April 22). Cord cutting will accelerate in 2019, skinny bundles poised to fail (report). *Variety*. Retrieved from: https://variety.com/2019/digital/news/2019-cord-cutting-data-1203194387/

Rubenking, B., & Bracken, C. C. (2018). Binge-watching: A suspenseful, emotional, habit. *Communication Research Reports*, 35(5), 381–391. doi: 10.1080/08824096.2018.1525346

Rubenking, B., Bracken, C. C., Sandoval, J., & Rister, A. (2018). Defining new viewing behaviors: What makes and motivates TV binge watching. *International Journal of Digital Television*, 9, 69–85. doi: 10.1386/jdtv.9.1.69_1

Shannon-Missal. (2013). Americans taking advantage of ability to watch TV on their own schedules. *Harris Interactive*. Retrieved from: http://www.harrisinteractive.com/NewsRoom/HarrisPolls/tabid/447/ctl/ReadCustom%20Default/mid/1508/ArticleId/1176/Default.aspx

Shoemaker, P. J., Tankard Jr, J. W., & Lasorsa, D. L. (2004). *How to build social science theories*. Thousand Oaks, CA: Sage. doi: 10.4135/9781412990110

Sung, Y. H., Kang, E. Y., & Lee, W. N. (2015, May). A bad habit for your health? An exploration of psychological factors for binge-watching behavior. Paper presented at *Annual International Communication Association Conference*, San Juan, Puerto Rico.

Tefertiller, A. C., & Maxwell, L. C. (2018). Depression, emotional states, and the experience of binge-watching narrative television. *Atlantic Journal of Communication*, 26(5), 278–290. doi : 10.1080/15456870.2018.1517765

Tukachinsky, R., & Eyal, K. (2018). The psychology of marathon television viewing: Antecedents and viewer involvement. *Mass Communication and Society*, 21(3), 275–295. doi: 10.1080/15205436.2017.1422765

U.S. Bureaus of Labor Statistics (2017, June). American time use survey summary. Retrieved from: https://www.bls.gov/news.release/atus.nr0.htm

Walton-Pattison, E., Dombrowski, S. U., & Presseau, J. (2018). 'Just one more episode': Frequency and theoretical correlates of television binge watching. *Journal of Health Psychology*, 23(1), 17–24. doi: 10.1177/1359105316643379

Weber, R., Mathiak, K., & Sherry, J. (2008). The neurophysiological perspective in mass communication research: Theoretical rationale, methods, and applications. In M. J. Beatty, J. C. McCroskey, & K. Floyd (Eds.), *Biological dimensions of communication: Perspectives, methods, and research* (pp. 41–71). Cresskill, NJ: Hampton Press.

West, K. (2014). Unsurprising: Netflix survey indicates people like to binge-watch TV. *CinemaBlend*. Retrieved from http://www.cinemablend.com/television/Unsurprising-Netflix-Survey-Indicates-People-Like-Binge-Watch-TV-61045.html

Wheeler, K. S. (2015). *The relationships between television viewing behaviors, attachment, loneliness, depression, and psychological well-being*. Honors Thesis. Georgia Southern University, Georgia, United States.

Zimmer, B. (2013, August). Binges: Lost weekends and lost seasons. *The Wall Street Journal*. Retrieved from: https://www.wsj.com/articles/SB10001424127887324635904578640423791473156

CHAPTER TWO

A Historical Perspective: The Evolution of Television Viewing and Audience Research

This chapter follows the evolution of television technology and research on television audiences, as they relate to binge watching and the current media landscape, from the late 1940s through modern day. The emphasis of this chapter explores how audiences view and select television content, with a later emphasis on timeshifting behaviors and the technologies that enabled them, which eventually led to more viewers ultimately having more control over their viewing options. Much of the early television research is descriptive and does not engage in hypothesis testing or apply social scientific theories. It should be noted that some early research does rely on either sociological or psychological theories, but in most cases the researchers are arguing that these types of theories can be applied to the study of television viewing. There is a pattern to the focus on new communication technology research. Initially, or in first-generation research, the focus in on how many units (of the new communication technology) were sold, who bought them, and how the new communication technologies were being used (Dobrow, 1990). These are all descriptive questions. In second-generation research, there is a shift to examine use patterns and the effects of using the communication technology. Dobrow (1990) discusses the third and final generation of research is placing the communication technology in the larger social/ cultural context, once it has reached saturation and existed long enough to generate first- and second-generation research. According to this model, early television research is almost entirely first generation, while some of the

VCR and cable research discussed later in this chapter could be characterized as second-generation research. Why are past viewing behaviors being discussed on a book about a new viewing behavior such as binge watching? Our reasoning is that television format, presentation of content, and limits of television technology all play a role in audiences' viewing options. Additionally, we seek to demonstrate that current TV viewing behaviors developed from past viewing patterns and habits. The next section will discuss the progression of television ownership, viewing behaviors, and the corresponding research on television.

Early Television Adoption, Users, and Uses

Early Television Growth

While television as a technology existed as early as the 1920s (Williams, 1974), it was not until after World War II that television content became available to a growing number of the American public. After WWII, there were six TV stations in the United States (Gomery, 2001). By 1948, there were four established television networks (e.g., NBC, CBS, ABC, and DuMont) broadcasting to 16 licensed stations. The majority of these networks migrated to television from radio.

The number of television sets proliferated after television networks were broadcasting content. In 1946 there were only 20,000 television sets, but in 1949 the number of television sets grew to approximately 3,000,000 sets in American homes and businesses. The number of homes with television more than doubled by 1950 to 7,000,000 (Gomery, 2001). While in England, television started broadcasting in 1946, with less than 15,000 homes having a television set (Silvey, 1947). However, it was not until 1960 that more than 80% of the British population owned a television set. The slower rate of television set ownership in England was attributed to the shortage of television sets production (Gorham, 1952).

Early television sets were pieces of furniture with two control knobs – one for volume and the second to tune the station. Television viewing required a person to turn on the power manually and to tune the station and often involved moving the antennae (e.g., rabbit ears). The antennae likely needed to be readjusted to view a different station. The next section profiles early television audiences and their viewing habits.

Profile of Early Audiences

Early Mass Communication research employed a mix of qualitative and quantitative research methods, including interviews, diaries, and surveys. The publication of scholarly research on television was new, and media scholars had few publications outlets. For example, the *Journal of Broadcasting* (later *Journal of Broadcasting and Electronic Media*) published its first issue in 1956. The vast majority of published studies before 1960 are descriptive. That is, their goal was to describe television households, the amount of time spent watching television, and viewing habits, including show preferences. This makes sense as the medium, and how people were using television, was so new. Comparisons of television and non-television households are also common.

Several sources refer to television viewing occurring initially in taverns (Bogart, 1956) because of the expense of television sets. However, there is some evidence that this route to diffusion did not occur in suburban communities and that middle-class families were some of the earliest adopters of television. The television audience was established and grew in the late 1940s in both urban and suburban America.

People who owned television sets in the late 1940s and early 1950s could be considered early adopters. Early adopters of television had several characteristics in common. They tended to live in cities or inner ring suburbs (Gomery, 2001), had families (Westley & Mobious, 1960), and were generally younger (Gomery, 2001). Interestingly, middle-class households were more likely than either upper-class or lower-class households to own a television (Westley & Mobius, 1960). However, there was a ubiquitous interest in television.

While the number of television stations was somewhat limited in the early days, the lack of programming choices did not dampen the audience's interest in viewing television. Bogart (1962) states, "the pastime character of television is demonstrated by the fact that the amount of time spent viewing bears little relationship to the variety of fare offered, as shown by the number of competitive channels within range of a particular community. Set usage is largely independent of the number of channels that can be viewed" (p. 37). In the United States, the Philadelphia broadcasting market was the first place where the television audience surpassed radio.

Most of early television's research publications focused on the exposure audiences had to television content. This was in part because new television stations were cropping up around the country. Many, if not most, stations were broadcasting for a limited number of hours per day. For example, stations offered limited programming during the day; provided morning, afternoon, and evening news; and shut down overnight. Researchers were highly curious about the differences between households with and without televisions sets for most of the 1950s. One area of comparison was how television impacted how people spent their leisure time.

Leisure Time

Early researchers often investigated the displacement of other leisure activities. Television viewing disrupted existing social interactions both within and outside of the home and impacted how families who owned a television set spent their time. By 1948, families with television sets were already engaging in fewer activities outside of the home (Coffin, 1948). As early as 1955, TV was "credited with increasing the family's fund of common experience and shared interests and blamed for decreasing its conversation and face-to-face interaction" (Coffin, 1955, p. 634). This is in part because the social life of the family was re-directed and assumed to be less interactive with the television, becoming the focus of the family's social life. In 1956, Hamilton and Lawless compared television and non-television households in order to assess the extent to which television was incorporated into the social matrix and influenced individual personalities. The researchers asked participants about why they liked television. Fifty percent of television households indicated the reason they liked it was that it keeps their family (including children, teens, and husbands) at home. It is worth noting that for television households, the second most frequent reason provided for liking TV was entertainment (19%). Hamilton and Lawless (1956) also report that television was incorporated into the social activities of households. Forty-two percent of television households reported TV viewing as the number one or primary family activity compared to 26.7 % of non-television households reporting that their family's primary activity was going to the movies. The second most common activity was pleasure driving (19.6%) for television households and (22.1%) for non-television households.

Robinson (1969) reported 28% of all leisure time was spent watching television with men watching a bit more spending 32% of their leisure time with television, while women spent less time, about 25%, of their leisure time with television. The average viewing time in the late 1960s was 2–3 hours of television viewing per day (Roper, 1969). In a similar timeframe, Robinson found just over two hours, and Nielsen reported just over three-hours of daily television viewing to be average. Robinson reports a positive relationship between the increase in the number of households that have television sets and viewing time. People were spending an increasing amount of their leisure time viewing television. Two to three hours of viewing time was a commitment because television content was only available live or aired at a particular time and required audiences to arrange their schedules to be able to view particular shows (appointment viewing).

In 1972, Robinson and Converse re-examined media use patterns as an allocation of leisure time. Their results showed that Americans were spending 40% of their leisure time viewing television, which was a 12% increase in less than three years. The amount of television viewing time continued to increase throughout the 1970s.

Csikszentmihalyi and Kubey (1981) examined television's impact on American life. They reported viewing times consistent with Robertson et al. (1972). The participants reported that TV viewing was the most relaxing of all activities inquired about (Csikszentmihalyi & Kubey, 1981), and TV viewing was linked to relaxation and lower cognitive investments. Leisure time continued to be dedicated to television viewing but appears to have stabilized sometime in the 1980s because Lin (1992) did not find the introduction of the VCR contributed to lessening leisure activities outside of the home.

Viewing Habits

Early research on viewing behaviors reported that individuals with a television set in the home are averaging approximately 3.4 hours of viewing per day (Gomery, 2001). In a study exploring children's use of "televiewing," Battin (1954) describes children's content preferences and viewing habits were well established within six months of owning a television set.

Once a television set was purchased for a home, the television was watched several nights a week. Gomery (2001) suggests that as early as 1950, the average time spent viewing was 3 hours and 24 minutes.

TV Viewing as Primary vs Secondary Activity

Today we associate multitasking with what is more precisely called Media Multitasking. We tend to think of multitasking as new phenomena, but humans have been engaging in some form of multitasking for eons. However, even with media, this behavior of attempting to attend to more than one activity is not new. People have been listening to music and doing homework, or listening to the radio and reading, or playing games (e.g., board, card, or video) and listening to music for several decades. McDonald and Meng (2008) discuss multitasking and media use as early as the 1930s, with audience members reporting engaging in various activities while listening to the radio. For example, listening to the radio and reading (Sorokin & Berger, 1939), cooking dinner or playing cards, and listening to the radio (Cantrill & Allport, 1935). Since television presents a visual image and early television screens were quite small, the TV demanded the audience's attention for a while. Evidence of media multitasking with television appears in the mid-1960s with researchers documenting primary and secondary activities, including television viewing. For example, talking and eating were identified as primary activities with viewing television being a secondary activity (Allen, 1965; Becthel et al. 1972). Eating in front of the television is something that can be traced back to the earliest days of television. The size of early television sets required they be placed in one of the larger rooms in a home. So, most households placed their television sets the sitting room or living room. The Swanson company introduced "TV dinners" in 1953. These frozen dinners came in an aluminium tray that could be heated in the oven – saving the homemaker time and effort and allowing more time for TV viewing.

The idea of primary and secondary activities resembles future media behaviors and suggests people have been using television to multitask since at least the 1960s. These same behaviors were confirmed by Csikszentmihalyi and Kubey (1981). They measured secondary activities and television viewing. Participants reported watching television as a secondary activity 67.4% of the time, meaning audiences attend to what was on the TV only 32.6% of the time. The participants' primary activities included eating, talking, and smoking.

We should note that most of these early results were found in studies focusing on leisure time or how people behave at home and were not an examination of multitasking. In the 1950s and 1960s there were a growing number of social science studies that focused on the consumption and effects of media, and the next section addresses television-related research.

Early Media "Effects" Research

The study of the effect of media messages grew out of the War Office established to develop messages addressing rationing and other World War II efforts. This body of work and research became the foundation for the discipline of Communication. A large multipart set of studies was published in 1949. Volume II, "Experiments on Mass Communication (Studies in social psychology in World War II)," details studies that explored how media messages, primarily films, impact audiences in the area of attitude formation. Schramm (1949) stated "but if there is a disappointing scarcity of empirical research bearing directly on the problems of communication effects, there is a considerable abundance of research and observation which is not aimed directly at communication effects but still contributes in an important way to our understanding of those effects and to the hypotheses we are able to frame concerning them" (p. 397).

Schramm then draws from the education, political science, advertising, psychology, and social psychology literatures to propose a line of further experimental investigations of mass communication. He draws from the findings of a series of studies conducted for the U.S. Army by Hovland, Lumsdaine, and Sheffield (1949). Schramm summarizes the findings of these extensive series of studies on film's influence on audience attitudes toward a variety of topics and messages and suggests

> any single communication impact must contend with deeply ingrained attitudes which are the products of years of the total environment. The 50 minutes of exposure to orientation films were therefore like a drop of water in the cave. Furthermore, they realized that the attitudes the films sought to teach were already the majority attitudes, and they were therefore trying to change the deviant minority who were confirmed in their position and clung to it. (p. 401)

The researchers reported that individuals who reported liking a film were the most affected by it.

Schramm (1949) outlines seven "Effects of Communications on the Individual." These seven insights served as the foundations for all media effects research: "Mass communication are capable of causing learning to take place and of changing attitudes and opinions in their audiences."

(1) The amount of opinion or attitude change may at times increase while the amount of faculty retention is decreasing (Hovland, 1949 p. 182–200).
(2) The amount of learning from mass communications, when other variables are controlled, is proportional to the intellectual ability of the member of audience.
(3) The amount of learning from mass communications, when other variables are controlled, is proportional to the degree of attention, and therefore motivation which compels the attention. Schram notes attention to mass media is lower than other learning situations.
(4) The amount of learning from mass communications, when other variables are controlled, tends to be proportional to the degree with which the individual can relate himself to the situation being presented, and therefore to the extent to which he can anticipate a reward for attention.
(5) The cumulative effects of mass communications are powerful. The communications blend into a form a large part of the individual's environment and contribute to the attitudes and opinions which remain as the facts are forgotten.
(6) The effect of mass communication on attitude and opinion tends to be reinforcement rather than change, modification rather than conversion.
(7) Persons are more likely to learn from a communication if they like it, than if they do not. Which of these two elements is cause, which effect, has not yet been determined? (Schramm, 1949, 404–405).

Schramm also addresses persuasion, media channels, public taste, and societal effects research. These lessons learned from experiments with film informed early media effects research. The influence of formal or structural features on learning and attitudes were also explored in the 1960s but did not generate a body of literature until the late 1970s.

Some early researchers were keen to understand the impact of media messages on individuals, and the process of identifying impact included early interest in cognitive processing or "finding out what went on in the mind of the respondent at the time he received the message" (Lazarsfeld, 1950, p. 265). Given their past experiences in the War Office, many media or mass communication scholars viewed media as having a powerful and direct effect on audiences.

By the end of the 1950s, we see the field start to investigate the impact of entertainment content on audiences. Many of these studies were still examining cinema-goers instead of television audiences.

While the majority of research was focused on the impact of news or advertisements on attitude formation, some researchers began to explore other phenomena that are likely quite familiar to us today. There are examples of studying viewers' identification with characters. Emery (1959) speculated that television audiences may experience a sense of "identification" with a media character.

> "In the viewing situation identification appears to be different. In identifying with a character in a story the viewer seems rather to experience, in some degree, the feelings of the character. He tends to suffer and to feel relief and affection as the figure is shown to be experiencing them. He feels the same way and not in a different although appropriately related way."…. "It is suggested that in the viewing situation that viewer temporarily loses his self-awareness and his self-identity is transformed into something like that of self-cum-hero. This suggestion is consistent with certain other observation facts and psychological formations." (Emery, 1959, p. 203)

There even were early discussions of sensations of being there, or telepresence. For example, Chein (1944) describes the experience of viewing motion pictures or films as not being *in* the cinema as "successfully identifying oneself with the characters in a motion picture one does not experience oneself as being in one's seat but as being there in the picture world and to do this successfully all directions must be appropriately experienced" (Chein, 1944, p. 308).

We also see the early origins of mood management. American audiences reported preferring television content that was entertaining and provided an escape (Paulu, 1955). In 1959, Pearlin published a report of his investigation into the impact of stress on television viewing. He interviewed 736 television owners asking them if "There are some programs that help us forget our personal problems and troubles while we watch them. What do you yourself think of this kind of program?" (p. 256). The respondents reported they enjoyed the programs very much (30%); that they liked them (59%); and 11% reported they did not particularly like them/or need them. Pearlin concluded it appears that one of the functions of television is to offer to its audience an opportunity to withdraw periodically from whatever strains and unpleasant experiences they might have. In this connection it is well to keep in mind that if people seek escape through television, it is not necessarily because the medium creates the need for escape. While television itself might help to generate the very needs to which it caters, the evidence suggests that the needs can also be created in experiences quite apart from the mass media. (Pearlin, 1959, p. 259)

While some researchers started to examine the effects that media was having on audiences, most television research was primarily in the area of media exposure. Troldahl (1965) described early television research as being in one of three categories: First, investigations into how television was displacing other media channels; second, the extent to which television was impacting participation in cultural and social activities; and third, the diffusion of information, primarily television news. As early as 1956, Danielson reported that 88% of the population first became aware of a news story via an electronic media channel (e.g., radio or television). Diffusion research dominated the 1960s, especially after John F. Kennedy's assignation.

The field of Mass Communication expands beyond these three categories and starts to explore audience perception of media content in the mid-1960s. For example, Carter and Greenberg (1965) explored mass media channels as primary news sources and perceived credibility with television content showing earlier signs of being highly believable. However, there is a shift in the research during the mid-1960s corresponding with the growth of Communication programs – particularly doctoral programs in Mass Communication. Wilbur Schramm started the first Mass Communication Ph.D. program at the University of Iowa, and the first graduate completed the program in 1947 (Rogers, 1994).

As the discipline of Mass Communication developed its own Ph.Ds, who were interested in studying media effects, we see the field start to diversify more. By the end of the 1960s, there is a growing number of researchers exploring the influence of TV content on children. There are extensive studies funded by the U.S. government focusing on the impact of media violence on children (U.S. Surgeon General's Scientific Advisory Committee on Television and Social Behavior, 1972). These large-scale media effects studies resulted in several significant developments in television history. First, the creation of the Children's Television Workshop (CTW), which was created using both public and private funds. CTW's first program was Sesame Street, which first aired in 1969 (Fisch & Truglio, 2001). Concern about the impact of media violence also leads to the creation of the Family Hour by the networks (a more detailed description of this is in Chapter 4). Other changes in the 1970s included the conversion to the majority of American households having color television sets. In 1970, color television sets outsold black and white only sets for the first time (Early Television Museum).

The early 1970s saw significant viewing behavior shifts. The average amount of television people were watching rose to over 6 hours per day in the 1970s. By 1984, Americans were watching 7 hours of television per day on average (Madrgial, 2018). The daily average time spent television viewing peaked in 2009–2010 with the average American household watching 8 hours and 55 minutes of TV per day (Madrgial, 2018). Communication technology developments also impacted viewing behavior in the 1970s, including the introduction of premium channels (i.e., pay to view stations) such as Home Box Office (HBO), which brought movies into our living rooms, and video game consoles such as Atari, and VCRs.

Characteristics of television, as presented to TV viewers, are largely connected to the organization of content. Traditionally, TV viewers saw content organized into networks, or channels (e.g., NBC, HBO, or Animal Planet). Channels organize content into programming and commercials, and commercials often promote programming using both internal and external messaging (Abreu, Nogueira, Becker, & Cardoso, 2017). Viewers often consumed television on one network for an entire evening. For example, in the 1974–1975 CBS Saturday line-up was *All in the Family; The Jeffersons; Mary Tyler Moore; The Bob Newhart Show*; and *The Carol Burnett Show*. TV viewers watched these shows back to back between 8 pm and 11 pm. All these shows were in the top 30 highest audience ratings (e.g., percentage of viewing audience) in September 1974 (Brooks & Marsh, 2009). Up until the late 1970s, TV viewers needed to be physically present to watch a particular program at a particular time. If the TV viewer missed an episode of *All in the Family*, then the viewer had to wait until the show was re-aired over the summer. Developments in communication technology (for more detail see Table 2.1), namely, the video cassette recorder (VCR), provided the option of recording a television show and watching it at the viewer's convenience. The introduction of the VCR began an interruption of the tradition flow of television audience viewing patterns.

Table 2.1: Evolution of Television Technology

TV broadcasting (beyond experimental) begins	1947
Networks start to broadcast color programming	1965
First sales in United States of VCR	1975
HBO begins	1975
Television ownership reaches 98%	1975
Television ownership reaches 99%	1980
Both cable television & VCRs available in more than half of US homes	1988
First sales in United States of DVR	1999
Netflix starts streaming service	2007
Hulu starts streaming service	2008
Disney+ starts	2019

Introduction of the VCR

After the introduction of television itself, the next technology that impacted viewers' behavior was the introduction of the VCR. Similar to the progression of television research, early research on VCRs initially focuses on descriptive questions: How many VCRs were sold, who bought them, and how VCRs were being used (i.e., first-generation research). Then there was a shift to examine use patterns and the effects of using VCRs. Next, we examine the first, second, and third generations of research on VCRs.

The VCR (video cassette recorder) was introduced in the mid-1970s. Ownership of VCRs increased dramatically in the early 1980s when VCRs became more affordable. In 1980, approximately 1.2 million households (1.5%) in the United States owned a VCR. By 1984 between 5.5 to 6.8 million households owned a VCR (6.2–7.7% of American households). We will not discuss the BETAMAX versus VCR war here (See Cusuamano, Mylandonis, & Rosenbloom, 1992). By the mid-1980s, many families had purchased a VCR and were using the devices to both record television content to view at a later time (we will discuss timeshifting later in the chapter) and to rent and watch movies at home. This section focused on the individual who recorded television content off the air.

In 1987, 50% of American homes had a VCR (Noble, 1987). This allowed for a comparison between viewing broadcast TV and VCR usage. Noble (1987) identified differences in viewing behaviors between households with VCRs and those without. The differences provide a glimpse into future viewing behaviors. VCRs offered (1) user control of programs; (2) user choice over programs; (3) user taste in programs; (4) user timing for program; (5) more freedom of choice; (6) controlled interruptions; (7) uncensored private taste supplied by users of video producers;

(8) audience chooses as individuals; (9) collective behaviors occur at different times; and (10) debatable consumer-oriented (p. 135). Some researchers argued VCRs offered television audiences an improved viewing experience by providing more control over the content viewed and when they watch their selected programs (Lin, 1993; Rubin & Bantz, 1987; Van den Bulck, 1999). In 1990, 60% of American households owned a VCR, and ownership increased to 80% by 1995 (Ironmonger, Lloyd-Smith, & Soupourmas, 2000).

Owning a VCR impacted other types of media consumption behaviors. For example, in a study comparing young teenagers (9th and 10th graders), those teens whose households owned a VCR consumed more media including watching more TV, going to more movies, and reading more print media (e.g., newspapers, magazines, and books) than those who did not own a VCR (Greenberg & Heeter, 1987). The average usage of VCRs reported in the early 1980s was between 3.3 to 3.4 hours of homemade tape viewing and 0.5 hours of pre-recorded tapes. Seventy-five percent of home taping was motivated by timeshifting (Levy, 1981). Henke and Donohue (1989) interviewed 485 VCR owners about their VCR usage and found that having a VCR displaced other media use. The overall conclusion was that owning a VCR influenced the owner's habits as well as their content preferences, but that in allowing television viewers the ability to timeshift resulted in more reach and higher frequency of taping for some types of programming content including network miniseries, local news programs, and regular network programming (Henke & Donohue, 1989). Other differences were reported between heavy and light television viewers who owned VCRs. Heavy viewers reported using their VCRs to concentrate their viewing on the favorite programs or genres., while lighter viewers reported using their VCRs to provide wider diversity of programming (Dobrow, 1987).

VCR functions contribute to the notion of the audience as active (Lin, 1990), as the ability to watch a program recorded off the air at a later time is highly consistent with the definition of an active viewer. The VCR was seen as freeing viewing from the restriction of needing to watch a show when it was broadcast live. However, other researchers suggested the VCR may also be a "time filling" device – especially for heavy viewers. It may reduce programming conflicts by allowing viewers to watch a program and record another at the same time, allowing the media user to watch more programming (Dubrow, 1990). While there was great enthusiasm for purchasing VCRs, some researchers argued that VCR use was not high enough to change TV viewing behaviors very much (Barwise & Ehrenberg. 1988; Van den Bulck, 1999). At least one researcher noted that the majority of recorded content (58%) was never watched (Levy & Fink, 1984).

VCR usage was also studied from a Uses and Gratifications perspective as the VCR gave the audience both more choice and control over when and what they viewed. VCR usage was impacted by needs to feel included, for affection, and to escape (Rubin & Rubin, 1989). Rubin and Bantz (1987) examined the perceived utility of VCRs. Participants reported that timeshifting and convenience were primary motivations in purchasing a VCR. They also argued that VCR adopters were more active and motivated in their TV viewing choices. VCR usage was associated with increased time spent with family and friends (Harvey & Roe, 1986; Roe 1987). Thus, some researchers saw the interpersonal and mass communication motives for using a VCR as being interconnected, as are motives for TV viewing and interpersonal communication (Rubin & Bantz 1987, 1988).

As VCR technology developed, VCRs allowed audience members to record a program repeatedly at the same day and time. This allowed for a single program to record several episodes of the same program over several weeks. Additionally, networks also began to sell full seasons of television shows on VCR cassette tapes. Recording several broadcast episodes or purchasing the box set of a television series allowed television audiences to watch several episodes back to back in one sitting. This viewing behavior was the beginning of what we now refer to as binge-watching. This type of viewing behavior was not possible before VCRs and became quite popular. So much that networks – especially cable networks – began to program marathons. The first TV marathons appeared in 1985 on *Nick at Nite* with vintage programs such as *The Donna Reed Show*. The next section addresses timeshifting and its lasting legacy on our viewing behaviors.

Timeshifting

VCR technology was promoted as a technology that would allow television audiences to be able to record a program and watch it later at a more convenient time (Finney, 1997; Levy 1980, 1981), freeing audiences from the confines of the broadcasting schedule. This type of behavior was described by Levy (1980), who suggested American households were using their VCR primarily to "timeshift." Timeshifting was defined as the "rearrange [ing] the broadcast schedule, making viewing more convenient or eliminating programming conflicts" (Levy 1980, p. 405). Levy, at least in part, sees this new viewing behavior as having the possibility of reducing the overall amount of TV viewing.

Levy also suggests that timeshifting allows viewers to be more active and to select desired programming instead of selecting from content that was available when audience members were able to sit down and view television (Levy, 1981).

Levy (1983) further suggested that timeshifting is "conceptualized as having two temporally-separated components, recording, and replay" (p. 267). He reported that 75% of VCR use was "re-broadcasting" television content at another time (Levy, 1980, 1981). Audiences engaging in timeshifting were seen as more active than audiences who selected what was available to them when they turned on the television. Levy (1987) argued that the extra effort it took to purchase the VCR and to set the unit to record a particular program was motivated by the audience member's needs and goals. The use of media technology to timeshift was influencing viewing behaviors to an increasingly greater extent over time. Morgan and Shanahan (1991) suggested that watching TV was different in the early 1990s. The penetration of VCR ownership and the timeshifting capabilities of VCRs allowed viewers to watch not only *what* content they wanted to watch but also *as often* as they wanted to watch (Morgan & Shanahan, 1991).

Van den Bulck (1999) deconstructed earlier definitions of timeshifting as recording a program and watching it at a later time. He argued that in the earlier definition, viewers were managing their time and viewing. However, Van den Bulck suggests there are three ways to see this definition:

> Firstly, people record programs they would like to watch, but which are broadcast at awkward hours, in order to watch them at a more appropriate time. Secondly, people may record programs which are aired while they are watching another program, thus avoiding program selection conflicts. The VCR may thus be used to manage differing family preferences. Finally, the VCR may serve as a technical improvement of the viewing experience. (p. 317)

Media researchers speculated on the impact of VCR usage. First, many researchers viewed the VCR as freeing television viewers from the restriction of needing to be available and present to watch a program or sometimes describe as being freed from the programming or broadcasting schedule (Morgan et al., 1990). Others suggested that the VCR may be a time filling device that would allow heavy viewers to view even more television programming (Morgan et al., 1990; Van den Bulck, 1999).

Over time there has been some suggestions that VCR usage led to program diversification. However, this was only true for some viewers. Others reported rarely using their VCR. (Lin, 1990). This assessment has been supported by more recent research suggesting most people did not use the VCR for timeshifting due to the challenge of setting the recording function (Darnell, 2015). In looking back, we can see that the introduction of the VCR and its usage by television audiences was the first step toward independence from the broadcasting schedule. We have continued to see the erosion of television audience's reliance on the broadcasting schedule through the introduction of on-demand content, streaming, and downloading.

Digital Timeshifting

As technology developed, the VCR gave way to the digital video recorder (DVR) introduced in 1999. DVRs are similar to a VCR allowing for timeshifting but with the additional functionality of allowing television viewers to pause and rewind live television content. DVRs were promoted to television viewers as being similar to VCRs in that they allow timeshifting, but some DVRs went beyond this and included a setting that allowed some systems to recommend content to viewers based on previous programming choices. Like the diffusion of other communication technologies, early DVR owners tended to be younger (Friedman, 2006); have more education, children, higher income levels (Story, 2007); and be heavier television viewers (Friedman, 2006) than non-DVR owners. DVR penetration was estimated at 17% of U.S. households in June 2007 (Steinberg & Hampp, 2007). Darnell (2007) observed ten people (six with DVRs and four without) in their homes using video recording equipment for at least six months. The video equipment was arranged to record both the individual and the content they were watching. The analysis reveals that the six participants with DVRs spent an average of 64% of their time watching DVR recorded programming, with two participants spending all their viewing time watching prerecorded content. This was a large step toward program personalization (Carlson, 2006).

Smith and Krugman (2009) investigated viewing behaviors and DVR usage through interviews and observations. Based on their data collection, they argue that DVR owners have a different relationship with television content, one in which the audience has more control over both the content viewed and when they view. Smith and Krugman call this the *timing of the viewing*. Additionally, DVR users were interested not only in controlling when they viewed their selected content, but were able to avoid undesirable content such as commercials. Since many households with DVRs included those with younger children, some scholars have speculated on how the use of menus instead of programming guides influenced children's perceptions of television content and viewing choices (Mittell, 2011).

More recently, Bury and Li (2015) collected data via an online survey from an international sample comprised of primarily English-speaking countries. Their results demonstrated that more than half (53.5%) of respondents reported watching a limited amount (20% or less) of television content "live" (Bury & Li, 2015). Further, their results supported past research which found that the extent to which audiences watch "live" television content is correlated with viewers' age. The younger the viewer, the less likely they are to watch live (Bury & Li, 2015; Nielsen, 2012). Viewers over 40 were more likely to use DVRs when they engaged in timeshifting than younger views who were more likely to stream content (Bury & Li, 2015).

Some DVR systems were designed to provide personal recommendations to viewers. One such device was TIVO. The programming recommendations or personalization were not all initially positive. There were pop culture stories about how TIVO would make recommendations that seemed deeply flawed. Zaslow (2002) reported that one owner reported their TIVO started recommending content with gay themes. In an attempt to "fix" the recommendations, the owner started to program war movies, which led to TIVO suggesting documentaries on the Third Reich.

While these types of stories were popular for a short while, this was not the typical experience with DVRs. In fact, Ferguson and Perse (2004) found that timeshifting was one of the most listed reasons for purchasing a DVR and was linked to greater satisfaction. The overwhelming majority of people reported their DVR empowered them to record programs and watch them at a more convenient time in the future (Consoli, 2005). However, the second most common reason for purchasing a DVR was to skip over commercials breaks. The next section will address how DVRs have impacted the traditional television business model of relying on advertisements.

DVRing and Advertising

The number of people using DVRs impacted the television business model of selling viewers to advertisers. As DVR technology became affordable, 79% of people reported they were purchasing DVRs specifically to skip past the advertisements (Consoli, 2005). Audiences were interested in taking advantage of the DVR's functions allowing audiences to record and fast-forward or zip through programming and thus reducing their exposure to commercials (Ghosh & Stock, 2010). Sixty-six percent of DVR owners reported fast-forwarding through commercials (Steinberg, 2007).

Wilbur (2008) identified four motivations of television viewers to avoid advertising embedded in television programming. First, viewers avoid ads when they have other activities to engage in while the advertisements are airing, such as changing the channel or talking to other people (Tse & Lee, 2001). Second, viewers tend to avoid ads that are not visually engaging (Woltman Elpers Wedel, & Pieters, 2003). Third, viewers dislike ads they have seen numerous times or that are worn out (Siddarth & Chattopadhyay, 1998). Fourth, ads for products that viewers deemed not relevant to them are also avoided (Alwitt & Prabhaker, 1994). Given these motivations, Wilbur (2008) concluded that most DVR owners were not watching commercials.

DVRs allow audiences to skip commercials in a variety of ways. Some DVRs allow audiences to skip ahead in 30-second increments. This duration was programmed to allow television viewers to skip a traditional 30-second commercial or two 15-second commercials. Other DVRs attempted to identify the commercial break and allow audiences to skip the whole advertising break (Bellman, 2010). The avoidance of advertisements was the primary reason people interacted with their TVs via the remote control (Bernoff, 2004; Darnell, 2007). Some researchers have argued that DVR owners may ironically be exposed to more ads than non-DVR users because in order to skip through the ads, the DVR users must monitor the ads to prevent missing programming content, while non-DVR users may simply leave the room.

Both broadcasters and advertisers need to understand why audiences avoid commercials. One goal of advertising is to create brand recognition, and ad avoidance was reducing television viewers' recall and recognition of ads. Research has demonstrated that skipping or zapping advertisements reduces the effectiveness of advertisements (Bellman, Schweda, & Varan, 2010; Gilmore & Secunda 1993; Stout & Burda 1989; Thorson & Zhao 1997). However, other researchers have argued that DVR usage (even with TV viewers skipping ads) is not necessarily bad for advertisers. The reason for this is that DVRs allow for targeted ads (Ghosh, Galbreth, & Shang, 2013). Further, Ghosh and Stock (2010) argued that DVR users were more likely to skip particular brands and view brands they see as more relevant to their interest. This would allow advertisers to collect data on ad viewership (Ghosh & Stock, 2010).

An increasing percentage of viewers are engaging in timeshifting, so why are some viewers still watching content live or engaging in appointment viewing? Kent, Mosely, and Schweidel (2019) suggest that some people watch live to avoid learning about what happens in an episode or what is commonly referred to as "spoilers." However, Kent et al. (2019) reported dramas were likely to be viewed on DVR with longer delays from the date the episode initially aired. Sports and reality programs had lower levels of delayed playback and may be more beneficial for advertisers to target time-sensitive information.

There has been a clear pattern demonstrating increasing numbers of people worldwide are using digital recording devices and other digital services to timeshift their viewing of preferred video content via mobile devices (Bury & Li, 2015; Madden, 2009; Nielsen Company, 2012; Purcell, 2010; Schonfeld, 2010; Serjeant, 2010).

Conclusion

This chapter detailed the context-relevant history of television from its introduction in the 1940s to current day digital television technologies. Research on television technologies follows a pattern of descriptive research describing the types of uses of the technology and the audiences engaging with each new television technology. Television viewing quickly became a leading leisure activity consuming an increasing amount of Americans' free time. Early Mass Communication research included studies on media effects and provided a road map for the growing field of Mass Communication. While both television viewing and the study of media effects of viewing have changed dramatically over time, early research points to familiar concepts. The research reviewed here touches on identification with characters, telepresence, mood management, displacement, and multitasking: all concepts explored elsewhere as relevant to today's viewing landscape and binge watching. The television viewing patterns we see today originated with the introduction of the VCR. The research discussed identifies that the VCR freed audiences from the requirement of watching a program when it was aired and allowed for timeshifting of television viewing. The ability to select the desired program and watch several episodes back to back informed both audiences and the television industry on possible future viewing behaviors we see commonly today – namely selecting a program on a streaming service and watching when it is convenient for the viewer. The importance of the ability to timeshift, as first afforded by the VCR, should not go understated. This can be viewed as the beginning of a trend that allows viewers more control and agency over when and what they watch. We can view binge watching as a critical component of that trend today.

References

Alwitt, L. F., & Prablhaker, P. R. (1994). Identifying who dislikes television advertising: Not by demographics along. *Journal of Advertising Research, 34*(6), 17–29.

Battin, T. C. (1954). A study of the televiewing habits of school children. *Western Speech, 18*(2), 101–108.

Bellman, S., Schweda, A., & Varan, D. (2010). The residual impact of avoided television advertising. *Journal of Advertising, 39*(1), 67–81. doi: 10.2753/JOA0091-336739010

Bernoff, J. (2004). *The mind of the DVR user: Media and advertising*. Cambridge, MA: Forrester Research.

Bogart, L. (1956). *Age of television: A study of viewing habits and the impact of television on American life*. New York: Frederick Ungar.

Bogart, L. (1962). American television: A Brief Survey of Research Findings. *Journal of Social Issues, 18*(2), 36–42. doi: 10.1111/j.1540-4560.1962.tb02196.x

Brooks, T., & Marsh, E. F. (2009). *The complete directory to prime time network and cable tv shows, 1946-present* (9th Ed). New York: Penguin Random House.

Bury, R., & Li, J. (2015). Is it live or is it timeshifted, streamed, or downloaded? Watching television in the era of multiple screens. *New Media & Society, 17*(4), 592–610. doi: 10.1177/1461444813508368

Carter, R. F., & Greenberg, B. S. (1965). Newspaper or television: Which do you believe? *Journalism Quarterly, 32*, 319–328. doi:10.1177/107769906504200104

Chein, L. (1944). Awareness of self and structure of ego. *Psychological Review, 51*, 303–314. doi: 10.1037/h0054270

Coffin, T. (1948). Television's effects on leisure-time activities. *Journal of Applied Psychology, 32*, 550–558. doi: 10.1037/h0061416

Coffin, T (1955). Television's impact on society. *American Psychologist, 10*, 630–641. doi: 10.1037/h0039880

Consoli, J. (2005). MindShare: Consumers buy DVRs to skip ads. *MediaWeek, 15*(46), 6–8.

Csikszentmihalyi, M., & Kubey, R. (1981). Television and the rest of life: A systematic comparison of subjective experience *Public Opinion Quarterly, 45*(3), 317–328. doi: 10.1086/268667

Cusumano, M., Mylonadis, Y., & Rosenbloom, R. (1992). Strategic Maneuvering and Mass-Market Dynamics: The Triumph of VHS over Beta. *The Business History Review, 66*(1), 51–94. doi: 10.2307/3117053

Danielson, W. A. (1956). Eisenhower's February decision: A study in news impact. *Journalism Quarterly, 33*, 433–441. doi: 10.1177/107769905603300402

Dobrow, J. R. (1990). *Social and cultural aspects of VCR use*. Hillsdale, NJ: Lawrence Erlbaum.

Early Television Museum (n.d). Early Color Television. Retrieved from https://www.earlytelevision.org/color.html

Emery, F. E. (1959). Psychological effects of the western film: A study in television viewing. *Human Relations, 12*, 195–213. doi: 10.1177/001872675901200301

Ephron, Erwin (1995), "What is recency?" Ephron consultancy. Retrieved from www.ephrononmedia.com

Ferguson, D. A., & Perse, E. M. (2004). Audience satisfaction among Tivo and Replaytv users. *Journal of Interactive Advertising, 4*(2), 1–8. doi: 10.1080/15252019.2004.10722082

Finney, R. G. (1997). *Time shifting*. In H. Newcomb (Ed.). *Encyclopedia of Television* (p. 1677). Chicago: Fitzroy Dearborn Publishers.

Fisch, Shalom M., & Truglio, Rosemarie T. (2001). *"G" is for growing: thirty years of research on children and Sesame Street*. Mahweh, NJ: Lawrence Erlbaum.

Friedman, W. (2006) Nets' study finds little difference in ad recall among DVR owners. *MediaPost*, Retrieved on November 8, 2019 from https://www.mediapost.com/publications/article/41938/nets-study-finds-little-difference-in-ad-recall-a.html

Ghosh, B. P., Galbreth, M. R., & Shang, G. (2013). The competitive impact of targeted television advertisements using DVR technology. *Decision Sciences, 44*(5), 951–971. doi: 10.1111/deci.12041

Ghosh, B., & Stock, A. (2010). Advertising effectiveness, digital video recorders, and product market competition. *Marketing Science, 29*(4), 639–649. doi: 10.1287/mksc.1090.0544

Gilmore, R. F., & Secunda, E. (1993). Zipped TV commercials boost prior learning. *Journal of Advertising Research, 33*, 28–38.

Gomery, D. (2001). Finding TV's pioneering audiences, *Journal of Popular Film and Television, 29*(3), 121–129. doi: 10.1080/01956050109601017

Gorham, M. (1952). *Broadcasting and television since 1900*. London: Andrew Daker's Ltd.

Greenberg, B. S., & Heeter, C. (1987). VCRs and young people: The picture at 39% penetration. *American Behavioral Scientist, 30*(5), 509–521. doi:10.1177/000276487030005006

Hamilton, R. V., & Lawless, R. H. (1956). Television within the social matrix. *Public Opinion Quarterly*, 20(2), 394–403. doi:10.1093/poq/20.2.394

Henke, L. L., & Donohue, T. R. (1989). Functional displacement of traditional TV viewing by VCR owners. *Journal of Advertising Research*, 29(2), 18–23.

Hovland, C. I., Lumsdaine, A. A., & Sheffield, F. D. (1949). *Experiments on mass communication*. (Studies in social psychology in World War II). Princeton, NJ: Princeton University Press.

Ironmonger, D. D., Lloyd-Smith, C. W., & Soupourmas, F. (2000). New Products of the 1980s and 1990s: The diffusion of household technology in the decade 1985–1995. *Prometheus, 18*(4), 403–415. doi: 10.1080/08109020020008514

Kent, B., Mosley, B. N., & Schweidel, D. A. (2019). Advertisements in DVR time: The shelf life of recorded television commercials in drama, reality, and sports programs. *Journal of Advertising Research*, 59(1), 73–84. doi: 10.2501/JAR-2018-042

Lazarsfeld, P. F. (1950). Research, argumentation and action in the media field. *Journalism Bulletin*, 27(3), 263–267. doi: 10.1177/107769905002700302

Levy, M. R. (1981). Home video recorders and time shifting. *Journalism Quarterly*, 58(3), 401–405. doi: 10.1177/107769908105800308

Levy, M. R. (1983). The time-shifting use of home video recorders. *Journal of Broadcasting*, 27(3), 263–268. doi: 10.1080/08838158309386491

Levy, M. R. (1987). VCR use and the concept of audience activity. *Communication Quarterly*, 35(3), 267–275. doi: 10.1080/01463378709369689

Lin, C. A. (1990). Audience activity and VCR use. In J. R. Dobrow (Ed.) *Social and cultural aspects of VCR use* (pp. 75–92). New York: Lawrence Erlbaum.

Lin, C. A. (1992). The functions of the VCR in the home leisure environment. *Journal of Broadcasting and Electronic Media*, 36(3), 345–352. https://doi.org/10.1080/08838159209364182

Lin, C.A. (2001). Television and the American family. In J. Bryant & J. A. Bryant (Eds.) *Television and the American family* (pp. 91–107). New York: Taylor and Francis.

Madden M (2009). The audience for online video-sharing sites shoots up. Retrieved from: http://fe01.pewinternet.org/Reports/2009/13-The-Audience-for-Online-VideoSharing-SitesShoots-Up.aspx

Madrigal, A. C. (2018). When did TV watching Peak? *The Atlantic* (May 30). Retrieved from https://www.theatlantic.com/technology/archive/2018/05/when-did-tv-watching-peak/561464/

McDonald, D. G., & Meng, J. (2008). The multitasking of entertainment. In S. Klienman (Ed.) *The Culture of Efficiency: Technology in Everyday Life* (pp. 142–157). New York: Peter Lang.

Morgan, M., Alexander, A., Shanahan, J., & Harris, C. (1990). Adolescents, VCRs, and the family environment. *Communication Research*, 17(1), 83–106. doi: 10.1177/009365090017001005

Morgan, M., & Shanahan, J. (1991). Do VCRs change the TV picture? VCRs and the cultivation process. *American Behavioural Scientist*, 35(2), 122–135. https://doi.org/10.1177/0002764291035002004

Nielsen Company (2012) Advertising & audiences: Part 2 by demographic. State of the Media.

Noble, G. (1987). The social significance of VCR technology: Television or not television? *The Information Society, 5*(3), 133–416. https://doi.org/10.1080/01972243.1988.9960054

Paulu, B. (1955). Audiences for broadcasting in Britain and America. *Journalism Quarterly, 32*(3), 329–334. doi: 10.1177/107769905503200307

Pearlin L. I. (1959). Social and personal stress and escape television viewing. *Public Opinion Quarterly, 23*(2), 255–259. doi: 10.1086/266870

Purcell, K. (2010). *The state of online video.* Retrieved from: http://pewinternet.org/Reports/2010/State-of-Online-Video.aspx

Robinson, J. P. (1969). Television and leisure time: Yesterday, today, and (maybe) tomorrow, *Public Opinion Quarterly, 33*(2), 210–222. doi: 10.1086/267692

Robinson, J. P., & Converse. P. E. (1972). The impact of television on mass media usage. In A. Szalai (Ed.) *The use of time* (pp. 197–212). Hague: Mouton.

Rogers, E. M. (1994). *A history of communication study: A biographical approach.* New York: The Free Press.

Roper, B. W. (1969). *A ten-year view of public attitudes toward television and other mass media 1959–1969.* New York: Roper Research Associates.

Rubin, A. M., & Bantz, C. R. (1987). Utility of videocassette recorders. *American Behavioural Scientist, 30*(5), 471–485. doi: 10.1177/000276487030005003

Rubin, A. M., & Rubin, R. B. (1989). Social and psychological antecedents of VCR Use. In M. R. Levy (Ed.) *The VCR age: Home video and mass communication* (pp. 92–111). New York: Sage.

Schonfeld, E. (2010) Live TV is for old people: Time shifting and online make up nearly half of all viewing. Available at: http://techcrunch.com/2010/08/30/video-time-shifting-online-half/

Schramm, W. (1949). The effects of mass communications: A review. *Journalism Bulletin, 26*(4), 397–409. doi: 10.1177/107769904902600403

Serjeant J (2010) Time-shifting on TV more than doubles in past year. Available at: http://www.reuters.com/article/2010/08/17/us-timeshifting-idUSTRE67G4IE20100817

Siddarth, S., & Chattopadhyay, A. (1998). To zap or not to zap: A study of the determinants of channel switching during commercials. *Marketing Science, 17*(2), 124–138. doi: 10.1287/mksc.17.2.124

Silvey, R. (1974). *Who's Listening?* London: George Allen and Unwin.

Sims, J. (1989). VCR viewing patterns: An electronic and passive investigation. *Journal of Advertising Research, 29*(2), 11–17.

Smith, D. C. (1961). The selectors of television programs, *Journal of Broadcasting, 6*(1), 35–44. doi: 10.1080/08838156109385990

Smith, S. M., & Krugman, D. M. (2009). Viewer as media decision-maker: Digital video recorders and household media consumption. *International Journal of Advertising. 28*(2), 231–255. doi: 10.2501/S0265048709200552

Steinberg, B. (2007). Networks compare apples to oranges when talking. *Advertising Age* (October 22), 26.

Steinberg, B., & Hampp, A. (2007). DVR ad skipping happens, but not always. *Advertising Age* (May 31).

Story, L. (2007) Viewers fast-forwarding past ads? Not always. *New York Times*. (Internet edition, 16 February), Retrieved November 8, 2019 from http://www.nytimes.com/2007/02/16/business/16commercials.html?ex=1329282000&en=ac19fdf65f3c4ef3&ei=5088&partner=rssnyt&emc=rss.

Stout, P. A., & Burda, B. L. (1989). Zipped commercials: Are they effective? *Journal of Advertising, 18*(4), 23–32. doi: 10.1080/00913367.1989.10673164

Thorson, E., & Zhao, X. (1997). Television viewing behavior as an indicator of commercial effectiveness. In W. D. Wells (Ed). *Measuring advertising effectiveness* (pp. 221–237). Mahwah, NJ: Lawrence Erlbaum.

Troldahl, V. C. (1965). Studies of consumption of mass media content. *Journalism Quarterly, 42*(4), 596–606. doi: 10.1177/107769906504200412

Tse, A. C. B., & Lee, R. P. W. (2001). Zapping behavior during commercial breaks. *Journal of Advertising Research, 41*(3), 25–29. doi: 10.2501/JAR-41-3-25-29

U.S. Surgeon General's Scientific Advisory Committee on Television and Social Behavior. (1972). *Television and growing up: The impact of televised violence* (DHEW Publication No. HSM 72-9086). Washington, DC: U.S. Government Printing Office.

Van der Bulck, J. (1999). VCR-use and patterns of time shifting and selectivity. *Journal of Broadcasting & Electronic Media, 43*(3), 316326. doi: 10.1080/08838159909364494

Westley, B. H., & Mobius, J. B. (1960). A closer look at the non-television household. *Journal of Broadcasting, 4*(2), 164–173. doi: 10.1080/08838156009385917

Wilbur, K. C. (2008). How the Digital Video Recorder (DVR) changes traditional television advertising? *Journal of Advertising, 37*(1), 143–149. doi: 10.2753/JOA0091-3367370111

Williams, R. (1974). *Television: Technology and cultural form*. Hanover: Wesleyan University Press.

Woltman Elpers, J. L. C. M., Wedel, M., & Pieters, R. G. M. (2003). Why do consumers stop viewing television commercials? Two Experiments on the influence of moment-to-moment entertainment and information value. *Journal of Marketing Research, 40*(4), 437–453. doi: 10.1509/jmkr.40.4.437.19393

Zaslow, J. (2002). If TiVo Thinks you are gay, here's how to set it straight. *Wall Street Journal* (November 26). Retrieved from http://www.tprophet.org/dialtone/linkedpics/TivoThinksGay.pdf

CHAPTER THREE

An Industry Perspective: Changing Competitors, Content, and Content Curation

Q: Did you watch TV last night? A: Yes/No (Select one).

The survey question above has only recently become more complicated to answer than it sounds. Does this include a Netflix drama viewed on a large screen TV in the living room? What about a Netflix original film? Does it include a half-hour long sitcom that aired last week on ABC, viewed on *Hulu* on a television screen? On a laptop? On a phone? What about professionally produced content on YouTube, Facebook, or Snapchat? What about user-generated content on the same platforms? From the industry side, are we including DTHT? OTT? IPTV? SVOD? VOD? UGM? Digital video? Film? Ads? A literal glossary of abbreviations is necessary to translate the relevant industry terms related to content types, sources, and delivery platforms.

Relatively current data on what people are viewing and via what platforms have been presented in Chapter 1 (i.e., Much of it is time-shifted, viewed on-demand, and across screens). A brief accounting of historically relevant details was presented in Chapter 2 (i.e., the importance of timeshifting enabled by the VCR). The goal of this chapter is to breakdown the relevant *industry competitors, content characteristics*, and *content curation strategies* that afford binge watching in today's media landscape. This is, of course, a difficult task to keep current on. This chapter attempts to situate binge watching among industry players and practices at the beginning of the 2020s. *Specifically, this chapter examines changes in television distribution, content, and audience flow strategies:* It attempts to understand who and what affords binge watching, and how they entice you to watch and binge watch.

1. *The Who – Industry Competitors*: From the national network and affiliate model to OTT services, we discuss the practices of those responsible for distributing and curating content for viewers.
2. *The What – Content Characteristics*: What content is treated as a premium in the current television viewing era? What structural and narrative characteristics make for the most-watched and most-binged television shows, and how are these characteristics evolving?
3. *The How – Curating Content*: We borrow Sorensen's (2014) turn of phrase to discuss how content is attained and then presented to audiences in a way to maximize audience flow. The last section discusses overlaps in practices to keep viewers watching, and preferably binge watching, among OTT services (namely Netflix) and the traditional network model' audience flow strategies.

The Who: Changes in Industry Competitors

In every "Introduction to Broadcasting" or "Mass Media" undergraduate course, we teach about broadcast networks (and later, cable) as the basis of commercial broadcasting in the United States. These networks are synonymous with 20th-century television, and their current role and relevance is at the heart of determining who retains power and financial control in a television industry that has decidedly and, rapidly, evolved. Netflix has become synonymous with binge watching in popular culture, and other over-the-top (OTT) streaming providers are also major players in today's television market (e.g., Amazon Prime Video, Hulu, HBO Now, Disney+). While Netflix may currently reign supreme as the OTT service to beat, some interesting data on *what* people are bingeing on the service signals that new options will present formidable competition. The traditional hold over consumers and advertising dollars that networks have had in the past is facing a direct threat from these OTT services. The current section discusses these audience-facing entities: networks, OTT services, and the new competitors on the horizon. Together, they constitute *who* affords binge watching for audiences. These make up a different, larger group of providers than were common in 20th-century television media, as we observe how the turn of the century and beyond can be described as a television industry shift from "Network TV" to "Networked TV" (Palmer, 2006), or to a "Post-Network Era" (Lotz, 2007), "Post-TV" (Strangelove, 2015), "Matrix TV" or "Post Broadcast Era" (Curtin, 2009). A variety of names have been offered and will continue to be offered in the coming years, to describe this switch from the traditional television model to current day practices.

There has been an undeniable shift from a network model, characterized as "a platform that has been created to enable video content to be pushed from a single point to a larger audience" (Cunningham & Silver, 2013). The new model is characterized as distinct from the unidirectional pushing of messages to mass audiences: It allows for interactive exchanges, a plurality of uses, and does not treat the audience as an undifferentiated mass (Curtin, 2009). It relies on ever-evolving networked distribution technologies that can send differentiated messages to niche audiences (Palmer, 2006). Lotz (2007) qualifies the current "Post-Network Era" as a decided break from traditional linear viewing options, one wherein viewers select what, when, and where to view from abundant options.

The Traditional Model: National Networks and Affiliates

The emergence of the "Big 3" networks during the early days of television's first Golden Age (1950s) was a smart solution to the encumbrance of analog video transmission, modeled after broadcast radio transmission before it. Since a single channel could only reach a geographically limited area, it made sense to build a network of stations nationally to reach larger audience shares. Likewise, every local station needed content to broadcast. Thus, networks gained affiliates in local stations across the country, and we all came to know ABC, NBC, and CBS, and later Fox, Telemundo, Univision, and the CW. For a time, there was an adequate amount of content for the Big 3 to fill primetime viewing across the country, and enough syndicated and local content to fill less-watched dayparts. That was the extent of television content, save for some local, independent programming and non-commercial content, which became somewhat networked later on. Studios sold pilots and seasons to broadcast networks, networks provided content and received advertising slots via affiliate agreements with stations across the country, and advertisers worked with networks and affiliates at the national and local levels. The growth of cable television in the 1980s, alongside widespread adoption of VCRs in homes, are the first two of many innovations that began a shift of viewing power and autonomy from networks to viewers.

Had television started with the technological innovations we have now – cable delivery, direct-to-home satellite delivery (DBS; e.g., Dish), digital transmission, the Internet, etc. – one can imagine that the national network and local affiliate model would not be a foregone conclusion. Other ways of distributing content may have emerged. The demand for high-quality content among geographically distant others would likely call for some networking of content, but other systems of monetization – such as we saw when cable emerged, may have proliferated.

However, local affiliates and national networks are still very much the structure of today's "broadcast" television. Local television markets operate within Nielsen's 210 DMAs (Designated Market Areas) across the country, as they have for decades. Each affiliate was built with offices, studios, engineers, transmitters, etc. for analog transmission, contributing to the relatively hefty infrastructure cost (Palmer, 2006). As compression technologies evolve, bandwidth and processing power increases, the availability of the Internet as a lower-cost alternative delivery system has been adopted by more and more households. Both traditional network content – carried on affiliates in different markets – and cable networks (e.g., ESPN, HGTV, USA) are now digitally transmitted to subscribers across the United States. Customers typically pay a systems operator or multiple systems operator (MSO) who offer multiple services, or systems, such as Internet and phone. An average viewer at home may or may not be aware of what networks are cable or broadcast. As professors of undergraduate media classes, and specifically of those large "Introduction to Broadcasting" courses mentioned, it is our experience that college students *studying television* are often unaware of broadcast network and cable network distinctions. If viewers are aware, it is even further unlikely that they are making daily entertainment viewing choices based on a network brand preference. A notable current-day exception to this would be cable network news viewing choices.

Broadcast and cable networks have seen a flurry of mergers in the late 2010s. There are a multitude of sources and important discussions on the downstream effects of media conglomeration and ensuing policy regulations (or, more recently, deregulation). The relevance here is smaller in scope: How do vertically integrated conglomerates (i.e., ones with stakes in content production and distribution) compete against OTT services? Who among networks and OTT services are better enabling viewers to access the content they want to watch – and want to binge? The relevance of networks has come under fire among industry commentators and academics alike. What, exactly, do network affiliates do for viewers (and hence, advertisers) if not what they were initially designed to do (i.e., reach large geographic swathes of the country)? In the United States, traditional "broadcast" networks and cable networks alike are subsidiaries of multi-conglomerate corporations.

Media content and distribution are vertically integrated into companies such as ABC/Disney, where production companies, networks, and MSOs operate within one company. Mergers and acquisitions have occurred at breakneck speed in recent years in direct response to OTT threats such as Netflix and Amazon (not to mention ventures by household names such as Google, Facebook, and YouTube). For instance, AT&T, a long-standing telephone company, acquired Time Warner media in 2018. This acquisition includes networks and content creators, including HBO, Turner Media, DC Comics, New Line Cinema, and multiple distribution channels in addition to cell service, including U-Verse cable offerings and satellite via Direct TV (Fortune, 2018; Mills, 2018). These types of mergers – where control over both content and distribution can fall under one company, and ultimately one bottom line – are increasingly common.

Are Networks Dead? On Branding, Screen Networks, and Disintermediation

Palmer (2006) makes the extreme claim that television networks, as we know them, are "brand-to-brand" brands, meaning they no longer function as consumer brands. They exist in the marketplace but are relatively meaningless to viewers at home. Indeed, "I can't wait to go home and watch ABC tonight" is not a common refrain. Palmer states that great *products* make great brands – not the other way around. Season after season, traditional broadcast networks produce multiple flops. Local affiliates work to brand their local news content, and cable networks are generally better at consistent, specific branding. This, of course, is aided by relying on more niche audience segmentation than mass audience desirability. While she notes that the traditional broadcast networks have succeeded in branding their news and sports content, the network itself is not a strong brand, which makes it more vulnerable to competition.

> You won't pick a broadcast network name from a list on your DVR or your VOD system, you'll pick a show name or show genre to explore. This will bode well for a branded network environment like Discovery or Disney, but it may be absolutely devastating (from a consumer branding perspective) for broadcast networks. The primetime entertainment divisions don't have the brand power to make the transition. (Palmer, 2007, p. 112)

The above quotation is from *2007*. VOD systems have expanded and evolved, and clearly OTTs have entered the equation. Importantly, Palmer makes this claim way before Netflix's noteworthy algorithms curate extremely targeted content not just to households, but to individual users on an account (which can, of course, be accessed from anywhere). This is not the first academic text to cite Netflix CEO Reed Hasting's famous (or infamous?) quote about broadcast television being like a horse, and "the horse was good until we had the car" (Hastings, 2014 cited in Doyle, 2016). The insinuation that not just OTT services, in general, but specifically Netflix could replace the broadcast network is one that many well-established players in the industry are not too keen on seeing come to fruition.

In a thorough monograph accounting of industry start-ups and shifts against a backdrop of lessons to be learned from television displacing the prominence of movie theaters, Cunningham and Silver (2013) describe what makes a successful "screen network." They use this term to move the idea of a "network" beyond traditional television networks. Indeed, the companies they discuss as potential top "screen networks" – Google/YouTube, Apple, Amazon, Yahoo!, Facebook, Netflix, and Hulu – are not television networks. They posit that Internet companies are uniquely better poised than today's television networks for success, while acknowledging the major push from traditional networks to maintain their staying power. All the above companies know much more about their audiences because their business model is fundamentally *not* built on mass appeal. This narrowcasting affordance is a clear advantage over broadcast networks. These companies face cheaper marketing costs (i.e., no local affiliate stations as intermediary).

An additional, critical advantage is that of *distribution*, not *content*. "Content is King" is an idiom in the industry – if you have the best content, you'll command the most viewers, and you can charge advertisers (or subscribers) higher rates. Cunningham and Silver (2013) claim this statement is a relic of the old broadcast television system. The authors maintain that if content is indeed "King," then *distribution* is "King Kong." They argue television is being reinvented "within an online, broadband-enabled, transnational if not global, paradigm" (p. 9). These researchers are hesitant of critical and social scientific media scholars who tend to espouse either extreme optimism about the opportunities new technologies (and especially Internet access) create or lament a crisis for the current industry that technology has created. Critical to the future, these new potential "screen networks" have not underscored or ignored international growth opportunities. In addition to these features, the authors hypothesize that ultimately successful screen networks will be able to credit their success to a number of other abilities that set them apart from traditional television networks, including reaching all major markets/ cities, procuring desirable content, distributing a slate of diverse programming from a central point, and marketing a brand based on quality content.

Strangelove (2015) takes the diminishing role of networks a step further, characterizing the new content distribution era as one of "disintermediation," where streaming services are cutting out the middlemen between producers and consumers. Instead of new screen networks emerging, as discussed by Cunningham and Silver, Strangelove's "Post-TV" era imagines audiences interacting directly with content producers. He describes Netflix as a "frenemy" of the television industry. They earn this title by being friendly with the content creation departments – purchasing most of their content from major studios such as Paramount, Sony, 20th Century Fox, MGM, and Time Warner, while likely taking away audiences from the distribution arms of these same conglomerate entities.

Of course, not all are so quick to question the staying power of traditional television networks. Broadcast networks have inertia on their side: Regulations and policy have long backed them, and despite rises in cord-cutting (discussed in

Chapter 6), consumers are used to paying a systems operator for broadcast and cable content, especially since the switch to digital television nearly 10 years ago in the United States. While cord-cutting and non-linear viewing has led to consistent declines in ratings for broadcast and cable in the late 2010s, networks with large, older audiences (e.g., CBS) and with mega events, such as the Superbowl and the Olympics (e.g., NBC in 2018), remain at the top in terms of overall viewership numbers (Schneider, 2018). In fact, CBS' strategy of non-risk taking, "meat and potatoes" fare, or the number of reliable, conservative crime shows that millions watch and critics largely ignore has paid off. CBS has topped annual ratings more than any other broadcast network in the past 10 years (VanDerWerff, 2016).

Despite some advantages and continued, smaller successes, no reputable industry, popular media, or academic sources are calling television in 2020 a "traditional network model." Indeed, networks continue to operate and distribute content, as some entity must. Quite simply, there will always be an interface between content and consumers. The brands, the technology, and the ways consumers view are all changing. The only way to finance content production and distribution (keeping in mind the cost-saving in distribution that OTT has capitalized on) is a model where consumers pay, either directly (via subscription or pay-per-view models) or indirectly (via advertising). Television networks' abilities to aggregate programs, operate with distinctive identities, and help viewers find content of interest are traditional network practices that still meet a need (Lotz, 2007).

What Comes Next Then? Looking Ahead

While networks may seem to be at odds with OTT services, the consumer demand for "TV Everywhere" has forced the hand of networks to move forward with online viewing options in one form or another. Many, if not all, broadcast networks and major cable networks are vested in online viewing platforms. Some networks are vested through different subsidiaries of the mega media conglomerates of which they are a member. Hulu, for instance, originated as a joint venture across media companies and major networks. However, between two major deals with Fox and then AT&T, Disney went from owning 33% of the venture to a dominating 66%, with Comcast owning the remaining third, across 2018–2019. These acquisitions are notable considering the recent launch of their own OTT service, Disney+ in November 2019 (Gartenberg, 2019). Bundling Disney+ with ESPN+ and Hulu could make the competition to services such as Sling TV and YouTube TV formidable, not to mention competition with Netflix. Netflix CEO Reed Hastings has said that they look forward to the strong competition and are used to it as they've been competing with Amazon for the past decade (BBC News, 2018). While the competition may be welcome (or, at least expected) for Netflix, many critics suggest that this move may add one more OTT services consumers must purchase in order to have access to the content they desire. How many streaming services is too many? How do households with regular cable television bills make these decisions differently than those relying on only OTT services? Time will tell what may serve as a tipping point for many consumers. Will content cease to be broadcast on linear digital television?

A case study of BBC3 going all online – and dropping their television broadcast station – was conducted by Doyle (2016), and the lessons revealed by her analysis are relevant here. The BBC3 channel is the more youth-oriented brand in the BBC's portfolio. The research goal was to identify whether this move made economic sense for an established channel. In short, it made no sense at all. Doyle cites viewing statistics from 2014 showing 69% of television viewing was done watching live, linear programming, and that a considerable share of viewers, or viewing minutes, are lost when moving exclusively online. As an established channel being part of the larger BBC organization, the move saved little money in distribution costs. While they were able to cut their content budget by 50%, this is counter to BBC's stated goals of extending the reach of their content and bringing in more creative content. Doyle (2016) concludes that linear channel delivery offers unrivaled ability to manage audience flow through bundling, programming strategies, and branding opportunities, and at the current time in the marketplace, online-only for an existing channel is not a good economic move. The BBC has had more success in *multiplatform* distribution through their regular BBC channel and the BBC iPlayer, which seems to meet viewers' growing need for complementary online viewing options. These notions of the advantages of network linear transmission – audience flow, bundling of new and old content or channels, and branding will become a theme in the ongoing discussion of distribution powerhouses.

Is the New Model Simply Netflix?

Netflix continues to globalize its brand and reach new customers to ensure growth, with a large international focus in recent years. Despite competition from homegrown streaming services in countries like France and India, and international competition from Amazon Prime (who were operating in Germany and India before Netflix), growth has been rapid and successful (Brennan, 2018).

> Netflix's global growth is a big factor in the company's success. By 2017 it was operating in over 190 countries, and today close to 73 million of its some 130 million subscribers are outside the U.S. In the second quarter of 2018, its international streaming revenues exceeded domestic streaming revenues for the first time. This is a remarkable

achievement for a company that was only in the U.S. before 2010, and in only 50 countries by 2015. (Brennan, 2018)

There are now more Netflix subscribers worldwide than all other streaming services combined. This success is due in part to their expansion strategies. When entering new markets, Netflix first entered those which were like its existing market(s); Canada was the second country that Netflix operates in. When launching the service, Netflix targets early adapters and then builds features over time to gain a wider audience (Brennan, 2018). As they accelerated the pace of their global reach, they also invested in improving the mobile experience for viewers, as mobile is the primary way that many parts of the world access the Internet.

Despite a negative cash flow of 690 million dollars over the third quarter in 2018, CEO Reed Hastings said they will continue their growth by "investing in content ahead of revenue" (BBC News, 2018). According to a tally by *Quartz*, Netflix debuted approximately 345 new titles (in the United States) in 2018, for a total of 90,000 minutes, or 1,500 hours of original productions. To view all of it would take 4 hours per day, every day, in 2018 (Rodriguez, 2019). And that is in just one of the 17 original content markets that Netflix operates in (Brennan, 2018).

All news on Netflix content acquisition bears out this business model. These investments have been part of a long-term plan on the part of Netflix, with an eye on future streaming service competition for titles. Recent and soon-to-be streaming services, discussed below, are mostly different from past competitors due to their Hollywood backing. With major studios and content ownership held by new competitors, much of Netflix's "library programming," or non-originals, may be up for expensive renegotiation, or pulled from the negotiating table in part or entirely. Many Netflix originals receive critical acclaim and serve to draw new subscribers, no doubt. Shows such as *House of Cards* and reappraising *Arrested Development* helped solidify Netflix's brand as it established itself as a premier streaming service. Titles since then have been well received by critics and viewers alike and dominated popular culture discussions of must-see TV since, including *Orange Is the New Black*, *The Crown*, *Tiger King*, and *Stranger Things*, etc. Time spent viewing original programming on the streaming service continues to grow. Not to mention their success with original feature-length films, including major A-List star power – Meryl Streep, Sandra Bullock, Will Smith, not to mention others, as well as showrunners, directors, and producers that are also household names. Netflix received a 2018 Best Picture Oscar nomination for *Roma* – which will likely not be their last. The Academy announced it will not introduce new rules pertaining to longer distribution windows of theatrical releases and streaming service eligibility for awards, despite considerable pushback from the film industry, including a vocal Steven Spielberg (Ha, 2019).

However, Netflix has quite a bit of competition headed its way. Three of Netflix's largest suppliers of content have recently introduced streaming services, including: Comcast's NBCUniversal, AT&T's TimeWarner, and Disney+. Nielsen data, as reported for *The Wall Street Journal*, recently shows that 72% of the time individuals spend watching Netflix is spent on library programming, or reruns (Flint & Sharma, 2019). While "reruns" may not be the first word that comes to mind when thinking about binge watching, the content that these major industry players are working so hard to attain and deliver while maximizing their financial investments is critical to the current discussion.

The What: Content Characteristics

Lotz (2007) states that the post network era can be characterized in large part by the changes in distribution windows available due to changing technologies. In the traditional network era, there were two options for successful primetime content after a first run: international distribution and domestic syndication. Channels, most often network affiliates across the country, would pay for exclusive rights to re-broadcast a show. These deals would include how many times they could air each episode and would often guarantee market exclusivity. Television shows typically had to reach 100 episodes to make it into syndication. How important are the shows created for and broadcast entirely on network television to current discussions of competition for viewers among old and new players? How relevant are older titles to larger discussions about binge watching? The case of *Friends* would suggest a clear answer: very much.

The "Most Binged" Shows Are Not What You Think They Are

Friends, which debuted in 1995 and enjoyed high ratings throughout its original run on NBC, did not go into syndication until 1998 (Lotz, 2007). Interestingly, we have noted how ubiquitous *Friends* fanship, or at least familiarity, is among *today's college students* both in our classrooms and in our research on television and binge watching. In our qualitative investigations of binge watching (presented in more detail in Chapter 5), we heard multiple instances of undergraduate participants talking about viewing *Friends* via a streaming service, typically as content that was easy to watch and complete other tasks, or "media multitask." Beyond that, when searching for a television show to use as an example in classroom discussions, or asking students to name their favorite television shows, *Friends* comes up more often than many other recent popular sitcoms, including *How I Met Your Mother* and *The Big Bang Theory*. The *Friends* series finale was broadcast in 2004. So, typical college students watched the show in some combination of syndication (A person could probably find an episode of *Friends* on right now, in any given market, across cable and broadcast syndication.), and OTT providers, namely Netflix. Beyond our anecdotal observations, recent data show that in 2018, *Friends* accounted for the second most viewing minutes across *all* Netflix titles – nearly 2% of all viewing minutes (Flint & Sharma, 2019)!

Why *Friends*? It's widespread availability in syndication, DVD sales, and availability on Netflix and VOD, paired with ten full seasons of content, has made it one of a handful of extremely visible syndicated sitcoms for years. It was at its height of popularity in a time when, despite competition from cable, network primetime offerings still commanded larger audience shares. The "reality TV" phenomenon was not in full swing. *Survivor*, often credited with starting the wave of reality content, premiered in 2000. Competition from streaming services was absent. Some may argue that OTTs and the declining power of the major television networks have led to less megahits, that more targeted niche content means a more fragmented audience, who select content from a larger pool of options. Aspects of the show itself may also be driving force: Co-creator of *Friends* Marta Kauffman commented recently that *Friends*' continued success, 15 years after going off the air, was a "glorious surprise." She commented that its endurance is related to its overall tone: "It's not dark, it's not twisted, it's not about corrupt people. It's comfort food" (Flint & Sharma, 2019).

Not twisted? *Not* dark? These are the very qualities that embody television shows that dominate popular discussion about binge watching. Binge watching is situated in discussions about suspenseful, engaging, compelling serialized dramas – which nearly always contain darker elements, conflicted, complicated characters, an antihero (or two), and nuanced portrayals of the complexities inherent to the human condition. No one can call Ross Gellar a dark, complicated antihero. He had a pet monkey. He thought they "were on a break." He bleached his teeth alarmingly white; he wore horrible leather pants – need we go on?

Why *Friends* and *The Office* Matter

Yet, *Friends* has continued to demonstrate its tremendous staying power specifically on Netflix – a service often viewed synonymously with binge watching. Netflix had previously scheduled *Friends* to leave the streaming service in January 2019. This sent Twitter into full "shock and awe" mode (Raftery, 2018). In a very quick turnaround, Netflix announced in December 2018 that they brokered a deal with the show's owners, Warner Media, for $100 million to keep the show for another year. According to off-the-record sources, this is more than a threefold jump from the $30 million Netflix has paid annually prior to the deal (Flint & Sharma, 2019; Raftery, 2018). The steep jump in price is an apt example of both Netflix's continued strategy to edge out any competition by acquiring an obscene amount of content, and perhaps of troubles ahead. The emergence of three Hollywood rivals launching their own streaming services means that their catalog of non-original content will likely become smaller, and cost more. Netflix's most watched show is *The Office*, a title owned by NBCUniversal, is under contract until 2021, and accounted for nearly 3% of all viewing minutes on Netflix in the United States in 2018. These viewing minutes data and those cited below come from a Nielsen analysis for *The Wall Street Journal* in Flint and Sharma (2019). It is quite likely that NBCUniversal will want to move *The Office* to their own streaming endeavor. As Hollywood rivals to Netflix jump into the streaming game, much of Netflix's non-original content is at risk of coming at enormous price increases or becoming available on other platforms instead of *Netflix*. Flint and Sharma's (2019) report examines the total minutes across programs, and then looked at the studios who hold those programs. A full 55% of Netflix's 2018 viewing minutes in the United States were of content owned by Disney, NBCUniversal and TimeWarner/ Warner Bros. Studios. All three of these entities had plans to launch their own streaming services in 2019/2020.

Across 12 months of 2017–2018, *Friends* accounted for 31.8 billion minutes of viewing time, *The Office* accounted for 45.8 billion minutes, in combination accounting for about 5% of all viewing time on the platform. In contrast, the second season of Netflix original *Stranger Things* accounted for 27.6 billion minutes of viewing (Flint & Sharma, 2019). According to data compiled by Nielsen for *The Wall Street Journal*, 8 of the 10 most viewed titles on Netflix were reruns in 2018, with *Orange Is the New Black* and *Ozark* – the only two originals cracking the top 10 shows with the most viewed minutes. While Netflix maintains a general policy of not commenting on outside viewing metrics (Flint & Sharma, 2019), and a well-known policy of not disclosing viewing data, a "most viewed minutes" approach clearly favors some content over others. There are 235 episodes of *Friends*; 201 episodes of *The Office*. Of the top 10 most minutes viewed shows in the Nielsen/ *The Wall Street Journal* analysis, the two Netflix originals that made the list contained the smallest number of available episodes to view. This is certainly a silver lining for Netflix, who has spent several years spending considerable amounts of money on new, original content.

Certainly, beyond time spent on a medium, there is the allure of big show and film titles that serve as an initial reason to sign up for an OTT service in the first place. Clearly, there are multiple measures to explore how the mix of reruns and original programming are viewed and perceived by Netflix viewers. It is crucial to keep in mind that owners of content including titles like *Friends* and *The Office* are undoubtedly motivated to promote the measures that paint their content in a positive light, while Netflix, like networks before it, is motivated to present their content viewing data in the most positive light. Indeed, in response to the Nielsen analysis presented by *The Wall Street Journal*, Netflix stressed that examining minutes viewed favors longer running shows, while many originals have only several seasons. This practice further underrepresents the draw of films, which are obviously constrained in length as compared to series. A Netflix spokesperson says that they prefer to look at *what* shows individuals watch, not only the time spent viewing each show. They maintain that Netflix has typically been well served by focusing on the *quality* of their original programming in recent years (Flint & Sharma, 2019). While Netflix has often become synonymous with binge watching, it has also been associated with the term "prestige TV," though to a lesser degree. Many of its original series, complete with drama, suspense, and some relative darkness, have garnered critical acclaim and popularity. However, they are not the only distributors who have contributed to an era of television some say is now squarely waning – in part due to Netflix's current content acquisition strategy.

"Binge-worthy" TV: How Content Has Changed How We Talk About TV

Often referred to as the new "Golden Age" of television, and later, "Peak TV" (Carr, 2014; Cowan, 2013), this era of "prestige TV" is often credited with beginning around the premiere of *The Sopranos* on HBO, in 1999, and was certainly underway when HBO released their next critically acclaimed hit, *The Wire*, in 2002. "Peak TV" characterizes a slightly different timeframe and has as much to do with the sheer quantity of programs as the quality of them. For students of television studies, the Golden Age of television may first spark a brief memory of textbook accounts of the 1950s television era – dominated entirely by the Big 3 networks (NBC, CBS, and ABC), in a time where television household penetration rates were saturated and several early "hits" are recognized. This new Golden Age is quite different. It is characterized as a change (almost exclusively for the better) in *quality* – one that "shift[s] away from the lower budget procedurals and toward often serialized and acclaimed television programs with cinema quality production values" (Franklin, 2018). The 2000s' Golden Age of television is characterized as building on some of the more niche programming successes of the 1990s and moving further away from the network procedural dramas that were quite successful in the 1980s and 1990s. Some television scholars and critics refer to the second Golden Age of television as the influx of procedural dramas on network television in the 1980s.

The newest (third) Golden Age of television boasts many titles seemingly *meant* for binge watching: It is more high-brow content with complexities that rival novels. Cowan (2013) quotes numerous industry sources who talk about television taking new risks, pushing the envelope, going beyond what you see major films doing, and providing much more character depth, with seasons to explore complex, novel characters. It is content that makes watching it late into the night an acceptable, or at least understandable, occurrence. Listicles of "what to binge next" from dozens of online sources include the seminal series of this era.

Television, Cowan (2013) notes, grew up in this new Golden Age, and we have *The Sopranos* to thank for revolutionizing television. The storytelling, characters, and production value – everything down to the dialogue is described as becoming more prestige, more film-like, and more authentic. *Boardwalk Empire* executive producer Terence Winter offers an interesting description of how dialogue has evolved:

> That is incredibly freeing to write those types of exchanges where you think, wow, this actually sounds like you're eavesdropping on a real conversation as opposed to "point, counterpoint, point-counterpoint, punch line," which is generally the type of dialogue that you'd get in a network show. (p. 2)

If the dialogue has become more true-to-life, and less "scripted" so to speak, characters have come to defy many scriptwriting conventions as well. These flawed and seemingly more authentic characters have contributed to the new ways we have water cooler discussions about what we watched on TV last night (Carr, 2014). He writes for *The New York Times*,

> The growing intellectual currency of television has altered the cultural conversation in fundamental ways. Water cooler chatter is now a high-minded pursuit, not just a way to pass the time at work. The three-camera sitcom with a laugh track has been replaced by television shows that are much more like books — intricate narratives full of text, subtext and clues.

Surely, this is a change in how television is perceived in a popular culture. It often has been just that: pop culture. "The boob tube," watched incessantly by the "couch potato," is blamed, largely speculatively, for any number of societal plights, from increased aggression due to exposure to violence, to increased obesity due to said couch potatoing. Carr notes "The idiot box gained heft and intellectual credibility to the point where you seem dumb if you are not watching it." Indeed, in his book on the "difficult men" who serve as the main characters in several prestige dramas of the era, Brett Martin writes that TV has become the "signature American art form" (Reese, 2018) "the equivalent of what the films of Scorsese, Altman,

Coppola, and others had been to the 1970s or the novels of Updike, Roth, and Mailer had been to the 1960s."

Increases in the quality and the quantity of content have allowed for many viewers to become more discerning. The sheer quantity of options allow viewers to indulge more niche interests. The quality of content improved greatly with this wave of series – across any number of indicators. Beyond dialogue, script-writing, and acting, the cinematography, special effects, and big budget productions of shows like *Game of Thrones* are a spectacle to view that is unlike any other era in television history. At the same time improvements in the quality of television are noted across critics and viewers alike in the early 2000s; we certainly have evidence that *not all* content is worthy of a "Golden Age" or "prestige" label. *Friends* and *The Office*, whose popularity continues, are funny, relatable, mass-appeal sitcoms. Much further down the continuum of "prestige," there are a host of reality programming options that also crop up during this period. MTV's *The Jersey Shore*, Bravo's *The Real Housewives* series, not to mention *Here Comes Honey Boo Boo*, and any number of other reality shows that run the gamut from guilty pleasure to exploitative. The increased quantity of content, alongside the proliferation of reality content ushered in by *Survivor* in tandem with prestige dramas and networks, is often left out of the conversation about content.

What Makes Content "Binge-Worthy?"

Central to nearly every look at this prestigious "Golden Age" of television are four shows: HBO's *The Sopranos* and *The Wire*, and AMC's *Breaking Bad* and *Mad Men*. A look at the similarities of these four shows sparks examples of other shows in the same vein. First, like many character-driven shows, many viewers started viewing *after* a season or two aired, as the shows generated positive word-of-mouth and media attention. On-demand or OTT services afforded many viewers the opportunity to catch-up or view these shows in their entirety. While many a television fan has viewed some or all these television shows, most did not start watching each from their first episode was broadcast, especially among younger audiences. *HBO* and *AMC* are also responsible for several other groundbreaking television shows over the years, including *Six Feet Under, Game of Thrones, Sex in the City*, and *The Walking Dead*. They remain in the hunt for prestige programming today. Continuing to secure such content guarantees network appeal.

These shows also pioneered the modern antihero. Martin (2013) chronicles the main characters of each of these four series and two others in his book, *Difficult Men: Behind the Scenes of a Creative Revolution: From The Sopranos and The Wire to Mad Men and Breaking Bad.* He characterizes them each as "unhappy, morally compromised, complicated, deeply human," and unlike any antiheros we've seen on television before. Martin makes the case for television to be an ideal format for the complex narratives surrounding the antiheroes he writes about:

> When you have the time to tell a 13-hour, 26-hour, 39-hour story, when you don't have to end artificially, that lends itself to serious work. Film in the last ten years, by and large, is more analogous to the networks--they still need a massive audience. I think there's something innate in television--the open-endedness--that makes it suited to evolve as long as the show can sustain, and that necessitates a dark view of life. One of the great themes of these shows is addiction and falling back into it. Nobody gets better. It keeps the story-engine moving. (quoted in Reese, 2013)

In addition to Tony Soprano, Omar Little, Don Draper, and Walter White, Martin chronicles two other well-known antiheroes: *Dexter's* Dexter Morgan and *Boardwalk Empire's* Nucky Thompson. And as for the similarities between all six of these leads? All of them are male. They are murderers, largely (sorry about the company you keep, Don). Certainly, they run the gamut from morally ambiguous to clearly immoral. Ross Gellar, these men are not! And yet, who wasn't rooting Walter White, right up to the electrifying, impossible end? Who didn't watch in delight every time Omar Little was on screen? Why are we drawn to these stories and these characters? Martin speculates that before Tony Soprano murdered someone on screen (with his bare hands, on a college visit with his daughter!), audiences just weren't ready or willing to invite that kind of hero into their living room (Reese, 2018). While the content of these shows has strayed from the procedural format, they haven't left the subject matter completely behind: Crime is central to nearly all these shows. They are dark. The character development required to root for – or even to be able to tolerate at some points in the tumultuous story arcs presented – do indeed require the longer storytelling window that Martin argues television is perfect for.

The antiheroes in these widely regarded prestige dramas are all men and present some very distinct versions of masculinity (Martin, 2013). While they are surrounded by powerful portrayals of women around them (e.g., Eddi Falco as Carmella Soprano; every female actor in *Mad Men*), we are slower to see the stories of difficult women. Rarer still are truly unlikeable and amoral women. In fact, the fan backlash to Walter White's wife, Skylar, in *Breaking Bad* is a prime example. Despite a handful of exceptions to the rule in well-received (but not era-defining) shows such as *Nurse Jackie*, *Homeland*, and *Killing Eve*, much of prestige television has been men's stories, told by men. Scholars far more expert in sex and gender portrayals in media have no doubt weighed in, as have the popular press. Nicholson (2018) notes in *The Guardian*,

The idea that women can be unlikable is becoming more of a given. As audiences, we are being presented again and again with characters' amorality. In part, that's because these need to be entertaining stories; people behaving well rarely lends itself to gripping drama.

Reverse Engineering Binge-Worthy Content

House of Cards, a Netflix original, has often also been discussed among the greats of "prestige" or the "Golden Age" of television. Its antihero, Frank Underwood, is no exception to the male antiheros discussed above. In an interesting critical analysis of the first several seasons of *House of Cards*, McCormick (2016) argues that the show is transformative in production, distribution, and in changing the narrative experience by "explicitly inviting the viewer to binge" (p. 101). This case study explores a fundamentally important question to us in this chapter: Is *content* changing to support binge watching and other new viewing behaviors? McCormick's (2016) analysis details numerous ways that *House of Cards* differs from the network and prestige dramas which preceded it. Two major themes throughout the storytelling are carefully created changes in temporality (1) and emotional intensity (2), which McCormick argues serve to further elicit viewer attention and immersion. This leads to continued binging. McCormick cites an analogy that a serialized drama, as told weekly in linearly viewed installments, is like a good relationship with friends we get to see once a week. Whereas, a drama made explicitly for binge watching is more of an intense affair.

How does *House of Cards* differ from a weekly serialized drama? Structurally, there are no recaps on what viewers missed last time – in this way the show assumes you just viewed the previous episode (McCormick, 2016). Episodes are labeled "chapters" with no indication of seasons between them – this continuity speaks to the serialized nature of the content. It also positions the series as akin to a novel, generally considered a more high-brow narrative media form than television. This show was among the first, and the most prominent, to be released in a now Netflix characteristic way: an entire season made available at once. Not all OTT services have followed suit (and Netflix hasn't either: They've recently begun delaying the release of several reality-based competition shows). Hulu, for example, also schedules weekly linear releases of its most acclaimed originals. The pressure to view multiple episodes in a short time frame was a popular culture discussion, particularly around the release of the second season of *House of Cards*. At the time, the actual President of the United States, Barack Obama, tweeted "no spoilers" ahead of the season 2 premier in 2014.

Content-wise, McCormick states that the often-ambiguous amount of time passage between episodes serves to keep viewers paying careful attention. Other features, such as the use of viewer surrogates, first-person address, among others – as well as themes of over-consumption, exhaustion, and addiction all serve to elicit binge watching as a preferred mode of viewing. Narrative peaks and wanes also do not follow the typical weekly drama pattern. The season 2 premiere of the show contains a sudden, unexpected death of a major character – precisely the kind of cliffhanger that season *finales*, not premieres, are known for. A season premiere with the sudden death of a major character serves to keep viewers watching the rest of the season. This is an excellent calculation of managing audience flow at a critical juncture.

Netflix itself has released data on what episode in a series' first season serves as a "hook" that results in viewers' likelihood of continuing with the series or season. They report that somewhere between episodes 2 and perhaps as late as 6 or 8, a "hook" occurs, where 70% of viewers will continue to finish the series' season. Netflix interprets this finding such that the "hook" always occurs later than the pilot – that is, more than one episode is needed to hook viewers for the long haul, which validates their distribution strategy of releasing entire seasons at once. Viewers are likely to give a show several episodes to prove itself, typically around three. The Netflix representative in one *Variety* article on the topic went on to note that "This won't have any direct effect on the creative process for our showrunners/creators" (Spangler, 2015), when speaking of the findings. What happens in one episode or the next to hook an audience? A follow-up to the original study found relatively universal content hooks across even more shows and geographically disparate audiences: It's usually something dark or deadly, or about love and family that hooks 70% or more of the audience to keep viewing (Netflix, 2016).

Show creators have taken notice of how changes in distribution could possibly enhance their storytelling, despite Netflix's claim that their "episode hook" data were not impacting content. Three creators of *Damages* (created for and initially aired on *FX*) and *Bloodline* (created for and initially distributed by Netflix) discussed changes in production and storytelling that they employed when creating their second show with a journalist at *Quartz*. *Bloodline* ran for three seasons between 2015 and 2017. First, they use flash-forwards, a change in temporality, to end the first several episodes with cliffhangers (Lynch, 2015). This seems a smart move, modeled after the Netflix data, and a play out of the *House of Cards* rulebook. The show creators talk of structuring the first season as a three-act play – where there wasn't a need to be as episodic, and by treating several episodes as an act, there was more time to delve deeper into characters (Lynch, 2015). Creator Daniel Zelman said of the more holistic approach to storytelling over a season:

> We know that the show can evolve before the audience's eyes, so it is not like every episode has to feel like the same, because they're all blending into each other.

The creators talk about creating a 13-hour story, with less of a need for repetition throughout episodes to catch up viewers who may have missed one. They talk optimistically about viewers sitting down to watch Netflix in an undistracted state to be entertained. In some circumstances, these seem like dangerous assumptions. Take a critic's review of *Love*, another show tailored specifically for Netflix, that claims its biggest mistake is wasting the first four episodes because of an assumption that viewers are binging the entire series. *Love* also ran for three seasons. Framke (2016) writes,

> So I get it, *Love*. You had 10 episodes to fill, and Netflix didn't restrict their running time, so you took that freedom and ran with it. But assuming that just because people have the opportunity to binge-watch, they'll stick with your show for a while — no matter what — is a dangerous trap. Airing on Netflix gives you more breathing room and flexibility, but it should in no way stop you from producing compelling, tightly edited work.

What made *House of Cards* a much-heralded, groundbreaking series, *Bloodline* a middling Netflix original drama, and *Love* such a drag? (The second two characterizations are, of course, absolutely up for debate.) While it is impossible to know all show creators' intentions unless they graciously spell them out as the *Bloodline* creators did, it is logical, even forward-thinking, to pay attention to how changes in distribution will influence viewing at home. Yet, there are clearly more moving parts in creating a successful television show. Whether television shows are becoming less episodic and employing different narrative arcs than were once the norm are empirical questions. They are interesting empirical questions that a large-scale content analysis could explore, but that does not seem to exist in the literature as of yet. If show creators are consciously changing the way they tell stories in a binge-watching television environment, examining those processes and looking at outcomes of shows would also be a worthwhile avenue of research.

The previous section reviewed the seminal prestige or Golden Age television shows that are often talked about in the same breath as binge watching – staying up all night to catch up on the previous season of *Breaking Bad*, watching the equivalent of a box set of new classics via HBO on demand – these anecdotes often are the public discussion of binge watching. And yet, as the Nielsen for *The Wall Street Journal* data reveal – *The Office* and *Friends* – two widely popular sitcoms created for network TV, as far as one can get from prestige drama, are the two most watched titles on Netflix. The amount of time spent watching them strongly suggests they're being "binged" – and with Netflix's autoplay features and suggestions as discussed below, that viewing mode is certainly encouraged by the platform. This is a practical example of the need for a clear and agreed-upon definition of binge watching: We don't believe having *Friends* on in the background while you do numerous other things and only sometimes pay attention is, in fact, binge watching.

Stories change when television distribution channels are different. This is evident everywhere from premium cable shows pushing the envelope more than broadcast shows, the trend toward shorter seasons, etc. Releasing complete seasons at one time rather than individual episodes may foster many of the content attributes described above, from having the time and space to play with time and character development, to playing with a traditional narrative story arc. And these attributes can make for more exciting, novel television. It may just be that they are not as much of a guarantee for successful audience reception as mass-appeal comedies.

Too Much Content? Peak TV and Post Peak TV

Following talk about the explosion of television content creating an industry "bubble" in 2014, FX Networks Chief Executive John Landgraf is credited with describing the industry as "Peak TV" the following year (Garber, Sims, Cruz, & Gilbert, 2015; James, 2015). Landgraf spoke at the 2015 Television Critics Association press tour with much of the industry listening:

> "My sense is that 2015 or 2016 will represent peak TV in America and that we'll begin to see decline coming the year after that and beyond." [The glut of shows] "has created a huge challenge in finding compelling original stories and the level of talent needed to sustain those stories …" [It has] "an enormous impact on everyone's ability to cut through the clutter and create real buzz." (Garber et al., 2015)

Indeed, the number of new shows in the early to mid-2010s released in the United States became staggering: 2013 saw 349 scripted series; 2014 saw nearly 400 (Malone, 2019). But growth continued, and headlines loved to decry that Peak TV had not yet reached its peak. The year 2016 saw 455 scripted television shows (Flint, 2016), and recent years have seen some tapering off, with 487 scripted originals airing in 2017 and 495 in 2018. In 2002, for comparison's sake, the total number of all scripted shows was 182 (Jeffery, 2018).

As compared to broadcast and cable networks, OTT services show the largest jumps in increasing numbers of original scripted series. Just 8% of scripted originals were from online sources in 2014, but in 2018, they accounted for 33% of all originals. Premium (pay) cable has held steady carrying 9% of scripted series across 2014 to 2018, while broadcast's share dropped 7%, and basic cable dropped 9% (Malone, 2018). The concern, perhaps most loudly articulated by Landgraf, is that there are not enough viewers nor content to sustain this level of production. Just several years ago, television critics noticed when Netflix dropped a new series with little-to-no fanfare or media marketing (*The OA*, in this example – Flint, 2016). Netflix does this weekly currently, and critics don't bat an eye. In fact, they're scrambling even harder to keep up with content. Critic David Carr (2014) complains of "the feast" of content on his DVR, and the negative consequences it has on the magazines, books, and films he wishes to read and see. Ultimately concluding that this rich golden age of television "leaves me feeling less like the master of my own universe, and more as if I am surrounded" (Carr, 2014). On one hand, it seems a bit of a paradox – business is good for television critics when it is good for television, right? But, between conversations with everyone from true television aficionados to casual viewers, there are several refrains we can all relate to.

The first is "Oh, yes, I've heard good things about [Show X], it's on my list to watch" or "Yes I watch it, but I'm not caught up on the current season." It isn't just television critics with full DVRs or notes in their phones about what to watch next on what platform. Most regular television fans – across genres, but especially of dramas – have a show or two on a list to check out when they have the time. How individuals manage these suggestions and decisions to view what, when, are likely great topics of research for the social scientific and culturally minded academics in the next decade of studying television. The second refrain we'll maintain is becoming a universally experienced one that is something along the lines of,

"What do you want to watch?" inevitably answered by,

"I don't know, what do you want to watch?"

Alternately, "Ugh, I just wasted 30 minutes scrolling through Netflix," Or, "There's nothing to watch."

How can these two refrains co-exist? We offer two explanations, which can help to explain these paradoxical refrains together. The first explanation is that there is, indeed, a record number of shows to choose from, but the perceived *quality* of these shows *has* peaked. More mediocre viewing options does not always make for a satisfied viewer. The second explanation is that we, fallible viewers at home, aren't great at making selections and need assistance. Again, and again, empirical studies have demonstrated humans' innate desire for some choice, but not infinite choice. These findings come up in television studies under "channel repertoire," studies, which report that in a given time period, individuals view only a handful of channels despite access to hundreds. More broadly, studies explore the "paradox of choice" across media studies, and find that too many choices overwhelm an individual, and a subset of choices to choose from are typically ideal. We argue that both explanations can be true, and we believe the networks of tomorrow will be the industry players who best meet the needs for content curation that frustrated or bored viewers experience when they don't know or can't find anything to watch.

The How: Managing Audience Flow

Considering *how* we binge watch, we explore the implications for viewing that an increase in *quantity*, but a likely decrease in overall *quality* brings (1) and how the industry's audience flow management strategies are evolving with changes in distribution, content, and viewer experiences (2). First, the industry's discussion of declining quality, and what it may mean for viewers eager to view, and/or eager to binge is addressed, followed by a discussion of the *curation* of content. Managing audience flow via programming strategies and using on-air promos to market new content are ways in which viewers receive some viewing choice assistance, and are common practices of traditional networks. How do new network competitors in today's media landscape manage audience flow? How do they ensure the success of new content? This final section explores *how* these industry players encourage you to watch and binge on the content types discussed in the previous section.

Post Peak TV and Netflix Strategy

The ongoing increases of available content are a product of greater competition between broadcast and cable, between all networks and existing OTT services, and will likely continue as more OTT competitors emerge. As the numbers above demonstrate, the rate at which new series are released is slowing, with the exception of Netflix original content acquired. Some have said this slowing down is past due. "Peak," after all, denotes that we're headed downhill.

Indeed, television critics have proffered opinions about Netflix going "post-prestige." Rubin (2019) reminds audiences of the critically acclaimed Netflix shows that first demonstrated the high quality of content a streaming service could offer. However, the strategy they're currently employing to obliterate the competition – not just edge out – includes a much greater *quantity* of shows, and in doing so, sacrifices *quality*. Rubin (2019) likens their business plan to the standard (i.e., network) programming strategy of tentpoling, which is the anchoring of two new or unproven shows with a strong one in between, creating a high point in the middle that can support the two new shows. He dryly notes, "Tentpoles are so 2017; these days, growth will come from niches, the small patches of ground left among the tents." The numbers demonstrate Netflix's strong commitment to producing a vastly greater amount of content than the competition; 80 original films and 700 series debuting in 2018 (Nguyen, 2018) was one estimate that seems too large to be true. However, they did launch 62 new programs (across movies, documentaries, and series) in May 2019 alone, and 345 titles across all show types in 2018 (Rodriguez, 2019). Netflix was projected to spend $13 billion on new content in 2019 after spending 8 billion in 2018. Meanwhile, Amazon spends half of that, and Apple TV+ spends about 2 million. The Disney+ platform likely won't reach 2 million for several years (Rubin, 2019). In the first four months of 2019, Netflix debuted nine comedies, with many more set to be released throughout the year. Some of the titles boast star power and interesting premises, while others appear to be very niche and have received less than kind reviews (Rubin, 2019). Not everything in the Netflix cannon can be a top hit, fairly enough.

The ballooning of digital platforms, and in particular Netflix, is driving the growing number of scripted programs debuting each year. Is it overwhelming for audiences, or is it more variety, which seems like a positive? One recent Netflix comedy, *I Think You Should Leave with Tim Robinson*, is described by Rubin (2019) as made for the fan of dark, off-putting sketch comedy – "the kind that uses the term "mud pies" scatologically … in multiple sketches … in its first episode." That sounds like an interesting show … for some audience. The question then becomes: Is appealing to the "small patches of ground left among the tentpoles" worth it? And, do you have a system for ensuring small niche audiences find your very, very niche content? With over 130 million Netflix subscribers worldwide (Rodriguez, 2019), there are many small patches in the ground to fill.

FX Chief Executive John Landgraf complains that individual shows get lost in the herd of Peak TV; that it is harder for any one show to stand out among the noise of so many middling quality shows (Jeffery, 2018). Landgraf was concerned with both shows getting lost in the fray, as well as the overall lack of creative talent to sustain so many shows, year after year. Landgraf isn't the only one vocal about his growing disappointment with the growing number of television shows. Film director Steve McQueen, who recently remade the 80s British TV show *Widows* into a feature-length film, says that television had its moment, but now there is just too much of it. McQueen is clearly in the camp that there should be concern about a lack of creative talent to sustain so many shows, saying "There's so much money and so little ideas," (Travers, 2018). He goes on to call Netflix's *Ozark* an example of this, labeling it a rip off of *Breaking Bad*. McQueen may be in the minority though, in believing that film can do much more than television. The film actors and filmmakers who have done short stints of prestige television across platforms and networks is no longer limited to a couple high-profile names and barely A list actors. It is now the norm for high profile actors to do high-brow television pieces.

The Competition and Industry Realities

Several industry giants – those that critics and scholars thought could surely become major players in streaming TV appear to be rethinking how and if to enter the market at large. YouTube launched YouTube Red and then rebranded as YouTube Premium in 2018, as its subscription-based service. At first, they seemed to be on a similar scripted program trajectory as others entering the market. They made rival streaming services take note after their *Karate Kid* spinoff, *Cobra Kai*, was viewed 5.4 million times in 24 hours. However, after debuting another original, the Google-owned company announced a shift in content strategy: holding original spending constant through 2020 (Jarvey, 2018; Jeffery, 2018). Although they still have a couple big budget pieces in production, YouTube has said that they do not see a gap in the scripted streaming market for them, and they are likely to instead focus on their ad-supported business (Jarvey, 2018). YouTube, which has nearly 2 billion unique users worldwide, has an incredible advantage in audience size. YouTube may not be the only ones shying away from jumping into the game, even as others continue to discuss launches coming soon. In 2018, Facebook Watch is said to have spent $1 billion or more on original content in news, entertainment, and sports (Spangler, 2018), and although they don't release viewing data, they enjoyed some critical success with *Sorry for Your Loss* in 2018 (Jeffery, 2018). At this stage, Facebook Watch is in an experimental phase, and although numbers are hard to come by, views of shorter fare, such as *Tasty* videos, seem to dwarf original content at the moment. With names like YouTube and Facebook looking for alternative content types to deliver, perhaps both the competitive market for viewers and for quality content have reached a peak.

How difficult is it to acquire content that is both high in quality and will appeal to a large enough, though still marketable niche audience? Certainly, an industry where the number of television series produced annually has doubled to tripled over five years has grown so quickly that there may be growing pains. Indeed, a thoroughly reported piece for *Vulture* spoke to many across the creative production industry to see how their work has changed and note that it's touched showrunners to actors, to crew members, and more (Adalian & Fernandez, 2016). They note,

> As so many networks and producers scramble again and again to make television that's great, finding standout ideas and then turning them into actual shows has perhaps never been more difficult. The effort that goes into securing top writers, actors, crew members, and soundstages these days is almost as challenging as coming up with the idea for the next *Mr. Robot* (para 4)

Across the industry, there is a fear that the non-stop jobs and calls for auditions and round-the-clock shoots could end abruptly at any minute. People on the inside are concerned it's a bubble. While the volume of shows characteristic of "Peak TV" may result in some dilution in quality, it has some other effects as well. We see bigger Hollywood names attached to television projects than ever before. This may signify the continued level of quality in the big budget pieces that streaming services and the handful of prestige TV cable networks – HBO, Showtime, AMC, FX, and Starz – are most interested in (Adalian & Fernandez, 2016). An interesting impact of so many shows is the shorter run times characteristic of prestige projects on these networks and streaming services. There are many 6, 8, or 10 episodes seasons, and sometimes entire series, as compared to the once-standard 22 and 13 episode cycles for broadcast and cable. While these shorter cycles allow for film actors to dip their toes in the prestige television waters, it means a shorter, less reliable work cycle for most actors, writers, showrunners, and crew positions. What does it mean for viewers? Well, with even the same amount of time devoted to television viewing, they're viewing more *different* programs than before. We've seen as detailed above what this can do to viewing metrics – where more viewing time is spent with Netflix's popular reruns than critically acclaimed, headline-grabbing originals. This leads to several relevant audience-centered questions, namely, how do they make viewing decisions?

Curating Content: Networks, YouTube, and OTT Services

In the network and affiliate television model of the previous century, industry and academics alike recognized the tools used by channels to manage audience flow. And yet, in a television viewing world heavily populated by, and perhaps soon to be dominated by OTT and on-demand options, discussions of how content is *curated* for audiences is lacking. Sorensen (2014) is among a growing number of scholars who talk about "content curators" in the context of multiplatform media distribution. She states that in addition to networks having an established market position, one of their premier advantages is their reputation for commissioning, creating, and broadcasting quality content.

With 72 hours of content uploaded to YouTube every *minute*, surely the problem is not the availability of something to watch in online video. The problem is identifying *high-quality* options (Sorensen, 2014). This problem for online viewers is exacerbated by text-heavy search engines. Sorensen's (2014) piece explores the distribution (and marketing) transition of two public service broadcasters into public service media providers of factual content (i.e. documentaries) in the United Kingdom via industry analysis and interviews. One interviewee from Channel 4 in the piece discusses the lack of gatekeeping function of YouTube: Content that violates copyright is removed. There are no arbitrators of taste, ethics, or factuality. This is both the downside and upside of user-generated content, right? That anyone can produce a "documentary" and upload it somewhere online where others can access it. When we want to hold content to some metric of quality – accuracy, or factuality, perhaps, YouTube is not curating that content. Sorensen's (2014) Channel 4 source says the lack of curation is the biggest problem the web has failed to address. In historical U.S. terminology, this framing of YouTube positions it as part common carrier – or, like telephone companies of the past, merely systems for others to use to convey their own information on.

There are, of course, some general distinctions to be made between "online video" and "television content." We would argue that the lack of curation on the part of YouTube, along with its monetization model and user-generated content options are major distinguishing features that currently differentiate it from OTT services. As described above, YouTube is not primarily in the business of acquiring professionally produced content and distributing it to audiences. OTT services, however, are held to a different standard of culpability for their content, and should be motivated to provide high-quality, targeted content. As Sorensen's sources reiterate, traditional networks have experience and time spent curating content on their side. Strangelove (2015) maintains that *scarcity* is an essential component of networks maintaining industry control. He states that TV networks need the status quo media business model to survive, and that is dependent upon scarcity of content and traditional windowing periods. Importantly, he maintains that YouTube blurs the lines of what television is defined as, while we maintain that YouTube is a separate distribution system (open source, search) and mix of content (professional, semi-professional, and user-generated). He defines windowing more specifically than the general management of the release sequence of content across time and platforms:

> Windowing is the studio process that sees a film or television show released in the U.S. market first and then gradually appear in cinemas and on television sets in other countries at a later date … windowing also involves isolating content on different platforms. (p. 183)

Indeed, we've already discussed how network content on Netflix and other OTT services is causing issues for both media conglomerates which own them and the OTT services which hope to maintain them at a reasonable cost. Strangelove (2014) makes two large arguments in his *Post TV* book worth discussing on this topic. The first thesis about scarcity and power players is one that the current authors find quite interesting. His analogy to what happened to the music industry with the introduction of the Internet follows in Chapter 6. The second is a claim about a current era of "disintermediation" where OTTs have cut out the middleman between producers and consumers. This seems mostly true of YouTube, less so for on-demand, pay-per-view services (iTunes, on-demand cable services) and simply not characteristic of OTT subscription-based services (e.g., Netflix, Hulu, Amazon). While these OTT services are markedly different as discussed above, they perform several functions as "middleman" that are critical here, such as creating a brand and *curating* content for audiences, albeit to niche (as opposed to mass) audiences. Scarcity is considered less of a premium here although scarcity and curation of content exist somewhat on a continuum. If no scarcity existed, every platform would have the curating power of YouTube, which is next to nothing.

The New Programming Strategies: Technology and Data

It is widely understood that network television programmers count on favorable windowing strategies and scarcity of quality, on-brand content as basics of managing audience flow. There are several programming strategies in terms of content placement still taught in broadcasting classrooms and employed by program directors across the country and world. In a linear viewing environment, strategies such as hammocking (placing a lower rated/ unproven show between two higher rated/ proven shows to increase its viewership) and tentpoling (placing a higher rated/ unproven in between to lower rated/ unproven shows to boost the other two) were classics. For a streaming platform, they are meaningless. *But* managing audience flow, or trying to keep viewers tuned in for longer to your content rather than the competitors' is a quite meaningful, consequential endeavor.

For several decades between Golden Ages of television, being on the network with the top rated nightly talk show (e.g., Letterman or Leno) was a twofold gift: It often resulted in a top-rated (or better rated than otherwise) morning national talk show because a television turned off after viewing channel 4 would turn back on to channel 4. This is news to today's electronic media students. Cable operators took control of what channel is on when a television is turned on some time ago. This is not a content-programming strategy, but clearly an audience-flow strategy. And it is not different from the many small structural choices that OTT services employ to keep viewers tuned in. Automatic starts of the next episode in a series after finishing viewing a previous episode is a great, effective example.

How else do OTTs and non-network providers of content attempt to manage audience flow? In many of the same ways as traditional networks, but often in additional ways that capitalize on the technology used. In Chapter 5, we present qualitative data from binge viewers that say time and again that the autoplay function used by streaming services is persuasive when the content is captivating. Autoplay is a function that works across viewing devices, while others depend on the platform being used. For example, when exiting the Netflix app on a smart TV, you're prompted with a question asking if you're sure you want to leave the Netflix app – imagine how frustrating that would be for a regular television channel to implement. If one watches Netflix on a laptop one can certainly "x" out of that browsing window, after likely exiting full screen mode, which necessitates another click. Making one more action, one more click, required in "changing the channel" from Netflix is of course a calculated move to manage audience flow. In 2018, Netflix introduced the "skip intro" feature, which allows audiences to skip opening credits and theme, getting them right back into the content even more quickly. It was a move that content creators may have been critical of, but one that many super fans seemed to appreciate (Nguyen, 2018). OTT services surely have an advantage over networks in giving more perceived control to audiences. There are ways to personalize watch lists, add ratings to content, etc. that just don't exist in a network television model. This added personalization and interactivity can be advantageous in bringing the viewer in as an active, involved viewer.

And of course, there are the personalized algorithms for each user on each Netflix account that provide viewing suggestions. While one won't see the term "viewing recommendation" anywhere on Netflix, every single thing one sees is a carefully placed recommendation based on tens of thousands of data points. It should not go understated how purposeful and measured every element of *your* viewing platform on Netflix is. While other OTT services also have similar search functions and viewing suggestions, it is Netflix, under the direction of Vice President Todd Yellin, who has pioneered these recommendation algorithms. Netflix viewing suggestion algorithms are personalized at three levels – the row (e.g., "Continue Watching," "Award-Winning Comedies"), the order of titles in each row, and the titles in each row (Netflix, no date). The algorithms used to determine which thumbnails for content you see (and where you see it) use weighted data based on three categories of information. The first is implicit and explicit viewer data, including ratings and previous viewing history. Previous viewing data includes not only what titles have been viewed and for how long viewers watched them, but also on what device and at what time of day they were viewed. The second source of data is carefully coded and tagged content characteristics. These content tags are as nuanced as you might imagine – is it set in outer space? Is there a corrupt cop? The third data point is what viewers watch in the same "taste groups" or "taste communities" as you (Nguyen, 2018; Plummer, 2017). How much each data point in all these categories and levels are weighted, is, of course, the 13 billion dollar question facing Netflix. And they certainly aren't releasing any of their best answers to the public.

More than 80% of what viewers watch on Netflix is through viewing suggestions. Netflix counts on viewers taking up to 90 seconds to decide on a title before they go elsewhere for their entertainment content, *and* viewers are spending an average of just 1.8 seconds on each title thumbnail before clicking or scrolling on (Nguyen, 2018). While many speculate about the billions of dollars Netflix has spent going into debt for new content, the second act of this business plan is just as essential: getting viewers to watch it and like it. Netflix's international reach with no time delayed distribution windows as well as extremely targeted niche audiences are attractive features to content producers (Nguyen, 2018). The ways Netflix manages audience flow through their interface design and suggestion algorithms faces a tougher battle when most of the titles are new, original content that audiences are unfamiliar with. For instance, *The Office* is an easier pitch when someone has binge watched *Friends* and *Parks and Recreation*. This isn't a new problem for program directors across broadcast and cable television. It is exactly why programming strategies like hammocking and tentpoling exist: to introduce new shows based on what people are already watching. The new approach is just a much, much more advanced, data-driven one. Nguyen (2018) notes that,

> Netflix ultimately needs to convince members that a subscription is worth paying for — and the best way to do that, after helping them find something to watch, is converting casual browsers into hardcore binge-watchers (para 5)

We agree! This goes back to the rule of thumb guiding many traditional television programming strategies as well; it is always easier to get a viewer to change the channel than to get them to turn on the television in the first place. In its data-driven quest to keep viewers watching, Netflix has made several missteps. In 2018, there was pushback about selecting thumbnail images with minor Black characters to display only to viewers Netflix had identified as having watched other content with Black characters. There was also a short-lived initiative to encourage young viewers to "collect patches" for watching certain episodes of kids programming (Nguyen, 2018). Will missteps of this scope be enough to allow one of the many competitors to get a leg up? The future remains quite difficult to predict.

Conclusion

About the only thing we can tell from the many sources who have speculated about the future of television is that everyone gets something wrong. Adalian and

Fernandez (2016), in a piece with dozens of interviews across all television creative functions, mention this in conclusion: "Plus, the streaming space is getting more competitive: CBS All Access and YouTube Red are ramping up production, while some in the industry expect that either AT&T or Verizon (if not both) will launch their own video services by decade's end." This isn't how the competition has shaken out, and this wasn't that long ago. Indeed, hindsight is 20/20. The same decisions in 2016 can be interpreted in many ways without knowing what we know now. For instance, Adalian and Fernandez (2016) quote one anonymous studio exec as saying that Netflix had just begun passing on expensive shows and concepts, which they hypothesize as a sign of tightening purse strings. Of course, we know now that this is not the correct interpretation – Netflix began looking at *more* content that was, on average, *less expensive*, not at less content acquisition.

Currently, it is a safe bet to consider Netflix the force to be reckoned with in the streaming OTT game. If – and it's a moderately sized if – other competitors with studio backing enter the OTT arena and take their content from Netflix in the process, seeing if the investment in original programming pays off will be fascinating to watch. Netflix is also the source to watch for innovations in managing audience flow. Their viewing data, audience reach, and advanced algorithms for making seamless viewing suggestions to viewers are unprecedented. Whether it is all enough to demolish the standard broadcast or cable network remains to be seen. However, their targeted appeals and quantity of content will certainly continue to erode the staying power of networks until some breaking point.

Popular discussions and academic investigations of binge watching seem entirely focused on dramatic narratives, identification with characters and suspenseful content. The Netflix data on *Friends* and *The Office* demonstrates we're "binging" – when binging is watching multiple episodes of a sequential narrative of more light-hearted fare at least as often. *How* content continues to evolve will also be exciting to watch – and an area ripe for both industry and academic research. In our perspective, none of the other big-picture discussions covered here – Networks vs. OTT services, what networks functionally do for viewers, who may win out in the end, and what the future tools of managing audience flow look like – are as up in the air as the question about how content evolves with changing distribution patterns. This is perhaps a tricky question because it is both relatively unknown and unstudied, but empirical in nature. Despite any number of confounding variables in how content evolves over time, isolating the influence of distribution strategy on television structure, form and content devices remains to be seen.

Keeping a watchful eye on audience flow strategies will surely reveal even more nuanced ways for content providers to try to keep eyes on screens. The general strategy of Netflix to encourage binge watching is one obvious strategy at managing audience flow. When a viewer is binging, they're watching the same series over an extended period in a single viewing session. We know that viewers are more likely to watch familiar content, and especially with Netflix's data on when viewers may become hooked on a series, binge watching as audience-flow strategy is a good one. However, the changing streaming wars landscape posits some problems for Netflix ahead as they will have to become more reliant on original programming. Recommendation algorithms, and electronic word-of mouth, or social viewing situations (discussed in greater length in the next chapter) are fascinating persuasive tools to keep viewers watching content.

References

Adalian, J., & Fernandez, M. E. (2016). The business of too much TV. *Vulture*. Retrieved from: https://www.vulture.com/2016/05/peak-tv-business-c-v-r.html

BBC News. (2018, November 9). Netflix chief Reed Hastings ready for Disney Plus battle (No Author). Retrieved from: https://www.bbc.com/news/business-46148040

Brennan, L. (2018, October). How Netflix expanded to 190 countries in 7 years. *Harvard Business Review*. Retrieved from: https://hbr.org/2018/10/how-netflix-expanded-to-190-countries-in-7-years

Carr, D. (2014, March 29). Barely keeping up in TV's new golden age. *New York Times*. Retrieved from: https://www.nytimes.com/2014/03/10/business/media/fenced-in-by-televisions-excess-of-excellence.html

Cowan, L. (2013, October 1). Welcome to TV's Second Golden Age. *CBS*. Retrieved from: https://www.cbsnews.com/news/welcome-to-tvs-second-golden-age/

Cunningham, S., & Silver, J. (2013). *Screen distribution and the new King Kongs of the online world*. New York: Palgrave MacMillan.

Curtin, M. (2009). Matrix media. In G. Turner & J. Tay (Eds.), *Television Studies after TV: Understanding television in the post-broadcast era* (pp. 9–19). New York: Routledge.

Doyle, G. (2016). Resistance of channels: Television distribution in the multiplatform era. *Telematics and Informatics*, *33*(2), 693–702. doi: 10.1016/j.tele.2015.06.015

Flint, J. (2016, December 21). Peak TV still going strong with 455 scripted shows in 2016. *The Wall Street Journal*. Retrieved from: https://www.wsj.com/articles/peak-tv-still-going-strong-with-455-scripted-shows-in-2016-1482350706

Flint, J., & Sharma, A. (2019, April 24). Netflix fights to keep its most watched shows: 'Friends' and 'The Office.' *The Wall Street Journal*. Retrieved from: https://www.wsj.com/articles/netflix-battles-rivals-for-its-most-watched-shows-friends-and-the-office-11556120136

Fortune. (2018). AT&T closes $85 billion Time Warner Deal after two year effort. (No Author). Retrieved from: http://fortune.com/2018/06/14/att-closes-time-warner-deal/

Framke, C. (2016, February 21). Netflix's Love makes a strong case against creating TV with binge-watching in mind. *Vox*. Retrieved from: https://www.vox.com/2016/2/21/11075740/netflix-love-review-judd-apatow

Franklin, G. (2018, October 26). Steve McQueen says 'Peak TV' era is over. *Dark Horizons* Retrieved from: http://www.darkhorizons.com/steve-mcqueen-says-peak-tv-era-is-over/

Garber, M., Sims, D., Cruz, L., & Gilbert, S. (2015, August 12). Have We Reached 'Peak TV'? *The Atlantic*. Retrieved from: https://www.theatlantic.com/entertainment/archive/2015/08/have-we-reached-peak-tv/401009/

Gartenberg, C. (2019, April 15). AT&T may have just signaled the end of Hulu as you know it today. *The Verge*. Retrieved from: https://www.theverge.com/2019/4/15/18312068/disney-hulu-att-sells-stake-comcast-control-streaming

Ha, A. (2019). The Oscars won't change their rules to exclude streaming. *Tech Crunch*. Retrieved from: https://techcrunch.com/2019/04/24/oscars-eligibility-netflix/?fbclid=IwAR0sk3QwI_dDZYowh1N5a1WjBW3fmCtYfm1LZxNTC1c3thVRbnsPRRej6PQ

James, M. (2015, December 16). 2015: Year of 'peak TV' hits record with 409 original series. *The Los Angeles Times*. Retrieved from: https://www.latimes.com/entertainment/envelope/cotown/la-et-ct-2015-peak-tv-new-record-409-original-series-20151216-story.html

Jarvey, N. (2018, November 27). YouTube to pull back on scripted in 2020 amid Ad-supported push. *Hollywood Reporter*. Retrieved from: https://www.hollywoodreporter.com/live-feed/youtube-pull-back-scripted-programming-ad-supported-push-1164256

Jeffery, M. (2018, June 12). Here's why the so-called Golden Age of TV might be coming to an end. *Digital Spy*. Retrieved from: https://www.digitalspy.com/tv/a25422929/golden-age-of-tv-peak-television-over-ending-netflix/

Lotz, A. D. (2007). *The television will be revolutionized*. New York: New York University Press.

Lynch, J. (2015, March 20). Here's the recipe Netflix uses to make binge-worthy TV. *Quartz*. Retrieved from: https://qz.com/367117/heres-the-recipe-netflix-uses-to-make-binge-worthy-tv/

Malone, M. (2018, December 13). Just shy of 500 scripted originals: FX survey. *Broadcasting & Cable*. Retrieved from https://www.broadcastingcable.com/news/just-shy-of-500-scripted-originals-says-fx-survey

Martin, N. (2013). *Difficult men – Behind the scenes of a creative revolution: From The Sopranos and The Wire to Mad Men and Breaking Bad*. New York: Penguin Random House.

McCormick, C. J. (2016). "Forward is the battle cry:" Binge-viewing Netflix's *House of Cards*. In K. McDonald & D. Smith-Rovey (Eds.), *The Netflix effect: Technology and entertainment in the 21st century* (pp. 101–115). New York: Bloomsbury.

Mills, C. (2018, June 16). Here's everything AT&T now owns, apart from your soul. *BGR*. Retrieved from: https://bgr.com/2018/06/16/att-time-warner-merger-brands-what-they-own/

Netflix. (2016, September 21). You're still hooked and Netflix knows why. (No Author). Retrieved from: https://media.netflix.com/en/press-releases/youre-still-hooked-and-netflix-knows-why

Netflix. (no date). How Netflix's recommendations system works. (No Author). Retrieved from: https://help.netflix.com/en/node/100639

Nguyen, N. (2018). Netflix wants to change the way you chill. *Buzzfeed*. Retrieved from: https://www.buzzfeednews.com/article/nicolenguyen/netflix-recommendation-algorithm-explained-binge-watching

Nicholson, R. (2018, July 26). From Sharp Objects to Killing Eve: TV's best antiheroes are women. *The Guardian*. Retrieved from: https://www.theguardian.com/tv-and-radio/2018/jul/26/sharp-objects-killing-eve-tv-antiheroes-women

Palmer, S. (2006). *Television disrupted: The transition from network to networked TV*. Oxford, England: Elsevier.

Plummer, L. (2017, August 22). This is how Netflix's top-secret recommendation system works. *Wired*. Retrieved from: https://www.wired.co.uk/article/how-do-netflixs-algorithms-work-machine-learning-helps-to-predict-what-viewers-will-like

Raftery, B. (2018, December 27). The streaming wars began in 2018 – and they'll only get worse. *Wired*. Retrieved from: https://www.wired.com/story/2018-streaming-wars/

Reese, H. (2013, July 11). Why Is the golden age of TV So dark? *The Atlantic*. Retrieved from: https://www.theatlantic.com/entertainment/archive/2013/07/why-is-the-golden-age-of-tv-so-dark/277696/

Rodriguez, A. (2019, January 1). Keeping up with Netflix originals is basically a part-time job now. *Quartz*. Retrieved from: https://qz.com/1505030/keeping-up-with-netflix-originals-is-basically-a-part-time-job-now/

Rubin, P. (2019, April 23). From sketch comedy to BDSM, Netflix burrows into every niche it can find. *Wired*. Retrieved from: https://www.wired.com/story/netflix-niche-programming/?fbclid=IwAR1MlsG7IoKv_bO2zvrjeho1IQu_MQdKwJdZUBDJ5W6_fWjKbKfOzL8LRdE&mbid=social_fb&utm_brand=wired&utm_campaign=wired&utm_medium=social&utm_social-type=owned&utm_source=facebook

Sørensen, I. E. (2014). Channels as content curators: Multiplatform strategies for documentary film and factual content in British public service broadcasting. *European Journal of Communication, 29*, 34–49. doi: 10.1177/0267323113504856

Spangler, T. (2015, September 23). Netflix data reveals exactly when TV shows hook viewers – And it's not the pilot. *Variety*. Retrieved from: https://variety.com/2015/digital/news/netflix-tv-show-data-viewer-episode-study-1201600746/

Spangler, T. (2018, June 14). Facebook bets $1 billion on content, but will it pay off? *Variety*. Retrieved from: https://variety.com/2018/digital/news/facebook-content-1202844037/

Strangelove, M. (2015). *Post-TV: Piracy, cord-cutting, and the future of television*. Toronto, Canada: University of Toronto Press.

Travers, B. (2018, October 25). Steve McQueen does not like TV one bit, and he'd never make his 2015 HBO pilot today. *IndieWire*. Retrieved from: https://www.indiewire.com/2018/10/steve-mcqueen-tv-is-bad-hbo-pilot-codes-of-conduct-1202015069/

VanDerWerff, E. T. (November 26, 2016). How NBC's This Is Us became the breakout hit of the fall Family dramas rarely hit the Nielsen ratings top 10 – but this one has. Vox. Retrieved from https://www.vox.com/2016/11/29/13769520/this-is-us-ratings-nbc

Welch, C. (2019, April 11). Disney confirms it will "likely" bundle *Disney+*, *ESPN+*, and *Hulu* for one price. *The Verge*. Retrieved from: https://www.theverge.com/2019/4/11/18306883/disney-hulu-espn-plus-streaming-service-bundle-deal-likely

CHAPTER FOUR

A Social Perspective: Family Viewing, Co-Viewing, and Content Curation

Binge watching presents a critical and consequential difference in viewing from the currently accepted assumptions under the existing methodological and theoretical framework employed in the academic study of media effects. This chapter explores macro-level phenomenon that are shaping these changing assumptions about television viewing. An exploration of the literature on situational determinants of television viewing, group viewing, and the crucial role of family in the broader picture of television in society is presented. The chapter then documents two relatively new television-related media behaviors that capitalize on old habits and interests: Social TV and Media Multitasking, or "second-screening." What we know and what we speculate about these phenomenon and binge watching are discussed throughout. As we discussed in Chapter 2, television has long been a shared activity with families, friends, and even fellow fans. This remains true as television continues to be the most common leisure activity in the United States (U.S. Bureau of Labor Statistics, 2015). Family viewing of television has been promoted since the early days of television and was embraced by the broadcast industry as seen in the promotion of content during "family hour." This chapter examines changes in viewing behaviors and discusses how changes in the original viewing unit – the family – have impacted current research on television viewing. Special attention is also paid to the role of coviewing over time and how technological changes have impacted how we view together. New technology allows television viewers to coview programming with others who are not physically present, or to "second-screen" with different tasks and streams of content on other devices. We use the term "social viewing" to broadly refer to the various literatures on coviewing, group viewing, and Social TV. The end of the chapter reviews media multitasking findings from industry reports and academic sources and approaches.

As we saw in Chapter 2, watching television has always included a social component. From its introduction, people have viewed with family, friends, and people in their communities (Pires de Sá, 2015). However, viewing with others has changed over time. This chapter will trace the history of viewing with others.

The Family and Television Viewing

The cost of television sets in the late 1940s and early 1950s meant households with TVs typically only had one television set, located in a common viewing space such as the family room or den. The industry promoted the use of television for family cohesion and created content catering to families. A decades-old industry practice of offering family friendly prime time programming demonstrates the critical role TV was assumed to have in family life.

From the mid-1970s onward, the first hour of prime time, the 8 pm to 9 pm hour (and two hours on Sundays from 7 pm to 9 pm) was commonly known as "Family Hour." The family hour was a time block on the broadcast networks (ABC, CBS, NBC, and eventually Fox), which programmed "family appropriate" content. This hour attracted one of the largest audiences of children and teenagers. In 1995–1996, Nielsen reported 6.5 million children and teenage viewers per program (1995–96 Nielsen ratings). The origin of "Family Hour" begins in the early 1970s with the broadcast industry attempting to self-regulate themselves to prevent government from doing so. The goal was to create a time frame featuring programming appropriate for all ages (Wiley, 1977). The broadcasting industry's commitment to the "Family Hour" waned in the 1980s in part due to legal challenges and court rulings that the policy violated first amendment rights (MacCarthy, 1995). Additionally, Rothman (2015) reported that the broadcast networks claimed that conforming to the family hour content resulted in lower ratings.

A content analysis of family hour programming comparing content broadcast in the family hour block from 1976, 1986, and 1996 found that the presence of and depiction of sexual content in "Family Hour" program steadily increased over time. Kunkel, Cope, and Colvin (1996) reported the increase was found both in the number of programs containing sexual messages as well as the frequency of sexual messages per episode.

> The amount of sexual interactions overall in 1996 was up 118 % since 1986 and 270 % since 1976. The largest part of this overall increase in sexual interactions involves the depiction of sexual behaviors, which have multiplied nearly five-fold from 1.1 interactions/hour in 1976 to 5.4 in 1996. The most common behavior, physical flirting and kissing, are hardly explicit. They account for more than 80% of all sexual behavior. Still, in the 1996 sample, 15 instances of sexual intercourse were depicted or implied across a sample of 84 hours of programs, representing 3% of all sexual behaviors presented. No examples of intercourse were included in the 1976 or 1986 programming analysis. (Kunkel et al., 1996, p. 33)

These changes in the content broadcast in the family hour led to a technological solution to provide parents a tool to try and protect their children from sex and violence in television content. The government mandated the inclusion of the V-Chip in the Telecommunications Act of 1996, requiring all television sets produced after 2000 to contain the electronic device. It allowed parents to monitor and restrict television content based on the rating of the program. The use of the V-chip by parents never gained any traction. Further, the amount of time spent viewing television as a family has decreased since 2000 for several other reasons which will be discussed later in this chapter.

Family Coviewing and Mediation

While broadcast networks continued their attempt to self-regulate with the creation of the family hour, they were also tapping into an established social ritual – television viewing with family. From the time television was introduced, it was promoted as a technology to keep families together because family members would sit together and view programs as a group. Several research studies have examined family interactions by conducting ethnographies of the role of television in families and households. Across most of these studies there is a common finding that television viewing plays a role in family life by providing structure to their interactions and organizing their time spent together and apart (Alexander, 1994; Courtis & Nelissen, 2018; Gauntlett & Hill, 1999; Goodman, 1983; Lull, 1980, 1990; Morley, 1986). In a highly cited research report, Lull (1980) identified two different types of relationships families can have to television. First, families that use television for companionship, for common ground or generally regulate their relationships, which Lull called "socio-oriented" (p. 328). Second, "concept-oriented" families rejected using television for companionship, but instead saw television as a way to transmit values and regulate children's behaviors by curating their programming.

Using television to regulate family interactions has been reported by several researchers. Bausinger (1984) found that individuals used television viewing to both spend time with family members and to create distance with family members. Other researchers have expanded on how television can be used to regulate family dynamics. Lindolf and Traudt (1983) asserted that for some families, the act of viewing television allows for the members of the family to create space in order to lessen tensions or conflict.

The idea of using television to create family interactions continued to expand in the late 1960s and early 1970s. The best example of this is *Sesame Street* which first aired in 1969. The goal of the show was to provide education and prosocial content for pre-school age children. Early experiments demonstrated that when children viewed with a parent or an adult their learning experience was increased compared with children who viewed the same content alone (Ball, 1970). The success of this type of pro-social children's programming continues today with other networks such as Nickelodeon and Disney producing content to entertain both parents and children. Initially, content for pre-schoolers was broadcast early in the morning. The popularity of such content led to Nickelodeon starting a channel just for pre-schoolers – Nick Jr – in 1999. Similarly, PBS Kids content provides television programming on non-commercial television in the United States, along with a host of online games and additional educational content.

The act of parents and children viewing television together is known as coviewing (Pires de Sá, 2015). Valkenburg, Krcmar, Peeters, and Marseilee (1999) have defined coviewing as "occasions when adults and children watch television together, sharing the experience, but not engaging in any discussions about the program" (p. 54). Research on parent-child coviewing has primarily focused on learning outcomes (Buijzen & Valkenburg, 2005; Nathanson, 2001, 2002; Warren, Gerke, & Kelly, 2002) and have provided continued support for earlier research findings suggesting when children view educational programming, their learning outcomes are greater when they view with adults and parents. Coviewing sometimes has also been examined to see if the prosocial benefits can be extended to reduce the less desirable or negative outcomes of media exposure (Austin 1993; Buijzen, Walma van der Molen, & Sondij, 2007; Nathanson & Botta, 2003; Schooler, Kim, & Sorsoli, 2006). The effect of lessening possible negative impacts of content has not yielded consistent outcomes, even when parents engage in mediation which has been defined as to talking with children about specific aspects of television content while viewing (Nathanson, 2002) rather than only coviewing. This type of coviewing behavior may take place across several hours per day. As discussed in

Chapter 2, the average amount of viewing time peaked at an average of approximately eight hours per day in 2009.

Changing Technology Habits

Over time and at an increasingly faster rate, both television technology and the traditional family structure are changing. Since the 1950s, there has been a steady increase in the number of television sets in the home (see Chapter 2). In the 1960–1970s, a traditional family setting included family gathering around the living room TV set. Today media choices abound and allow individualized media diets resulting in audience fragmenting (Chaffee & Metzger, 2001). Research suggests this pattern started in the 1990s with an increase in "bedroom culture." Bedroom culture refers to the use of screen media, including televisions and personal computers, being used by teens in their bedrooms rather than in shared family spaces (Livingstone, 2007). It should be noted that before moving technologies into their bedrooms, teens spent less time watching television content with the family than family members of different ages for a variety of reasons, including socializing and talking on the telephone. However, most teens did have not access to a telephone line in their bedrooms. This pattern accelerated with the introduction of more affordable personal laptops, tablets, and smartphones, while older generations tend to view television and use computers in communal viewing spaces.

Even with the increase in media choice and technological devices, viewing is still a social activity, and parents and children still coview TV (Nelissen & van den Bulck, 2018). The presence and the age of children living in a household impacts the amount of coviewing engaged in by a family. Courtis and Nelissen (2018) surveyed 288 Belgian households. Households with children had different viewing patterns with a higher likelihood of coviewing in households with younger children and single-parent households. Additionally, solitary viewing increases when there are TV sets present in bedrooms, while intergenerational viewing is more likely to occur in a communal space such as a living room. Courtis and Nelissen (2018) concluded that "in spite of the firmly diversifying media landscape, family viewing persists, especially concentrating on content genres such as soaps, series, films, and newscasts" (p. 687). All of these content types except news have been linked to binge viewing. The perception of family closeness was impacted in interesting ways. Siblings who watched television together reported a stronger familial bond. Families also reported that when a family member was not at home to view with the group, the experience felt incomplete or that they had a limited sense of family closeness (Courtis & Nelissen, 2018). Television appears to continue to fulfil a social function and provide a platform for family togetherness (Saxbe, Graesch, & Alvik 2011).

Television viewing can also have an impact on our personal relationships. Osborn (2012) examined the television viewing habits of 392 married couples. The goal of Osborn's research was to examine the intersection between TV viewing and romantic relationships. His research tested cultivation theory – to compare media relationships to the real-world relations of the couples in the study. The results of the study concluded that media content can play an important role in the interpersonal realms and should be considered when examining factors that impact relational outcomes. Familial relationships have been found to impact the behaviors of individuals while watching television. One example is Walker and Bellamy's (2001) examination of remote-control use while families are viewing television. They reported that some remote control behaviors (grazing and multiple program viewing) resulted in a negative impact on the desire to view as a familial unit. Potentially agreeing to watch a single program may lead to longer coviewing time and perhaps include binge watching.

Changing Family Structures and Living Arrangements

Changing technology habits, as detailed above, demonstrate both a fragmentation in viewing among family members in a household while still demonstrating how television viewing can fulfill important interpersonal needs among family members. While far more experienced sociologists have weighed in, a discussion of the role of television in the family unit over time would be remiss to not include a brief discussion of how the family unit itself has changed over time. Pew Research Center reports that family life is changing: Since 1960, there has been both a trend toward smaller family sizes and a rising diversity in family structure, in which a two-parent (in their first marriage) home with several children is no longer the dominant family norm (Pew Research Center, 2015). The trend toward smaller family size is driven by two changes over time. First, there has been an increase in single parent households: In 1960, 9% of children lived in single parent households, and in 2014, 26% of children did. It is also driven by a decreasing birthrate, which is likely due to a combination of factors, including increased educational attainment, labor force participation, a general trend away from marriage, and improvements in contraception (Pew Research, 2015). Changing family dynamics and average size of families likely interact with television viewing and media behaviors in interesting ways.

At the same time families are getting smaller; individuals are delaying marriage and having children (United States Census Bureau, 2018). The median age at first marriage rose by over 2.5 years for both men and women from 2003 to 2018, to 29.8 years old and 27.8 years old, respectively. In 2018, 29% of those 18–34 year olds were married and living with a partner. In 1978 – at the height of the family hour – that number was nearly 60%. While those 18–34 are now more likely to live with an unmarried partner than they have been in the past, they are also more likely to live at home with their parents. A full 54% of those ages 18–24 live with a parent, while 16% of those ages 25–34 do. Changing dynamics such as these have led both researchers and lay pop culture commentators to discuss the concept of extended or delayed adolescence (Stretka, 2017; Twenge & Park, 2019). An analysis of seven large nationally representative surveys of U.S. adolescents between 1976 and 2016 (N = 8.44 million; between 1976 and 2016) found that teens are delaying a number of adult activities. Basically, the 18-year olds of today are like the 15-year olds of 25 years ago. They have sex later, they drink less, use tobacco and drugs less – but they are also less likely to drive, work part-time, go out without their parents, and date (Twenge & Park, 2019). Twenge and Park's (2019) analysis ruled out the influence of increased time spent on extracurriculars or studying (this amount of time has remained relatively flat) and examined time spent online. The decline in adult activity participation began prior to widespread adoption of the Internet, although the authors note it may play a role in the continued decreases observed over the 2000s. Other research analyses have demonstrated that adolescents are indeed spending more time with media – with a pattern of social media and online activities displacing time spent with books and television (Twenge, Martin, & Spitzberg, 2019).

Today's 20 somethings – whose cord-cutting, shaving and never-ing are discussed in Chapter 6 – have grown up amid increasingly diverse family norms, and are more likely to have an extended young adulthood. These environmental factors have likely shaped them into different television content consumers than generations past. More time as a young adult – with the help of cost-reduced living at home and absent the responsibilities of partnership and children could certainly lead to speculation about an increase in time to binge watch television. Representative, time-lagged studies on media use are rare enough (Twenge et al., 2019), that empirical studies of these changing factors' influence on media consumption patterns remain a far-away goal at the moment.

Situational Determinants of TV Viewing

As documented throughout this text, there are competing approaches to studying television audiences. Taneja and Viswanathan (2014) discuss perspectives on understanding television viewing audiences. Historically there was tension between seeing audiences as active who watch TV to satisfy their needs (e.g., Uses & Gratifications) and the influence of situational factors or determinants such as media environment, audience availability, and group viewing. Individual determinants (micro-level) of television viewing and binge viewing, as well as the Uses and Gratifications approach are discussed in greater detail in Chapter 5. The next section details situational determinants of television viewing.

Situational determinants have been shown to have an impact on television viewing behaviors. Taneja and Viswanathan (2014) suggest that situational determinants explain media use even in contemporary high-choice media environments. The continued influence of situational determinants is attributed to people's strong media habits, particularly those that influence viewing practices (LaRose, 2010; Taneja & Viswanathan, 2014). Specifically, Taneja and Viswanathan (2014) argue, "situational determinants explain an impressive proportion of variance in viewing patterns, yet fail to provide insights into the mechanisms responsible for these patterns" (p. 2137).

More recent studies attempt to combine both individual and situational factors (Cooper & Tang, 2009; Wooneberger, Schoenbach, & van Meurs, 2009). This attempt is not new to media studies. In 1982, Webster and Wakshlag proposed an integration of both perspectives. Their model

> suggests that a viewer's traits, needs, and preferences for a type of program influence his decision to watch a certain program type. However, the viewer should be available and choose that program over competing programs. Moreover, the viewer's companion(s) should not restrict him or her from watching that program. In other words, this framework suggests that individual needs and preferences are moderated by situational factors. (Taneja & Viswanathan, 2014, p. 2137)

Wooneberger et al. (2009) examined the effect of having multiple platforms available for audience selection. They measured both situational and individual factors and tested the interaction of the two. Their results demonstrated that "individual characteristics and needs (age, education, and viewing motivations) are moderated by situational factors such as audience availability, and group viewing" (p. 2152). The next section will detail these situational factors. There have been numerous studies exploring reasons why people watch TV and the specific programs they select. While demographic and socio-economic characteristics of television viewers can impact why certain shows are watched (Rao 1975; Webster 1986), and re-watched (Bentley & Murray, 2016), the focus of the next section of this chapter is how changes in media technology have impacted our viewing behaviors.

Media Environment

The changing media landscape is influencing television viewing behaviors. The structure of television content offerings and having access to different media forms, as well as the constant addition of new media platforms are impacting how people are watching TV. Over time, we find an increasing number of people watching alone with newer and more mobile technology. Newer technology devices have increased the amount of synchronous coviewing experiences. In 2012, 62% of TV viewers reported using social media while viewing (Ericcson ConsumerLab).

Another reason for changes in viewing behaviors is media ownership, including the number of television sets typically owned by families. In 2005, there were more television sets per household on average (2.93) than the average number of people per household (2.54) (Perry, 2010). However, more recently there has been a decline in the number of television sets per household. Lott (2017) has reported the Energy Information Administration's (EIA) assessment of Residential Energy Consumption Survey (RECS) revealed the percentage of homes without a television increased from 1.3% to 2.6% between 2009 and 2015. Likewise, the same trend was reported for the percentage of homes with more than two televisions over the same period. There was a decline to less than 39% of homes reporting three or more TV sets in 2015 down from 44% a high in 2009. In this same period, 68% of U.S. adults owned a smartphone, an increase from 35% in 2011, and 45% among adults reported owning tablet computers (Anderson, 2015). The number of devices connected to the Internet per household continue to increase. As these ownership trends suggest, television viewing has expanded to include displays which allow for viewing content in multiple and mobile locations outside of the home (Bondad-Brown, Rice, & Pearce, 2012). A thorough look at cord-cutting, cord-shaving, and cord-never-ing is in Chapter 6.

Audience Availability

Audience availability is the time people have in their daily lives to spend time watching television content. Work or family obligations impact the amount of free time people have available in their daily lives and often result in individuals having the same time blocks being free each day.

Some researchers view audience availability as being related to ritual or habitual viewing (Cooper, 1996; Rosenstein & Grant, 1997; Webster, 1985) and that audience availability precedes program choice. Evidence that people watch TV content at the same time regardless of what programs are on TV supports this position. Other researchers examine a subset of audience availability: audience duplication. Audience duplication is defined as the size of the audience common to two different programs on different days. Duplication research asserts that people are more connected to the time a particular program is broadcast and to the channels on which they are aired, rather than the content of the programs (Goodhardt, Ehrenberg, & Collins, 1975). In audience duplication research, program exposure is an attribute of programs, and the program is the unit of analysis. Individuals display strong program loyalty, repeat viewing, and duplication of some programs. Even when people have an almost unlimited choice of programs, we continue to see audiences engaging in repeated viewing of well-loved movies and TV shows.

If we consider the changing media landscape, then we might consider how audience availability is impacted by the increasing mobility of media offerings. With more streaming services reintroducing the airing of single episodes each week – and thus creating an extended timeline for the viewing of the program, sometimes audience members arrange their schedule to be available during the time a show is airing live (Bury, 2017), similar to how people viewed TV programming before streaming services, on-demand viewing, or VCRs. Other audience members may have increased availability due to using multiple media at once, discussed below. Interestingly, researchers continue to see viewing patterns that are "guided by both patterns of availability as well as the practice of watching TV as a group" (Taneja & Viswanathan, 2014, p. 2153).

Group Viewing

Morrison and Krugman (2001) assert that television is a social activity often viewed in the company of others. Numerous researchers have examined group practices across the decades and offered several explanations as to the longevity of this activity. While entertainment is often identified as a primary motivation, Lull (1980) described group/family viewing as contributing "to structuring of the day" (p. 202). Some researchers have studied families as groups and examined the media choices of these groups. Specifically, content choices were explored to understand viewing patterns. Webster and Wakslag (1982) compared the viewing patterns of individuals and groups. Previously, patterns of program choice were understood to be directly related to individual program choice. Researchers had found this pattern when studying the viewing habits of people who were viewing TV alone. Solitary viewers were the most likely to watch or avoid particular types or genres. However, Webster and Wakslog (1982) found that when people viewed TV in the company of others, individual program type loyalty was diminished. An individual may watch content preferred by the group and not consistent with their own preferences and needs. Group viewing transforms program choice from an individual preference into a socially negotiated choice (Taneja & Viswanathan, 2014).

Ducheneaut, Moore, Oehlberg, Thornton, and Nickell (2008) observed physically separated viewers who knew each other and who were connected via an audio link. This arrangement allowed the groups to interact while watching the same TV program. The researchers observed the viewing groups and categorized their comments while viewing. Five types of comments were identified: (1) Content-based comments refer directly to the show's content; (2) Context-based comments refer to the show in broader context but not the specific episode being viewed; (3) Logistical comments refer to the television watching experience but not the program; (4) Non-sequiturs are comments or social exchanges not related to the TV program; and (5) Phatic responses are emotional and involuntary reactions to the content. Ducheneaut et al. (2008) concluded that "interactions between television viewers are tightly interwoven with the structure of the show they are watching" (p. 147).

Chaney, Gartell, Hofman, Guiver, Koesnigstein, Kohli, and Paqut (2014) examined group viewing patterns with a large data set using peoplemeter and paper diaries collected in June 2012 by the Nielsen Company. Similar to Webster and Wakslog, Chaney et al. concluded that groups are more complex than the sum of their parts and that viewing habits shift significantly between individual and group preferences.

Group viewing program preferences. Group viewing impacts the type of content watched, and group preferences may evolve. Groups who watch together regularly develop a shared program type loyalty that emerges over time and is similar to individual program loyalty (Webster & Wakslog, 1982). Research has found that group viewing increases the likelihood of watching news programming even for people uninterested in the news (Wonneberger et al., 2011). News viewing allows viewers to participate in both viewing of and conversation about the television content, whereas the complex plots of some narrative content do not afford conversation as well.

In a survey investigating social interactions during group viewing situations, (Ducheneaut et al., 2008) asked participants about the type of programming participants were likely to watch in a group setting. Participants reported animation, sports events, documentaries, reality television, and poor-quality movies. These television program genres are not typically identified as ones that people are frequently binge watching. We have suggested that limiting the term "binge watching" to narrative content reflects the most popular usage, as most people think of binge watching compelling, serial dramatic shows (See Chapter 5 for a fuller discussion). It appears that the types of television programming we are enjoying watching with others may not be the same content we would select to re-watch (unless we are watching a film or TV series to show it to others) or even to binge watch. Indeed, the connotation of a binge watcher viewing episode after episode while sitting alone on the couch is the opposite of watching a live sporting event at a restaurant with a large group of others or hosting friends for a presidential candidate debate at one's home. What makes sports, documentaries, reality television, and news content enjoyable to watch with others? The next section about group viewing – with known and unknown others via communication technologies and apps investigates the content viewed with others, and what conversations and effects this mode of viewing engenders.

New Patterns in Group & Coviewing: Toward Defining Social Viewing

The influence of coviewing on viewing patterns and viewer behavior is of interest to both academics and media industries. Mediated "Social TV" practices permit television viewers to connect with, monitor, and express themselves to entire communities during viewing (Cohen & Lancaster, 2014, p. 512). Much of the coviewing experiences revolve around the actual content generated in online channels (e.g., live-tweets) while watching live TV programs (Ji, 2019). Like conversations with others in the same room (direct sociability), sharing comments via social viewing includes comments on the content of the program, thus allowing water cooler talk to take place in real-time instead of the next day (indirect sociability) (Krämer, Winter, Benninghoff, & Gallus, 2015). Television viewing has expanded and now includes sharing content via displays across locations and media users (Bondad-Brown, Rice, & Pearce, 2012). Some researchers have characterized this virtual coviewing as a more active viewing style with audiences engaging in content-producing and content-sharing (Jenkins, 2006; Shirky, 2010).

Over time, the terminology used to describe viewing with others – whether family members or friends – has evolved from using the term "group viewing" to the introduction of the term "coviewing." The meaning of the term "coviewing" also has changed. Initially coviewing was used to describe situations where parents and children viewed television together. While this definition is still used, it more commonly refers to a broader range of viewing situations where individuals are viewing content together. Coviewing has been defined as the "shared consumption of an entertainment product whether in public, with a stranger, or privately with a friend, and has many implications for how viewers select and respond to media entertainment" (Banjo et al., 2017, p. 609). The definition of coviewing has also been stretched to include individuals watching the same programming in different physical locations.

As researchers stretched the term "coviewing" to include viewing together in different physical locations, some people argued a new term was needed. As early as 2012, Doughty, Rowland, and Lawson defined virtual coviewing as a "shared or co-viewing experience afforded by the use of a second screen during television viewing sessions" (p. 80) and suggested that social networking communities could be analogous to coviewing experiences. However, some researchers have suggested that this virtual coviewing may have negative impact by weakening family ties by bringing virtual others into family spaces and quality time (Harboe, 2009, 2010).

There have been several attempts to create technology that allows people in different locations to coview programming in a connected manner. The term some researchers used to describe new technologies connecting people watching TV who are not in the same physical location is "SocialTV" (Almeida, Ferraz, Pinho, & Costa, 2012; Chorianopoulos & Lekakos, 2008; Jin, Xie, Wen, & Xie, 2013; Weisz et al., 2007; Wu, Zhang, Wu et al., 2013). "Social television" was defined by Harboe (2009) as "any technology that supports social practices associated with TV" (p. 6). The term "Social TV" has also been defined as "a shared viewing experience in which different media technologies and platforms are integrated into traditional television viewing" (Ji, 2019, p. 169). This integration allows live interactions of various types ranging from voice to text-only exchanges among viewers who are in different physical locations. One example of a Social TV technology is Danmaku which is a "real-time commentary system that displays user-generated comments specific to the current playback time of the video as streams of moving subtitles overlaid on the video screen" (Chen, Gao, & Ra, 2017, p. 731). Ji (2019) reports that the adoption rate and consumer use of technology designed specifically for this function are quite low.

The term "Social TV" has also been applied to coviewing using social media channels and messaging apps with both known and unknown others or as people connecting with each other via social media formats while consuming other types of media content (Gorkovenko & Taylor, 2016; Schirra, Sun, & Bentley, 2014; Trilling, 2015; Wohn & Na, 2011).

For example, Lin, Sung, and Chen (2016) assert "social television, brought about by the integration of TV and digital technology to support sociable, computer-mediated group viewing experiences, has made the act of TV viewing a communication, interactive, and engaging experience" (2016, p. 171). While, Hwang and Lim (2015) define Social TV as "real-time backchannel communication on social networking sites (SNSs) during a live television broadcast" (p. 756). Most commonly, this type of behavior is defined as an act of using social technologies to communicate with other while viewing television content (Harboe, 2009; Kim, Merrill, & Yang, 2019; Raney & Ji, 2017).

While the use of technologies intended to create Social TV experiences are quite low, audiences have adapted technology designed originally for other uses such as tablets, mobile phones, and laptops to create connections to other TV viewers. In 2014, Nagy and Midha reported 85% of primetime-active twitter users regularly tweeted about TV programs while watching live. Over time, the social media channel used to communicate during viewing television has changed. Currently, the most common device for engaging in Social TV is with a smartphone using IMS (primarily WhatsApp) or private communication channels, such as text messaging. Newer technologies, including apps, allow for user comments to be time-synchronized (Chen, Gao, & Rau, 2017).

Other researchers have referred to virtual coviewing as second screening (Lochrie & Coulton, 2012), connected viewing (Holt & Sanson, 2014), and social viewing (Lee & Choi, 2017). However, the most comprehensive definition comes from Lee and Choi (2017), who suggested the term "social viewing." Social viewing *"emphasizes that social viewers can partake in a virtually communal experience of television viewing with other co-viewers through the use of online media (e.g., blog, comments, chatting, messenger, etc.) pre, post, and during television viewing"* (Lee & Choi, 2017, p. 302). This definition also extends to the viewing experience, program selection, discussion of program content, and the impact of the program that occur in the post-viewing phase. It is the term and definition that we endorse because it provides a clear definition while incorporating the whole process. The term "social viewing" is used throughout the remainder of this chapter, where the media behavior discussed fits into this definition – even when the author(s) did not use this term in the original research report.

How is social viewing different from other definitions? In order to be considered "social viewing" instead of second-screen viewing requires individuals to be engaging with virtual coviewers and not just using another screen (smart phone, table, or laptop) to engage with separate content such as shopping or a game. Social viewing is also different from coviewing where viewers' sense of connectedness is bound to the physical presence of others, while social viewers are connected virtually and thus not limited to a small group or even the same group twice.

Social viewing occurs on a continuum of private to public communication (Marwick & boyd, 2011). The private includes people known to the audience member who they are engaging in social viewing, whereas the public participants may not be known. Research has shown that individuals tend to engage in Social TV viewing more in public platforms than private ones (Kim, Merrill, & Yang, 2019).

Content of Social Viewing Messages

To understand how social viewing connects television audiences, the messages of social viewing posts were examined by researchers. The majority of these studies are descriptive qualitative studies. In 2011, Wohn and Na analyzed and compared tweets sent during either a reality TV program or a televised political event. The tweets were categorized into four categories of comments: First, attention-seeking messages which were attempts to bring attention to oneself. Second, informational messages primarily relating information about the program. Third, emotional messages, which included subject references to self and how the audience member felt. The fourth category was opinionated messages, including subjective opinions about the program content.

Other types of television content have yielded similar findings. McPherson et al. (2012) conducted a mixed-methods study, including a content analysis of the tweets posted during the television show Glee and conducted qualitative interviews. The participants reported sending live-tweets about episodes, specific show related events, as well as more general show-related comments. The type of programming impacted the conversations more than being physically or virtually co-located (Oehlberg, Ducheneaut, Thomton, Moore, & Nickell, 2006). This was supported by Ji and Zhao (2015), who content analyzed 4400 tweets sent during various programming content. The programming genres included a drama, an award show, and a sports game. Different patterns of social viewing were found, largely depending on the program *content* being discussed. Posts made during sports broadcasts were related to the judgment of the scene or action in the game. Tweets during an award show were primarily related to judgmental comments about actors and included the most tweets with mentioned names of individuals (mostly celebrities). What we see when considered all together is that live posting is a building block of Social TV (Ji, 2019).

Genre Differences in Social Viewing

Researchers have examined several types of television genres and how audiences engage in social viewing. Some genres appear to lead to higher levels of participating in social viewing than others. Notably, dramas may not be suitable for live/synchronous connected viewing (Vanattenhoven & Geerts, 2017), but have generated much social media content post-viewing (Lozano Delmar & Bourdaa, 2015; Slade, Narro, & Givens'-Carroll, 2015). Over the past decade, audiences have engaged in social viewing with political content in addition to narrative content. Gil de Zuniga and Liu (2017) reported that social viewing during the broadcast of political content and political or presidential debates is quite common. Additionally, Selva (2016) conducted interviews with 31 people who met the criteria of tweeting during a political televised debate and who regularly tweet while watching television content. The interviewees reported that their primary motivation for engaging in social viewing while watching political content was the perception of being a good citizen and providing information to other viewers.

Sports are an activity that people will go to great lengths to experience with a group. So, it is not surprising that this genre generates some of the highest numbers of social viewing interactions. For example, in Feb 2016, more than 27 million tweets were shared via twitter during the Superbowl (Flynn, 2016), while the 2014 FIFA World Cup semi-final match between Germany and Brazil was tweeted about more than 35.6 million times during the game (Dredge, 2014). Two other studies, discussed in the section below about second screening, also report that viewers spend the most time talking with others – and performing a number of other tasks on connected devices – during sports content viewing, and they spend the least amount of time on social viewing and multitasking during dramatic content (Rubenking, 2016; Voorveld & Viswanathan, 2014).

Motivations for Engaging in Social Viewing

Motivations for engaging in social viewing were examined by McDonald, Lin, Anderegg, Na, and Dale in 2014. The reported motivations for viewing TV impacted the type of tweets sent by the viewers. Participants who reported instrumental (more active, intentional) motives tended to send more detailed tweets, which were posted typically after the broadcast and not during the broadcast; while participants who reported more ritualized motives (more passive, medium-based) tended to post live during the broadcast. Some studies found that social viewing experiences, primarily via Twitter, usually occur without communication between viewers. Wohn and Na (2011) suggested that digitally connected social viewers who were tweeting live during the television program were not seeking to connect directly with anyone in particular, but were more interested in conversing about the program. This appears to be particularly true of newer media formats that are providing audiences more opportunities to consume their preferred content (Dutta-Berghman, 2004).

While perhaps using Twitter is not the best channel to connect directly with specific, known, individuals, Cohen, Bowman, and Alexander (2016) suggest that people are drawn to using twitter for social viewing because of a sense of belonging with no strings attached. Some researchers defined this behavior as needing to belong. Early and traditional television viewing research found that individuals with a greater need to belong may appreciate television viewing with at least one other person. Currently, having a higher need to belong may also be predictive of social networking sites and mobile phone use (Cohen et al., 2016).

A greater need to belong may be a predictor of engaging in social viewing. Lin et al. (2016) found that viewers who interact with programs and other viewers through social viewing reported greater satisfaction and investment toward a favorite program. The participants described that they feel the interaction they experience via social viewing is "an extension of their viewing experience" (p. 176). Additionally, Hwang and Lim (2015), who examined the impact of social viewing and viewer engagement, found that social viewing allows viewers to feel a sense of being together or social presence. They identified three motivations for engaging in social viewing – convenience, excitement, and information. These three motivations resonate with the traditional needs for sharing, feeling, and belonging (Hwang & Lim, 2015). While researchers reported a variety of motivations for engaging in social viewing, the need to belong is unique in being reported in nearly all studies on the motivation to engage in social viewing (Cohen & Lancaster, 2014; Haradakis & Hanson, 2009; Kim, Merrill, & Yang, 2019). More recently, researchers have started to explore the motivations for engaging in social viewing and live posting or sending tweets while a program is live on air. Ji (2019) reported five motivations. First, social viewing provides participants with a sense of social presence or being a part of a community. Second, social interaction with virtual others was considered as a substitution for real live interaction. Third, social viewing was reported to be cathartic because participants report needing to express their arousal reaction or emotional response to the content. Fourth, participants reported that social viewing allowed them to engage with content because they share and receive information on the program. Fifth, they engaged in social viewing because it was entertaining and fun. Ji (2019) concluded that social viewing experience is integrally linked to the actual content that viewers generated in online channels (e.g., live-tweets) while watching live TV programs (Ji, 2019).

Effects of Social Viewing

There are several studies that have examined the effect of social viewing. Numerous researchers report individuals feel connected to a larger group or experience a feeling of belonging when they engage in social viewing while watching television content (Chen, Gao, & Rau 2017; Cohen & Lancaster 2014; Han & Lee, 2014; Kramer et al., 2015). This is consistent with the psychological and relational benefits previously associated with television coviewing with others physically present. Television viewing in the presence of others provides opportunities to converse (Fallis, Fitzpatrick, & Fristad, 1985; Finucane & Horvath, 2000; Gantz, 1985), and provide comfort to others (Zillmann, Weaver, & Mundorf, 1986).

Entertainment & Enjoyment. Entertainment has long been identified as a motivation for TV viewing (Rubin, 1984) as well as an outcome of watching television (Raney & Bryant, 2020; Vorderer, Klimmt, & Ritterfeld, 2004). It should come as no surprise that researchers have found that entertainment is central to audiences' motivations and response to engaging in social viewing (Smith, Pegoraro, & Cruikshank, 2019). Mora, Ho, and Krider (2011) reported that individuals who frequently engaged in social viewing were more likely to spend more time with media entertainment than people who viewed on their own. A fuller discussion of enjoyment/entertainment is in Chapter 6.

Emotional Contagion. Physically coviewing is theorized to heighten affective reactions to content because the presence of others permits emotions to spread contagiously (Hocking, 1982; Wenner & Gantz, 1998). This spreading of emotional response is also called emotional contagion. Emotional contagion is defined by Cohen and Lancaster (2015) as the tendency to pick up on experience or express another person's mood or emotions. Other researchers had argued that group viewing and coviewing inhibits emotional reactions (Harris & Cook, 2010) while Banjo et al. (2015) found in-group and out-group differences of emotional reactions with more emotional contagion when in-groups viewed programs together. When examining social viewing, Cohen and Lancaster found that participants who reported greater susceptibility to catching others' emotions tend to engage in social viewing more often. However, emotional contagion did not lead to more frequent social viewing.

Engagement. Lim, Hwang, Kim, and Biocca (2015) proposed three levels of social viewing engagement. Specifically, they identified functional, emotional, and communal engagement. Lim et al. define functional engagement as online users' "real-time participation in a social media platform to modify the format and content of such mediated environments" (p. 159). Emotional engagement is defined as the feelings a viewer has toward commentators, actors, athletes, and the events of the program. Lim et al. also include feelings toward other social viewers as being part of emotional engagement. The sense of feeling connected to others is communal engagement. Lim et al. concluded that emotional engagement increased channel commitment and led to channel loyalty. Ultimately, Lim et al. argue that emotional engagement is required to have more "bonding relationships" with the program and with other social viewers (p. 165). Social viewing increases a sense of social presence with other social viewers (Kim et al., 2019).

Social trust. Patulny (2011) examined the associations between trust and media use. The results demonstrate that when people spend most of the time with others they know (e.g., friends, family), it leads to lower levels of trust in people outside of these groups, while more time spent with others (e.g., strangers) correlates with higher levels of trust in people in general. The time spent with virtual others also leads to higher trust levels of people in the real world. Lee and Choi (2017) found that TV viewers who engage in social viewing are more likely to have social capital with other social viewers, and they have more contact with others who hold divergent opinions.

Social Viewing and Binge Watching

The investment in creating technologies specifically designed to connect viewers who are not physically co-located demonstrates the desire for companionship in many viewing situations. The technologies and apps created specifically for individuals to connect over shared television content are just a recent development in television history and highlights the prevalence of socializing while viewing. These communication technologies have not, however, created the desire to connect with others while viewing. Using twitter to talk about an exciting series premier, text messaging a friend about a performance at an awards show, or posting about your favorite teams' horrendous performance in the big game on Facebook is merely today's version of the family hour or water cooler interactions. Due to changing family structures and living situations, the rise of "bedroom culture," and the increased time we spend physically alone but always within arm's reach of a connected device, it only follows we continue to enjoy watching with others.

However, in social viewing situations, what *we're doing while we watch*, and *what content* we are watching may be quite distinct from when we are binge watching. The content genres most discussed in social viewing situations are not the ones most selected in binge-watching situations, and the experiential components of binge watching, such as feeling absorbed and transported into the story, do not lend themselves to simultaneous polite conversation. However, there are similarities: Many of the effects of social viewing, for example, entertainment, enjoyment, experiencing emotions, and engagement are common to both modes of viewing. Further studies examining both ways of watching television should be explored. A third mode, or common way of viewing, is watching television while media multitasking or "second screening." Like social viewing, multitasking enables more time to be spent watching television. A review of the literature and its relevance to binge watching are discussed below.

Media Multitasking

Multitasking (introduced in Chapter 2) across media is one way individuals are coping with a limited amount of viewing time while having so many different media device and content options. Nielsen reports that U.S. adults spend nearly 10.5 hours per day consuming media, and much of that is spent simultaneously watching television and interacting with a digital device (Knight, 2018). A 2018 survey found that 36% of the respondents said that they use television and a digital device simultaneously "very often," 28% said they "sometimes" do, and 9% said that they "always" do. Only a combined 27% reported rarely or never engaging with a secondary digital device while viewing television. Other research demonstrates this commitment to engaging with other devices while viewing television: Between 68% and 80% of U.S. adults report multitasking with other devices while watching TV, and estimates place the total percentage of media usage that is split between two devices to be between 40% and 65% (Clement, 2019; Interactive Advertising Bureau (IAB), 2015; Nielsen, 2012; Pilotta, Schultz, Drenik, & Rist, 2006). The IAB reports that more than two-thirds of smartphone users regularly conduct other activities while on their phone during television viewing.

Our interest in media multitasking as it relates to binge watching is both general and specific. At a more macro-level, there has always been multitasking while watching television, as documented in Chapter 2. However, the seemingly endless potential combinations of *media* multitasking have increased over time, as has a more general cultural shift to splitting one's attention across multiple tasks or media being a norm. This may be especially true during one's downtime, which can be spent watching television. A second, more closely related tie between binge watching and media multitasking is the paradox of today's television watching landscape (also briefly discussed in Chapter 6). There has never been as much premium, compelling, well-done narrative television content available to binge, *and* there also has never been as many mediated distractions which can serve to pull us away from being engrossed in them.

A Multitasking Distinction: Dual Tasking vs. Task Switching

Media multitasking is a broad term which encompasses several distinctions and many combinations. One such distinction is between dual tasking, where two tasks are being completed concurrently (Lee & Taatgen, 2002) and task switching, which is when one alternates attention and effort across tasks serially. Yeykelis, Cummings, and Reeves (2014) reviewed the communication literature on media multitasking and found that 34 of 54 studies in communication and related fields approach media multitasking as concurrent use of two or more devices. They smartly contend that exploring between and within device multitasking is important. Yeykelis et al. (2014) used screen capture software to monitor switching tabs over hours of time among college students that, with the permission of students, captured screenshots of their computers every 5 seconds. They found that a switch occurred every 19 seconds on average, much shorter than previous research had demonstrated. Given the technological convergence that has followed digitization, we're now using less devices to complete just as many or more tasks. How we manipulate and switch between content streams or apps on one device has become of even more practical relevance. This becomes of keen interest in relation to binge watching, since the prevalence of watching on devices that allow quick and easy tab/ window switching – such as laptops and mobile devices – is drastically on the rise, especially among younger viewers.

The focus on between-device multitasking is likely due in part to the multitasking combinations and downstream effects that drive communication and media research investigations into multitasking. Many are concerned either with the effects of multitasking or "multiscreening" in regard to media planning and assuring exposure to advertising messages (Pilotta, Schultz, Drenik, & Rist, 2006; Segijn, Voorveld, Vanderberg, Pennekemp, & Smit, 2017), while many others explore these behaviors as they relate to students' academic performance (Calderwood, Ackerman, & Conklin, 2014; Rosen, Carrier, & Cheever, 2013). Generally, multitasking results in negative cognitive outcomes, or performance outcomes related to a primary task (Jeong & Hwang, 2012; Ophir, Nass, & Wagner, 2009; Wang & Tchernev, 2012).

Indeed, some research finds that individuals may be giving up performance and cognitive-based outcomes for emotional, or entertainment-based ones. One study of gratifications sought and obtained while multitasking found that cognitive motivations were often a gratification sought, yet not obtained while media multitasking (Wang & Tchernev, 2012). However, emotional gratifications, which were not being sought, were often being obtained. It may simply be worth the trade-off to multitask when the primary task is challenging or boring. Several other studies suggest that multitasking may serve to augment or enhance experiences when a primary task is dull or boring but overstimulate or overload an already enjoyable primary task. In a study by Chinchanachokchai, Duff, and Sar (2015), where the primary task was simply viewing advertisements, participants in two and three task conditions reported greater enjoyment than those in the single task condition. Those in the dual and three task conditions also expressed more positive brand attitudes toward the brands featured in the advertisements being viewed. The pendulum can swing the other way as well. In a study where the primary task was watching a sitcom of the participants' choosing and the secondary task was interacting on Facebook (which included low and high multitasking conditions), the opposite was found. Participants in the multitasking conditions reported less enjoyment and engagement with the television show, and the effect was even more pronounced among self-reported heavier multitaskers (Oviedo, Tornquist, Cameron, & Chaippe, 2015). A separate study found no effect on enjoyment between multitasking and single task conditions when the primary task was viewing either positive or negative television shows. However, there was an effect when the television show being viewed was boring/ neutral such that less enjoyment was reported in the multitasking condition (Rubenking, 2017). These studies demonstrate that the nature of a primary task and multitasking may interact in different ways when trying to establish enjoyment of the viewing experience.

Media Multitasking Combinations

Certain media multitasking combinations are more likely to occur than others. One study of Dutch adults found that about 60% were using multiple screens simultaneously for an average of 30 minutes per day (Segijn et al., 2019). The study further investigated the prevalence of multitasking across different platforms in their diary-based study: TV, smartphones, laptops, tablets, PCs, gaming devices, and e-readers among self-report "multiscreeners." The top three combinations all included multitasking while watching TV. In order, they were: television and smartphone; television and laptop; and television and tablet (the fourth most common combination was laptop and smartphone). Similarly, a widely cited study of teens and multitasking reports that teens are spending more time with television than any other platform: a number that is increasing due to more time spent multitasking while watching television (Foehr, 2006; Rideout, Foer, & Roberts, 2010). They report television and listening to music to be the platforms that are most likely to be used alongside a second device/ mediated activity.

A network analysis of data gathered on the Media Multitasking Index (Ophir, Nass, & Wagner, 2009) sought to determine the most frequent multitasking combinations reported (Wiradhany & Baumgartner, 2019). In contrast to the studies reported above and several others, they did not find TV viewing to be among the most common activities reported when two media activities were being carried out concurrently. Listening to music, browsing, and texting/IM-ing were the most prominent media tasks used in conjunction with others. Wiradhany and Baumgartner (2019) suggest that this finding is reflective of an overall shift, especially among younger individuals, away from traditional media consumption, such as watching television and reading books, and toward more "new" and social media use. They state that this could indicate that media which were traditionally consumed in a ritualistic, passive fashion is also changing: from television viewing to texting and browsing social media. Another result reported in this network analysis was the finding that all the most commonly used devices during multitasking were no more likely to be a primary or secondary task. That is, participants were just as likely to report that they were primarily engaging in texting/ IM'ing, or they were engaging in the same media behavior as a secondary task. Overall, this study suggests a more fluid and evolving story of media multitasking. We think that this example of the fast-pace of change in new media behaviors and how they relate to the relatively "old" media behavior of television watching should be carefully considered by researchers moving forward.

Second Screening

While "new media" multitasking combinations may be exceedingly popular, those in the industry and academics alike have been particularly interested in multitasking while television viewing. This has been dubbed "second screening" by some – which denotes the second content stream being concurrently used alongside television viewing on a second device, or screen. A second screen could be any second screen, including a laptop while one is watching television on a television, or mobile device or tablet while one is watching television content on a desktop or laptop. In addition to the downstream effects that second screening can have on entertainment and cognitive outcomes, other questions surrounding what types of devices are being used, what people are doing on that second screen, and qualities of primary screen content that may encourage or discourage second screen usage are all relevant questions with empirical answers perceived to be quite valuable.

An eMarketer report (Chadha, 2018) reports a combination of studies from YuMe, Nielsen, and PwC on devices used to second screen most frequently. In 2017, 177.7 million U.S. adults simultaneously used a computer and/ or mobile device and television at least monthly, and that number was predicted to grow between 4% and 5% in 2018 and 2019. Chadha (2018) found that 68% of younger audiences (ages 20–36) fell into this second screening group, and they were equally likely to use a smartphone or a desktop/ laptop to do so. Older age groups were slightly less likely to second screen but were more likely to do so on a laptop/ desktop than on a mobile device. It may also be helpful to know if the technology being used to view television has an impact on the prevalence or devices used to multitask while viewing. Rubenking (2016) found college students' primary technology used to watch television had no impact on the frequency or extent of multitasking while viewing. However, that study did reveal that access to more technologies – a laptop, tablet, and smartphone – was predictive of greater multitasking while viewing television than having regular access to fewer media technologies.

What else are viewers doing online on their second screens while watching television? In order, one study reports that over 50% of U.S. adults report checking email, using social media, looking up information about what is on TV, playing games, and online shopping. Other less frequent activities include online banking, watching videos, reading the news, taking pictures/ selfies, ordering food, and listening to music/ podcasts (Clement, 2019). The IAB (2015) also reports that "browsing online" is the most common second screen activity. It is also of interest to know if multitaskers are likely to do so when viewing different types or genres of programming. Voorveld and Viswanathan (2014) hypothesized that television content which required more cognitive effort to process would lead to less multitasking than content which demanded less. They found support for this prediction, such that the lowest levels of second screening were reported during dramatic content, and the most second screening behavior was found during sports content, which is often studied in social viewing contexts. Another study that examined multitasking across five television genres also found the most multitasking during sports content (17.76 minutes of every hour) and the least during dramas (12.90 minutes of every hour) (Rubenking, 2016). In order, the most multitasking during an average hour of viewing was reported for sports content, news, premium cable content, sitcoms, and dramas. The limited capacity theories that guided the (data supported) hypotheses in both Voorveld and Viswanathan (2014) and Rubenking (2016) are discussed in the following section.

Theoretical Approaches to Multitasking

In addition to emotion, enjoyment, and an array of new technologies and apps, there is one very clear determinant of multitasking not yet discussed: cognitive load and ability. Many studies exploring media multitasking apply limited capacity theories to hypothesize about when and how people will multitask (Lang, 2000, 2009). Basically, an individual possesses a singular, fixed pool of cognitive resources. Through both automatic, bottom-up and controlled, more deliberate modes of processing, these resources may be allocated to various tasks while engaging with media. As media (or the environment) demand more and more resources, and the demand exceeds availability, a point of cognitive overload is reached. This results in poor encoding and memory for content and can result in a shift in focus from the primary task to the secondary task, or a response similar to shutting down and not attending to any of the stimuli available. Evidence of individuals maintaining a desirable level of cognitive involvement are found in the Chinchanachokchai et al. (2015) and Oviedo et al. (2015) pieces that found multitasking can improve a boring task (i.e., when a task is not involving enough because of lost cognitive demands) as well as lessen the entertainment value when an acceptable level of cognitive resources are being demanded and allocated to a task at hand (i.e., watching a television show).

There simply are limits to the human perception and cognition systems, and these need to be primary considerations when studying humans multitasking with media. Lang and Chrzan (2015) maintain that these limits shape possible multitasking combinations, making some easier and some impossible. For instance, combinations with tasks that do not demand a high level of resources should be more common than those which demand high ones. We see evidence of this in the recent study by Wiradhany and Baumgartner (2019). However, reading an online article and being engaged in a conversation on the phone simultaneously is an impossible feat to do successfully. The human cognitive system cannot listen to, process, and respond to two or more different streams of symbols systems, i.e. language (Lang & Chrzan, 2015). One could pause reading an article, or a television episode to take a phone call, for instance, but you could not listen to two separate streams of language and understand both. If we believe this to be true, multitasking while television viewing is typically a task-switching endeavor: We switch out attention to read a text and then switch right back to the screen we're watching television on. It isn't news that television can be used as background noise, or as a secondary task; however, it is often not referred to in this way in the second screen or multitasking research.

Due to resources being limited, others have noted the tendency of individuals to avoid cognitively taxing situations. Coined the "law of less work" (Allport, 1954; Kool, McGuire, Rosen, & Botvinick, 2010; Wang, Irwin, Cooper, & Srivastava, 2015), researchers have previously noted that except when highly motivated, our primary goal is to conserve resources. Based on this rule and limited capacity models and bottleneck models of cognition, Wang et al. (2015) proposed 11 basic dimensions of media multitasking behaviors that affect resource demand and allocation and can be used to predict both behavioral performance in multitasking situations as well as multitasking combinations employed. The 11 dimensions are categorized into four areas, where the two modalities or technologies to be used concurrently are evaluated upon how task relevant they are, how information is presented to the user, if feedback is required, and along with user differences. Evaluations of previously published research and two empirical studies uniformly supported the predictions along these dimensions: Technologies with greater consistency, user-controlled information flow, and less feedback capabilities or demands were more likely to be used concurrently.

Media Multitasking and Binge Watching

What does this mean for binge watching? It is clear that like binge watching, media multitasking is not a trend set to disappear. Multitasking while viewing can have both positive and negative outcomes for learning and entertainment at the individual level. The cognitive resources demanded, enjoyment/ interest in the tasks, and the relationship between the two tasks all impact outcome variables. This does suggest that we should perhaps be more wary of using video capture/ viewing data from OTT services as evidence of binge watching, if so much of the time we are spending "watching TV" is spent doing other things or with our attention allocated elsewhere. This speaks to the larger issue of defining binge watching as a qualitatively distinct experience, and not just by the number of episodes viewed.

If viewers are spending as much time as they report with other devices while viewing television, and we know that engaging with unrelated secondary tasks either creates a task-switching environment or one that at least hurts cognitive resources being allocated to viewing television, those in the industry that are operating with an advertising supported economic model are on the losing side of this equation. Delivering audiences to advertisers in a multiscreen environment is much harder task. Subscription-based services, including most OTTs, are less affected by this than traditional networks and advertisers. Despite viewers engaging with other tasks while viewing their content, there is no reason to believe that viewers think they're getting a worse deal for the subscription prices they're paying. In some ways, the more secure footing that OTT services have in the marketplace, the stronger a guarantee that the ease of binge watching for most people is safe for the moment. However, one should not assume that all time spent multitasking while watching television serves to draw people away from the content and advertising on television.

Conclusion

This chapter has discussed how our viewing habits have been influenced by situational determinants such as the media environment, the time we have available, and media technologies. The introduction of mobile technologies that allow us to engage more than one source of entertainment at a time (multitasking) has made a significant impact on our viewing behaviors. Additionally, changes in our lifestyle have resulted in more people having access to watch television content on their own. We are viewing less in group settings with friends. While it is occurring less frequently than in the past, group viewing is still occurring in families, especially those with young children. Yet we still crave social interaction about and during television viewing, and many people have started to engage in social viewing using mobile devices (primarily smart phones) to connect to others who are watching the same programs. What the actual impact of these changes viewing behaviors have on binge watching has not yet been determined but is certainly an area worthy of future research.

References

Alexander, A. (1994). The effect of media on family interaction. In D. Zillmann, J. Bryant, & A. C. Huston (Eds.), *Media, children, and the family: Social scientific, psychodynamic, and clinical perspectives* (pp. 51–59). New York: Routledge.

Allport, G. W. (1954). *The nature of prejudice*. New York: Addison Wesley.

Almeida, P., Ferraz, J., Pinho, A., & Costa, D. (2012). Engaging viewers through social TV games. In *Proceedings of the 10th European Conference on Interactive TV and Video* (EuroITV '12). ACM, New York, NY, USA, 175–184. doi: 10.1145/2325616.2325651

Anderson, M. (October 29, 2015). *Technology Device Ownership: 2015*. Pew Research Center Report. Retrieved from https://www.pewinternet.org/2015/10/29/technology-device-ownership-2015/#fn-14935-1

Austin, E. W. (1993) Exploring the effects of active parental mediation of television content. *Journal of Broadcasting & Electronic Media, 37*(2), 147–158. doi: 10.1080/08838159309364212

Ball, S. (1970). *The first year of Sesame Street: An evaluation*. Final Report. Education Testing Service, New Jersey, U.S. Technical Report. Vol 3 (III), 1–439.

Banjo, O. O., Appiah, O., Wang, Z., Brown, C., & Walther, W. O. (2015). Co-Viewing effects of ethnic-oriented programming. *Journalism & Mass Communication Quarterly, 92*(3), 662–680. doi:10.1177/1077699015581804

Banjo, O. O., Wang, Z., Appiah, O., Brown, C., Walther-Martin, W., Tchernev, J., Hedstrom, A., & Irwin, M. (2017). Experiencing racial humor with outgroups: A psychophysiological examination of co-viewing effects. *Media Psychology, 20*(4), 607–631. doi: 10.1080/15213 269.2016.1234396

Bausinger, H. (1984). Media, technology, and everyday life. *Media, Culture, and Society, 6*(4), 343–352. doi: 10.1177/016344378400600403

Bentley, F., & Murray, J. (2016). Understanding video rewatching experiences. *Proceedings of the ACM International Conference on Interactive Experiences for TV and Online Video* (TVX '16). ACM, New York, NY, USA, 69–75. doi: 10.1145/2932206.2932213

Bondad-Brown, B.A., Rice, R.E., & Pearce, K.E. (2012) Influences on TV viewing and online user-shared video use: Demographics, generations, contextual age, media use, motivations, and audience activity. *Journal of Broadcasting & Electronic Media, 56*(4), 471–493. doi: 10.1 080/08838151.2012.732139

Buijzen, M., & Valkenburg, P. M. (2005). Parental mediation of undesired advertising effects. *Journal of Broadcasting & Electronic Media, 49*(2), 153–165. doi: 10.1207/s15506878jobem 4902_1

Buijzen, M., Walma van der Molen, J. H., & Sondij, P. (2007). Parental mediation of children's emotional responses to a violent news event. *Communication Research, 34*(2), 212–230. doi: 10.1177/0093650206298070

Bury, R. (2017). *Television 2.0: Viewer and fan engagement with digital TV.* New York: Peter Lang.

Calderwood, C., Ackerman, P. L., & Conklin, E. M. (2014). What else do college students "do" while studying? An investigation of multitasking. *Computers & Education, 75*, 19–29. doi: 10.1016/j.compedu.2014.02.004

Chadha, R. (2018, January). Millennials favor smartphones for second-screening. *eMarketer.* Retrieved from: https://www.emarketer.com/content/millennials-favor-smartphones-for-second-screening

Chaffee, S. H., & Metzger, M. J. (2001). The end of mass Communication? *Mass Communication and Society, 4*(4), 365–379. doi: 10.1207/S15327825MCS0404_3

Chaney, A. J. B., Gartrell, M., Hoffman, J. M., Guiver, J., Koenigstein, N., Kohli, P., & Paquet, U. (2014). A large-scale exploration of group viewing patterns. In Proceedings of the ACM International Conference on Interactive Experiences for TV and Online Video (TVX '14). ACM, New York, NY, USA, 31–38. doi: 10.1145/2602299.2602309

Chen, Y., Gao, Q., & Rau, P.-L. P. (2017). Watching a movie alone yet together: Understanding reasons for watching Danmaku videos. *International Journal of Human–Computer Interaction, 33*(9), 731–743. doi: 10.1080/10447318.2017.1282187

Chinchanachokchai, S., Duff, B. R., & Sar, S. (2015). The effect of multitasking on time perception, enjoyment, and ad evaluation. *Computers in Human Behavior, 45*, 185–191. doi: 10.1016/j.chb.2014.11.087

Chorianopoulos, K., & Lekakos, G. (2008). Introduction to Social TV: Enhancing the shared experience with interactive TV. *International Journal of Human–Computer Interaction, 24*(2), 113–120. doi: 10.1080/10447310701821574

Clement, J. (2019, January). Second screen usage-Statistics & Facts. *Statista.* Retrieved from: https://www.statista.com/topics/2531/second-screen-usage/

Cohen, E. L., Bowman, N. D., & Alexander, L. L. (2016). R u with some1? Using text message experience sampling to examine television coviewing as a moderator of emotional contagion effects on enjoyment. *Mass Communication and Society, 19*, 149–172. doi:10.1080/15 205436.2015.1071400

Cohen, E. L., & Lancaster, A. L. (2014). Individual differences in in-person and social media television coviewing: The role of emotional contagion, need to belong, and coviewing orientation. *Cyberpsychology, Behavior, and Social Networking 17*(8), 512–518. doi: 10.1089/cyber.2013.0484

Cooper, R. (1996). The status and future of audience duplication research: An assessment of ratings-based theories of audience behavior. *Journal of Broadcasting & Electronic Media, 40*, 96–116. doi: 10.1080/08838159609364335

Cooper, R., & Tang, T. (2009). Predicting audience exposure to television in today's media environment: An empirical integration of active-audience and structural theories. *Journal of Broadcasting & Electronic Media, 53*(3), 400–418. doi: 10.1080/08838150903102204

Courtois, C., & Nelissen, S. (2018). Family television viewing and its alternatives: Associations with closeness within and between generations. *Journal of Broadcasting & Electronic Media, 62*(4), 673–691. doi: 10.1080/08838151.2018.1523907

Doughty, M., Rowland, D., & Lawson, S. (2012). Who is on your sofa? TV audience communities and second screening social networks. In *Proceedings of the 10th Association for Computing Machinery (ACM) European Conference on Interactive Television and Video* (pp. 79–86). New York, NY: ACM Press.

Dredge, S. (2014). World Cup was biggest event yet for Twitter with 672m tweets. *The Guardian*. Retrieved from https://www.theguardian.com/technology/2014/jul/15/twitter-world-cup-tweets-germany-brazil

Ducheneaut, N., Moore, R. J., Oehlberg, L., Thornton, J. D., & Nickell, E. (2008). Social TV: Designing for distributed, sociable television viewing. *International Journal of Human–Computer Interaction, 24*(2), 136–154. doi: 10.1080/10447310701821426

Dutta-Bergman, M. J. (2004). Complementarity in consumption of news types across traditional and new media. *Journal of Broadcasting & Electronic Media, 48*(1), 41–60. doi:10.1207/s15506878jobem4801_3

Ericcson ConsumerLabs (2012). *TV and video: An analysis of evolving consumer habits*. Retrieved from https://www.ericsson.com/assets/local/news/2012/8/tv_video_consumerlab_report.pdf

Fallis, S. F., Fitzpatrick, M. A., & Fristad, S. A. (1985). Spouses' discussion of television portrayals of close relationships. *Communication Research, 12*, 59–81. doi: 10.1177/009365085012001003

Finucane, M. O., & Horvath, C. W. (2000). Lazy leisure: A qualitative investigation of the relational uses of television in marriage. *Communication Quarterly, 48*(3), 311–321. doi: 10.1080/01463370009385599

Flynn, K. (2016, February 8). For Super Bowl 50, Twitter Inc. (TWTR) touts 4.3 billion views, not tweets shared. *International Business Times*. Retrieved from http://www.ibtimes.com/super-bowl-50-twitter-inc-twtr-touts-43-billion-views-not-tweets-shared-2299339

Foehr, U. G. (2006). *Media multitasking among American youth: Prevalence, predictors and Pairings*, 7592. Menlo Park, CA: Henry J. Kaiser Family Foundation.

Gantz, W. (1985). Exploring the role of television in married life. *Journal of Broadcasting & Electronic Media, 29*, 65–78. doi: 10.1080/08838158509386564

Gauntlett, D., & Hill, A. (1999). *TV Living*. London: Routledge.

Gil de Zúñiga, H., & Liu, J. H. (2017). Second screening politics in the social media sphere: advancing research on dual screen use in political communication with evidence from 20 countries. *Journal of Broadcasting & Electronic Media, 61*(2), 193–219. doi: 10.1080/08838151.2017.1309420

Goodhardt, G. J., Ehrenberg, A. S. C., & Collins, M. A. (1975). *The television audience: Patterns of viewing*. Westmead, England: Saxon House.

Goodman, N. (1983). *Fact, fiction, and forecast*. Boston: Harvard University Press.

Gorkovenko, K., & Taylor, N. (2016). Politics at home: second screen behaviours and motivations during TV debates. In *Proceedings of the 9th Nordic Conference on Human-Computer Interaction* (NordiCHI '16). ACM, New York, NY. doi: 10.1145/2971485.2971514

Han, E., & Lee, S-W. (2014). Motivations for the complementary use of text-based media during linear TV viewing: An exploratory study. *Computers in Human Behavior, 32*, 235–243. doi: 10.1016/j.chb.2013.12.015

Harboe, G. (2009). In search of social television. In P. Cesar, D. Geerts, & K. Chorianopoulos (Eds.), *Social Interactive Television: Immersive Shared Experiences and Perspectives* (pp. 1–13). New York: Information Science Reference.

Harboe, G. (2010). Introduction to Social TV. In A. Marcus, A. C. Roibás, & R. Sala (Eds.), *Mobile TV: Customizing Content and Experience* (pp. 21–24). New York: Springer.

Haridakis, P., & Hanson, G. (2009). Social interaction and co-viewing with YouTube: Blending mass communication reception and social connection. *Journal of Broadcasting & Electronic Media, 53*(2), 317–335. doi: 10.1080/08838150902908270

Harris, R. J., & Cook, L. (2010). How content and co-viewers elicit emotional discomfort in movie going experiences: Where does the discomfort come from and how is it handled? *Applied Cognitive Psychology, 25*, 850–861. doi:10.1002/acp.1758

Hocking, J. E. (1982). Sports and Spectators: Intra-audience Effects. *Journal of Communication, 32*(1), 100–108. doi: 10.1111/j.1460-2466.1982.tb00481.x

Holt, J., & Sanson, K. (2014). Introduction: Mapping Connections. In J. Holt, & K. Sanson (Eds.), *Connected Viewing: Selling, Streaming and Sharing Media in the Digital Era* (pp. 1–15). New York: Routledge.

Hwang, Y. C, & Lim, J. S, (2015). The impact of engagement motives for social TV on social presence and sports channel commitment. *Telematics and Informatics, 32*(4), 755–765. doi: 10.1016/j.tele.2015.03.006

Interactive Advertising Bureau (IAB). (2015, April). *Critical changes in consumers' TV viewing driven by connected TV, multiscreen activities and 'Better Ad Experience' in digital video, according to IAB research*. Retrieved from: https://www.iab.com/news/critical-changes-in-consumers-tv-viewing-driven-by-connected-tv-multiscreen-activities-better-ad-experience-in-digital-video-according-to-iab-research/

Jenkins, H. (2006): *The convergence culture: Where old and new media collide*. New York: New York University Press.

Jeong, S. H., & Hwang, Y. (2016). Media multitasking effects on cognitive vs. attitudinal outcomes: A meta-analysis. *Human Communication Research, 42*(4), 599–618. doi: doi.org/10.1111/hcre.12089

Ji, Q. (2019). Exploring the motivations for live posting during entertainment television viewing. *Atlantic Journal of Communication, 27*(3), 169–182. doi: 10.1080/15456870.2019.1610762

Jin, Y., Xie, T., Wen, Y., & Xie, H. (2013). Multi-screen cloud social TV: Transforming TV experience into 21st century. *Proceedings of the 21st ACM international conference on Multimedia*, 435–436. doi: 10.1145/2502081.2502257

Kim, J., Merrill, K., & Yang, H. (2019). Being social during the big dance: Social presence and social TV viewing for March Madness in public and private platforms. *The Social Science Journal.* doi: 10.1016/j.soscij.2019.04.004

Knight, S. (2018, December). *TechSpot.* Nearly half of the population use secondary devices while watching TV. Retrieved from: https://www.techspot.com/news/77899-nearly-half-population-use-secondary-devices-while-watching.html

Kool, W., McGuire, J. T., Rosen, Z. B., & Botvinick, M. M. (2010). Decision making and the avoidance of cognitive demand. *Journal of Experimental Psychology: General, 139,* 665–682. doi: 10.1037/a0020198

Krämer, N. C., Winter, S., Benninghoff, B., & Gallus, C. (2015). How "social" is Social TV? The influence of social motives and expected outcomes on the usage of Social TV applications. *Computers in Human Behavior, 51,* 255–262. doi 10.1016/j.chb.2015.05.005

Kunkel, D., Cope, K. M., & Colvin, C. (1996). *Sexual messages on family hour television: Content and context.* Report Prepared for Children Now and Kaiser Family Foundation.

Lang, A. (2000). The limited capacity model of mediated message processing. *Journal of Communication, 50,* 46–70. doi: 10.1111/j.1460-2466.2000.tb02833.x

Lang, A. (2009). The limited capacity model of motivated mediated message processing. In R. Nabi, & M. B. Oliver (eds.), *The Sage handbook of mass media effects* (pp. 193–204). Thousand Oaks, CA: Sage.

Lang, A., & Chrzan, J. (2015). Media multitasking. *Communication Yearbook, 39,* 99–126. doi: 10.1080/23808985.2015.11679173

LaRose, R. (2010). The problem of media habits. *Communication Theory, 20*(2), 194–222. doi:10.1111/j.1468-2885.2010.01360.x

Lee, J., & Choi, Y. (2017). Shifting from an audience to an active public in social viewing: Focusing on the discussion network. *Computers in Human Behavior, 75,* 301–310. doi: 10.1016/j.chb.2017.05.027

Lee, F. J., & Taatgen, N. A. (2002, August). Multitasking as skill acquisition. In *Proceedings of The 24th annual conference of the Cognitive Science Society* (pp. 572–577). doi:10.1016/S1389-0417(01)00049-3

Lim, J. S., Hwang, Y., Kim, S., & Biocca, F. A. (2015). How social media engagement leads to sports channel loyalty: Mediating roles of social presence and channel commitment. *Computers in Human Behavior, 46,* 158–167. doi: 10.1016/j.chb.2015.01.013

Lin, J-S., Sung, Y., & Chen, K-J. (2016). Social television: Examining the antecedents and consequences of connected TV viewing. *Computers in Human Behavior, 58,* 171–178. doi: 10.1016/j.chb.2015.12.025

Lindlof, T., & Traudt, P. (1983). Mediate communications in families: New theoretical approaches. In M. Mander (Ed.), *Communications in Transition* (pp. 260–278). New York: Praeger.

Livingstone, S. (2007). From family television to bedroom culture: Young people's media at home. In E. Devereux (Ed.), *Media Studies: Key Issues and Debates* (pp. 302–321). London: Sage.

Lochrie, M., & Coulton, P. (2012). Sharing the viewing experience through second screens. *EuroITV '12 Proceedings of the 10th European Conference on Interactive TV and Video, 199–*202. doi: 10.1145/2325616.2325655

Lott, M. C. (2017). Is television ownership on the decline? *Scientific American*, February 28. Retrieved from https://blogs.scientificamerican.com/plugged-in/is-television-ownership-on-the-decline/

Lozano Delmar, J., & Bourdaa, M. (2015), Case Study of French and Spanish Fan Reception of Game of Thrones. *Transformative Works and Cultures, 19*. http://dx.doi.org/10.3983/twc.2015.0608

Lull, J. (1980). The social uses of television. *Human Communication Research, 6*, 197–209. doi: 10.1111/j.1468-2958.1980.tb00140.x

Lull, J. (1990). *Inside family viewing: Ethnographic research on television's audience*. London: Routledge.

MacCarthy, M. (1995). Broadcast self-regulation: The NAB codes, family viewing hour, and television violence. *13 Cardozo Arts & Entertainment Law Journal*, 667–696. Retrieved from https://ssrn.com/abstract=3093311

Marwick, A., & boyd, d. (2011). To see and be seen: Celebrity practice on Twitter. *Convergence, 17*(2), 139–158. doi: 10.1177/1354856510394539

McDonald, D. G., Lin, S.-F., Anderegg, J. J., Na, K., & Dale, K. R. (2014). *Time, tweets, uses, and gratifications: The dynamic nature of television viewing orientations*. Paper presented to the annual conference of International Communication Association, Seattle, WA.

McPherson, K., Huotari, K., Cheng, F., Humphrey, D., Cheshire, C., & Brooks, A. L. (2012). Glitter: A mixed-methods study of twitter use during glee broadcasts. In *Proceedings of the ACM 2012 Conference on Computer Supported Cooperative Work Companion*, 167–170.

Mora, J., Ho, J. & Krider, R. (2011). Television co-viewing in Mexico: An assessment on people meter data. *Journal of Broadcasting & Electronic Media, 55*(4), 448–469. doi: 10.1080/08838151.2011.620905

Morley, D. (1986). *Family television: Cultural power and domestic leisure*. London: Routledge.

Morrison, M., & Krugman, D. M. (2001). A look at mass and computer mediated technologies: Understanding the roles of television and computers in the home. *Journal of Broadcasting & Electronic Media, 45*(1), 135–161. doi: 10.1207/s15506878jobem4501_9

Nagy, J., & Midha, A. (2014). The value of earned audiences: How social interactions amplify TV impact. *Journal of Advertising Research, 54*(4), 448–453. doi:10.2501/JAR-54-4-448-453

Nathanson, A. I. (2001). Parent and child perspectives on the presence and meaning of parental television mediation. *Journal of Broadcasting & Electronic Media, 45*(2), 201–220. doi: 10.1207/s15506878jobem4502_1

Nathanson, A. I. (2002). The unintended effects of parental mediation of television on adolescents. *Media Psychology* 4(3), 207–230. doi: 10.1207/S1532785XMEP0403_01

Nathanson, A. I., & Botta, R. A. (2003). Shaping the effects of television on adolescents' body image disturbance: The role of parental mediation. *Communication Research, 30*(3), 304–331. doi: 10.1177/0093650203030003003

Nelissen, S. & Van den Bulck, J. (2018). When digital natives instruct digital immigrants: active guidance of parental media use by children and conflict in the family, Information. *Communication & Society, 21*(3), 375–387, doi: 10.1080/1369118X.2017.1281993

Nielsen. (2012). *State of the media: Cross-platform report q2*. Retrieved from https://www.nielsen.com/us/en/insights/report/2012/state-of-the-media-cross-platform-report-q2-2012/

Oehlberg, L., Ducheneaut, N., Thomton, J. D., Moore, G. E., & Nickell, E. (2006). Social TV: Designing for distributed, sociable, television viewing. *Proceedings of the European Conference on Interactive Television – EuroTV 2006, 251–262.*

Ophir, E., Nass, C., & Wagner, A. D. (2009). Cognitive control in media multitaskers. *Proceedings of the National Academy of Sciences of the United States of America, 106*(37), 15583–15587. doi:10.1073/pnas.0903620106

Osborn, J. L. (2012). When TV and marriage meet: A social exchange analysis of the impact of television viewing on marital satisfaction and commitment. *Mass Communication and Society, 15*(5), 739–757. doi: 10.1080/15205436.2011.618900

Oviedo, V., Tornquist, M., Cameron, T., & Chiappe, D. (2015). Effects of media multi-tasking with Facebook on the enjoyment and encoding of TV episodes. *Computers in Human Behavior, 51*, 407–417. doi: 10.1016/j.chb.2015.05.022

Patulny, R. (2011). Social trust, social partner time, and television time. *Social Indicators Research, 101*(2), 289–293. doi: 10.1007/s11205-010-9649-9

Perry, M. J. (2010). More TV sets (2.93) than people per U.S. households (2.54)' average TV sets per home set new record. *Carpe Diem.* Retrieved from https://www.aei.org/carpe-diem/more-tv-sets-2-93-than-people-per-us-household-2-54-average-tv-sets-per-home-sets-new-record/

Pew Research. (2015, December). *The American family today.* Retrieved from: https://www.pewsocialtrends.org/2015/12/17/1-the-american-family-today/

Pilotta, J. J., Schultz, D. E., Drenik, G., & Rist, P. (2006). Simultaneous media usage: A critical consumer orientation to media planning. *Journal of Consumer Behaviour: An International Research Review, 3*(3), 285–292. doi: 10.1002/cb.141

Pires de Sá, F. (2015). The co-viewing 2.0: Detaching from history and applying in the new media age. *Культура/Culture, 5*(11), 55–64.

Raney, A. A., & Bryant, J. (2020). Entertainment and enjoyment as media effects. In M. B. Oliver, A. A. Raney, & J. Bryant (Eds.), *Media Effects: Advances in Theory and Research* (4th Edition, pp. 324–343). New York: Routledge.

Raney, A. A., & Ji, Q. (2017). Entertaining each other? *Human Communication Research, 43*(4), 424–435. doi: 10.1111/hcre.12121

Rao, V. R. (1975). Taxonomy of television programs based on viewing behaviour. *Journal of Marketing Research, 12*, 355–358. doi: 10.2307/3151237

Rideout, V. J., Foeher, U. G., & Roberts, D. F. (2010). *Generation M2: Media in the lives of 8-to 18-year-olds.* Menlo Park, CA: Kaiser Family Foundation.

Rosen, L. D., Carrier, L. M., & Cheever, N. A. (2013). Facebook and texting made me do it: Media-induced task-switching while studying. *Computers in Human Behavior, 29*(3), 948–958. doi: 10.1016/j.chb.2012.12.001

Rosenstein, A. W., & Grant, A. G. (1997). Reconceptualizing the role of habit: A new model of television audience activity. *Journal of Broadcasting & Electronic Media, 41*(3), 324–344. doi: 10.1080/08838159709364411

Rothman, L. (June 11, 2015). The reason TV was allowed to get dirty any time of day. *Time.* Retrieved from https://time.com/3917142/the-reason-tv-was-allowed-to-get-dirty-any-time-of-day/

Rubenking, B. (2016). Multitasking with TV: Media technology, genre, and audience influences. *Communication Research Reports, 33*(4), 324–331. doi: 10.1080/08824096.2016.1224167

Rubin, A. M. (1984). Ritualized and instrumental television viewing. *Journal of Communication, 34*(3), 67–77. doi: 10.1111/j.1460-2466.1984.tb02174.x

Saxbe, D., Graesch, A., & Alvik, M. (2011). Television as a social or solo activity: Understanding families' everyday television viewing patterns. *Communication Research Reports, 28*(2), 180–189. doi: 10.1080/08824096.2011.566104

Schirra, S., Sun, H., & Bentley, F., (2014). Together alone: Motivations for live-tweeting a television series. *Proceedings of the SIGCHI Conference on Human Factors in Computing Systems,* 2441–2450. doi:10.1145/2556288.2557070

Schooler, D., Kim, J. L., & Sorsoli, L. (2006). Setting rules or sitting down: Parental mediation of television consumption and adolescent self-esteem, body image, and sexuality. *Sexuality Research & Social Policy, 3*(4), 49–62. doi: 10.1525/srsp.2006.3.4.49

Segijn, C. M., Voorveld, H. A., Vandeberg, L., Pennekamp, S. F., & Smit, E. G. (2017). Insight into everyday media use with multiple screens. *International Journal of Advertising, 36*(5), 779–797. doi: 10.1080/02650487.2017.1348042

Selva, D. (2016). Social TV and the participation dilemma in NBC's The Voice. *Television & New Media, 17*(2), 108–123. doi:10.1177/1527476415616191

Shirky, C. (2010): *The cognitive surplus: Creativity and generosity in a connected age.* New York: Penguin Press.

Slade, A., Narro, A. J., & Givens-Carroll, D. (2015). *Television, social media, and fan culture.* Lanham: Lexington Books.

Smith, L. R., Pegoraro, A., & Cruikshank, S. A. (2019). Tweet, retweet, favorite: The impact of Twitter use on enjoyment and sports viewing. *Journal of Broadcasting & Electronic Media, 63*(1), 94–110. doi: 10.1080/08838151.2019.1568805

Stetka, B. (2018, September). Extended adolescence: When 25 is the new 18. *Scientific American.* Retrieved from: https://www.scientificamerican.com/article/extended-adolescence-when-25-is-the-new-181/

Taneja, H., & Viswanathan, V. (2014). Still glued to the box? Television viewing explained in a multi-platform age integrating individual and situational predictors. *International Journal of Communication, 8,* 2134–2159.

Telecommunications Act of 1996, Public Law 104-104 Sec. 551. Parental Choice in Television Programming, February 8, 1996

Trilling, D. (2015). Two different debates? Investigating the relationship between a political debate on TV and simultaneous comments on Twitter. *Social Science Computer Review, 33*(3), 259–276. doi: 10.1177/0894439314537886

Twenge, J. M., Martin, G. N., & Spitzberg, B. H. (2019). Trends in US adolescents' media use, 1976–2016: The rise of digital media, the decline of TV, and the (near) demise of print. *Psychology of Popular Media Culture, 8*(4), 329–345. doi: 10.1037/ppm0000203

Twenge, J. M., & Park, H. (2019). The decline in adult activities among US adolescents, 1976–2016. *Child Development, 90*(2), 638–654. doi: 10.1111/cdev.12930

U.S. Bureau of Labor Statistics (2015). Available from https://www.bls.gov/opub/mlr/2015/home.htm

U.S. Census Bureau. (2018, November). U.S. Census Bureau releases 2018 families and living arrangements tables. Retrieved from: https://www.census.gov/newsroom/press-releases/2018/families.html

Valkenburg, P. M., Krcmar, M., Peeters A. L., & Marseille, N. M. (1999). Developing a scale to assess three styles of television mediation: "Instructive mediation," "restrictive mediation," and "social coviewing." *Journal of Broadcasting & Electronic Media, 43*(1), 52–66, doi: 10.1080/08838159909364474

Vanattenhoven, J., & Geerts, D. (2017). Social experiences within the home using second screen TV applications. *Multimedia Tools and Applications, 76*(4), 5661–5689. doi: 10.1007/s11042-016-3646-1

Voorveld, H. A., & Viswanathan, V. (2014). An observational study on how situational factors influence media multitasking with TV: The role of genres, dayparts, and social viewing. *Media Psychology, 17*, 1–28. doi:10.1080/15213269.2013.872038

Vorderer, P., Klimmt, C., & Ritterfeld, U. (2004). Enjoyment: at the heart of media entertainment. *Communication Theory, 14*(1), 388–408. doi: 10.1111/j.1468-2885.2004.tb00321.x

Walker, J. R., & Bellamy, R. V. (2001). Remote controller devices and family viewing. In J. A. Bryant (Ed.), *Television and the American family* (pp. 75–89). New York: Routledge.

Wang, Z., Irwin, M., Cooper, C., & Srivastava, J. (2015). Multidimensions of media multitasking and adaptive media selection. *Human Communication Research, 41*(1), 102–127. doi: 10.1111/hcre.12042

Wang, Z., & Tchernev, J. M. (2012). The "myth" of media multitasking: Reciprocal dynamics of media multitasking, personal needs, and gratifications. *Journal of Communication, 62*(3), 493–513. doi:10.1111/j.1460-2466.2012.01641.x

Warren, R., Gerke, P., & Kelly, M. A. (2002). Is there enough time on the clock? Parental involvement and mediation of children's television viewing. *Journal of Broadcasting & Electronic Media, 46*(1), 87–111. doi: 10.1207/s15506878jobem4601_6

Webster, J. G. (1985). Program audience duplication: A study of television inheritance effects. *Journal of Broadcasting & Electronic Media, 29*, 121–133. doi:10.1080/08838158509386571

Webster, J. G. (1986). Audience behavior in the new media environment. *Journal of Communication, 36*(3), 77–91. doi:10.1111/j.1460-2466.1986.tb01439.x

Webster, J. G., & Wakshlag, J. J. (1982). The impact of group viewing on patterns of television program choice. *Journal of Broadcasting, 26*(1), 445–455. doi: 10.1080/08838158209364012

Weisz, J. D., Kiesler, S., Zhang, H., Ren, Y., Kraut, R. E., & Konstan, J. A. (2007). Watching together: Integrating text chat with video. *Proceedings of SIGCHI 2007*, 877–886. doi: 10.1145/1240624.1240756

Wenner, L. A., & Gantz, W. (1998). Watching sports on television: Audience experience, gender, fanship, and marriage. In L. A. Wenner (Ed.), *MediaSport* (pp. 233–251). New York: Routledge.

Wiley, R. (1977). Family viewing: A balancing of interests. *Journal of Communication, 27*(2), 188–192. doi:10.1111/j.1460-2466.1977.tb01847.x

Wiradhany, W., & Baumgartner, S. E. (2019). Exploring the variability of media multitasking choice behaviour using a network approach. *Behaviour & Information Technology*, 1–14. doi: 10.1080/014429X.2019.1589575

Wohn, D., & Na, E. (2011). Tweeting about TV: Sharing television viewing experiences via social media message streams. *First Monday, 16*(3). doi: 10.5210/fm.v16i3.3368

Wonneberger, A., Schoenbach, K., & van Meurs, L. (2009). Dynamics of individual television viewing behavior: Models, empirical evidence, and a research program. *Communication Studies, 60*, 235–252. doi:10.1080/10510970902955992

Wu, Y., Zhang, Z., Wu, C, Li, Z., & Lau, F. C. M. (2013). CloudMoV: Cloud-based mobile social TV. *IEEE Transactions on Multimedia, 15*(4) 821–832. doi: 10.1109/TMM.2013.2240670

Yeykelis, L., Cummings, J. J., & Reeves, B. (2014). Multitasking on a single device: Arousal and the frequency, anticipation, and prediction of switching between media content on a computer. *Journal of Communication, 64*(1), 167–192. doi: 10.1111/jcom.12070

Zillmann, D., Weaver, J. B., Mundorf, N., & Aust, C. F. (1986). Effects of an opposite-gender companion's affect to horror on distress, delight, and attraction. *Journal of Personality and Social Psychology, 51*(3), 586–594. doi: 10.1037/0022-3514.51.3.586

CHAPTER FIVE

Motivations to Binge Watch

Thus far, this text has provided context about the current television technologies and industry strategies which afford binge watching (Chapter 3) as well as how the social viewing landscape further encourages it (Chapter 4). This chapter and the next shift the focus to the user, or viewer, side of the equation. Recently, the academic literature from communication, mass media, health studies, psychology, information systems, and other fields has seen a surge in social scientific studies on various forms of binge watching. The theoretical perspectives vary, as do the methodological approaches (although focus groups and surveys are quite common). Together, these chapters aim to identify what we already know and how to move forward around two central questions: *Why do people binge watch television* (Chapter 5) and *to what effect* (Chapter 6)? These two questions have motivated most of the social scientific work on binge watching to-date, hence the number of academic theories explored here and in the closely related following chapter.

On an individual level, at the point of decision-making and viewing, what makes a viewer opt to reward oneself or indulge in binge-watching session, or slide from watching one episode into multiple episodes in an unintentional way? We highlight two broad theoretical perspectives that provide groundwork for attempting to answer this question. These approaches are grounded in theories that share many assumptions about humans, media, and their interactions. However, they vary primarily in whether they see binge watching as largely *intentional*, explained by goal-directed, conscious choices, or as a combination of *intent and habits*.

The uses and gratifications approach assumes that active users binge watch for a number of goal-directed reasons and is often employed to explain what motivates users of new media technologies and platforms. Uses and gratifications (Katz, Blumler, & Gurevitch, 1974) views audiences as active, aware of their needs, and able to meet them by making informed choices about media to satisfy specific gratifications. The second approach assumes that binge watching is less intentional, and along with other frequent media behaviors, it is an outcome of both intentions and habits built over time. This habit-based perspective on binge watching assumes, in some small part, a more passive viewer more likely to default to automatic processing when making media choices, and hence a reliance on tried and true habits. Habits can be a result of deficient self-regulation and self-control that turns initially goal-driven behaviors (e.g., watching entertainment television) into less conscious behaviors (e.g., continuing to view past the point of intent, or binging, on entertainment television). Several new research studies cite the large umbrella framework of social cognitive theory, SCT, (Bandura, 2001a) as well as a model of media attendance and media habits (LaRose, 2010; LaRose & Eastin, 2004), which provides well-articulated theoretical links between SCT, habit, and uses and gratifications traditions. In addition to these two larger approaches, a number of research articles have explored individual differences, and the roles that various viewing experiences – such as identification with characters, feelings of regret, and transportation into narratives may also play in binge viewing behaviors. By delving first into the active audience, goal-directed approach, we review what theory and current empirical data suggest are the conscious motives to engage in binge watching. Following is a look at the middle ground of a continuum of intentionality where media habits also determine binge-watching behaviors.

Binge Watching as Goal-Directed

A Background on Uses and Gratifications

A uses and gratifications approach ushered in the "active audience" phase of mass communication theory development in the 1970s. The idea that audiences are active and make goal-directed selections of media to fulfill specific needs, or gratifications, is the central tenant of uses and gratifications theory (Katz et al., 1974). Mass communication theory had previously been dominated by a limited effects model (Berger, Roloff, & Ewoldsen, 2016), which replaced the dominant, all-powerful effects model in the early days of communication research. Prior to the active audiences paradigm in Mass Communication, the limited effects models (such as Agenda-Setting) had reigned after replacing the "magic bullet" and "hypodermic needle" theories of the all-powerful effects paradigm. This active audience approach made audiences the more active agent among audiences and media. Instead of concerning itself with what the media was doing *to* audiences, uses and gratifications was among the first to focus on what audiences were doing *with* media. This approach provided a welcome departure from theories based on assumptions of a passive, mass audience. Blumler and Katz (1974) outline a continuum that runs between active, rational audiences and passive, complacent audiences. Under this approach, audiences are viewed as aware of their needs and capable of meeting them through media or other options. Theory development by Rubin (1983) further discussed two general modes of television viewing: instrumental and ritualistic. Instrumental media use was seen as content-driven, conscious, and very active; it is characterized by users operating at the far end of rational, active endpoint of the audience activity continuum. Ritualistic media use is conceptualized as being motivated both by an affinity of the medium and less conscious processing, or automaticity, existing largely at the other end of the continuum.

The fulfillment of needs is a motivator in the selection of a particular media channel and the media content. In this perspective, motives are dispositions that influence people's behaviors enacted to fulfill a need or want (Papacharissi & Rubin, 2000). Others worked to further refine the theory by isolating and clarifying the relevant concepts to media choices. Palmgreen, Wenner, and Rosengren (1985) introduced a distinction between gratifications *sought* and gratifications *obtained*, which can be separated from a measurement perspective to look at both motives and outcomes of media use. While a person may actively select a program to watch to gain information, or to relax and escape, those goals are not always met by a given media choice. Anecdotally, we can all think of a time in which we learned information instead of being entertained, or selected a film to view and relax, and were disappointed by content that didn't elicit the desired responses we intended for ourselves. Gratifications sought are operationalized as measures of the goals going into media choices, while gratifications obtained are those desired outcomes, or unintentional other outcomes of media use. When gratifications sought and obtained do not match up, it is likely alternative choices will be made in the future. Likewise, when the gratifications sought are obtained, the media choice was successful, it is likely to be made again in the future. With repetition of this pattern, the media behavior may become a media habit. For example, whenever I want to watch television to relax/escape, I choose content in the science fiction or fantasy genre, because it always has the desired effect.

Gratifications and Television

Research has explored different gratifications (sought and obtained) from different media. Even prior to the shift to active audience theories and the formalization of uses and gratifications theory, researchers examined motives for reading newspapers (Berelson, 1949) and listening to the radio (Mendelsohn, 1964). Foundational pieces in the uses and gratifications tradition have explored motives to view television (Rubin, 1983) and use the Internet (Ruggerio, 2000). Rubin (1983) has argued that viewing motivations produce television viewing patterns. He and others have identified typical television viewing motives, such as, *pass time/ habit, entertainment, companionship/ social, information-seeking, relaxation*, and *escapism* (Greenberg, 1974; Rubin, 1983). These are the standard television viewing gratifications sought (and/or obtained) that are recognized throughout the larger mass media/ audience analysis fields of research. Additional and often complementary gratifications related to new media and the Internet, such as *diversion, social utility, personal identity*, and *surveillance* have also been identified (Ruggerio, 2000). Studies of various mobile devices, social media apps, YouTube, etc. often use a combination of Ruggerio and Rubin's gratifications when studying why people use a new technology.

Exploring "new media" uses in the typical uses and gratifications way has some advantages and disadvantages. A typical, thorough uses and gratifications study starts with a review of academic and industry research on the new "use" (e.g., *Facebook, Snapchat, Netflix*). Often, a qualitative component – focus groups or interviews – are conducted to search for the greatest breadth of possible gratifications afforded by the new "use" of interest. Then, several items are created by researchers, and participants are asked to indicate how much (on a Likert scale) they agree with each statement regarding their behavior, attitudes, feelings toward the "use." An exploratory factor analysis is completed, a factor solution is decided upon, and researchers label each "factor" based on the items it includes. These factors become some variation of the ones mentioned abov. This method certainly meets the Ockham's razor criteria of producing the most direct, obvious answer. If a researcher's basic research question is "what motivates individuals to _____?", then simply asking them to indicate their agreement with every motive you could think of is certainly a direct way of approaching the problem. It is parsimonious. It is not unnecessarily complicated and part of a complex mediation/ moderation model with dozens of predictors and non-linear relationships, which can be a pitfall of some current media/ audience research. However, as discussed below, several pitfalls are created when this is the *only* way that social scientific research explores a new media behavior.

Binge Watching Gratifications/ Motives

Several studies have sought to identify motives to binge watch under a uses and gratifications perspective. One study often cited in the emerging empirical literature on binge watching is based on a survey administered to a snowball sample of binge watchers which revealed a five-factor solution to dispositions related to binge watching, including *engagement, relaxation, pass time, hedonism,* and *social motives* (Pittman & Sheehan, 2015). While the latter four motives are traditionally found in uses and gratifications studies of television viewing (and were, indeed, based on previous such studies' measures), the engagement factor was based on both measures used in previous TV uses and gratifications studies (Papacharissi & Mendelson, 2007) *and* several items derived from popular press discussions of binge watching being more interesting, entertaining, and engaging way to watch television. Pittman and Sheehan (2015) also found that of all five factors of motives to binge watch, engagement was the only significant predictor of greater binge-watching frequency. The authors conclude that the motives found for binge watching television are a combination of established gratifications sought when using television and the Internet, which thus "extends U&G into hitherto uncharted territory" (p. 10).

Another study utilized the uses and gratifications perspective in a field experiment, where half of the student sample was instructed to binge watch half of a season of a specified, popular television show, and half were instructed to watch the show in an appointment viewing format (Pena, 2015). Since the viewing modes were assigned, this study explored the gratifications *obtained* from viewing, not *sought*. Across 10 motives obtained, there were differences across viewing conditions, such that those who binge watched reported greater endorsement of obtaining the gratifications of: "It passed the time," and "It allowed me to forget about my life for awhile," while those in the appointment viewing condition reported greater endorsement of obtaining the gratifications of "It was habit," and "I could talk to others about it." There were no differences across the two viewing conditions for gratifications related to: entertainment, "knowing what was going on," learning, relaxing, attaining information, or identifying with characters. The gratification items were based on those used in previous studies of television viewing.

The results from Pena (2015) do not show a difference in engagement that Pittman and Sheehan (2015) did, and interestingly, the two items related to habit (i.e., pass time, habit) were split across the two viewing modes, indicating that habitual nature of both appointment viewing and binge watching. Since Pittman and Sheehan (2015) didn't measure gratifications related to appointment viewing, or another mode of television viewing, direct comparisons cannot be made – and the combinations of measures from various factors that were labeled "entertainment" leave the uniqueness of binge-watching gratifications, as compared to general television viewing gratifications, undetermined. An alternative interpretation of these findings would focus on the differences between gratifications sought and obtained. Users may be seeking entertainment motives when binge watching and are instead left with feelings related to it "passing the time," and forgetting about the world for at least a little while.

Several studies after the oft-cited Pittman and Sheehan (2015) piece are quite similar. Shim and Kim (2018) based a scale of binge-watching viewer motivations on recurrent themes found in focus groups they conducted on the topic. An EFA revealed a five-factor solution for their 19-item scale, explaining 69% of the variance in the model. The dimensions of their motives scale were labeled *enjoyment* (based on fun and entertainment items), *efficiency, recommendations from others, perceived control,* and *fandom*. Of these, three predicted greater engagement in binge watching: *enjoyment, efficiency,* and *fandom* (Shim & Kim, 2018). Sung, Kang, and Lee (2018) start with the same research question, that is, "What motives are associated with binge watching," and the same survey and factor analysis approach. They found seven dimensions of binge watching: *social interaction, entertainment, passing time, relaxation, escape, information,* and *habit*. They found the Entertainment motive predictive of binge watching among both "high" and "low" binge watchers, following a median split and regression analysis, and "passing time" as predictive among the "high" binge watchers. A similar approach found scales measuring social engagement, escape, access, and advertising influence motives to be related to greater intention to engage in binge watching, but no significant effect of enjoyment, stress relief, quiet, boredom, or price motivations to be related to binge watching (Panda & Pandey, 2017).

Flayelle et al. (2019) take a somewhat different approach and present validation of two scales: A "Watching TV Series Motives" and "Binge-watching Engagement and Symptoms" questionnaires. They do so to explore and isolate problematic binge-watching behaviors from those characterized as highly involving, engaging, or passionate. Their second scale consists of two larger factors, indeed identifying a high involvement dimension and a problematic viewing dimension. Their problematic viewing factor was associated with more escapism/ coping viewing motives, as identified with the first scale. They argue, quite convincingly, that the functionally impairing nature of engagement that comes with problematic binge watching is a better qualifying factor for "binge watching" than simply the number of episodes viewed.

Altogether, the empirical uses and gratifications research on binge watching demonstrate related, but slightly different, gratifications associated with binge watching. There seems to be a trend that greater enjoyment/ entertainment and social motives are related to greater binge watching. However, we are hesitant to draw conclusions based on the inconsistency of definitions used – both of binge watching and characterizations of gratification items. The entertainment/ enjoyment concept is especially muddled, as is the case with these terms in the broader literature. Further, although several studies do offer a point of comparison (e.g., Flayelle et al., 2019), the bulk of the research *fails to demonstrate if the motives related to binge watching differ from any other type of television watching*. In doing so, the "proof of concept" piece is missing: Research doesn't demonstrate that these motives are unique to binge watching when they don't have a benchmark employed for comparison.

Qualitative Examinations of Motivations and Binge Watching

There are also several exploratory qualitative studies that do not explicitly frame their research in the uses and gratifications tradition, yet seek to uncover general motives for binge watching, albeit with small, non-representative samples. These studies generally look at gratifications obtained, by asking retrospectively about what motivates viewers to binge watch, or how they feel after binge watching. For example, Mikos' (2016) "group discussions" with 16 binge watchers revealed that individuals reported binge watching to stay caught up with what others recommend or discuss (representing a social dimension). Mikos (2016) also found that several qualities of television content were important to binge watching, such as complex narratives, thorough character development, suspense, and emotionally identifying with characters. Devasagayam (2014) found support that binge watching is motivated by three different factors: relationships, addiction, and dependence on media stimulation in a focus group. The participants stated that they felt connected to a certain character, had a hard time stopping their viewing habits at one episode, and binge watched when bored, respectively.

Consistent with some of the previous research, a focus group of seven French individuals also reports that immersion, entertainment, and social reasons are paramount motives for binge watching (Flayelle, Maurage, & Billieux, 2017). Their quite thorough analysis reveals that anticipation and a "hooking" effect of content – including suspense at the end of one show – drives binge-watching behavior among participants. Emotional connections with characters, as well as feelings of extreme emotions, and most often extremely positive emotions, were reported as consistently rewarding experiences of binge watching (Flayelle et al., 2017). The authors structure their focus group analyses according to three themes: In addition to the motives described, a second theme is concerned with engagement/ addiction to viewing, and a third is concerned with the structural characteristics of the television shows that individuals report binge watching. The structural characteristics contain two subthemes related to the content of shows being viewed: high-quality, suspenseful narratives that display a continuity that makes it difficult not to see what happens next in a next episode, and characters that engender a high degree of identification and liking. The availability of shows – the sheer abundance and volume available, paired with the ease of access, was a third related subtheme.

The current authors' own research reflects many of the preliminary findings reported in Flayelle et al. (2017). Rubenking et al. (2018) report data from 11 focus groups of American university students. Uses and gratifications, habituation research, and Webster, Phalen, and Lichty's (2000) model of media exposure are presented as guides to the exploratory work on binge watching. Webster et al.'s model discusses media use as co-determined by media/ structural factors and individual level of factors. We found four general themes in the responses, identified using Owen's (1984) thematic analysis method, focusing on recurrence, repetition, and forcefulness of dialogue. These emergent themes include *anticipation*, characterized by the cycle of suspense one experiences when binge watching as one views a dramatic arc and can satiate the desire to continue being engaged with content by beginning the cycle again immediately. Participants talked about binging suspenseful, dramatic content, and many mentioned the use of cliffhangers as effective in keeping them watching. *Mood management and excitement* was a second theme related to motives to binge watch and encompassed a range of moods. Some reported watching to feel better about a break-up, or to feel something out of the ordinary. A related, yet distinct, third factor was *procrastination and escapism*, which referred to the general idea that users binge watch television to put off undesirable or monotonous daily tasks, such as homework or housework. The frequency with which participants reported that they use binge-watching content as an excuse to put off less fun tasks was unexpected. The final motive revealed here were *social* ones. This broad factor included coviewing, but also viewing to participate in discussions with friends and make and take recommendations from others, as well as identifying with characters and companionship.

The Rubenking et al. (2018) piece sought to make a strong case for binge watching as a unique way of television viewing; *a distinct phenomenon* as compared to other types of viewing. Beyond identifying motivations to binge watch, it revealed that participants considered binging to be a heavier time commitment than is typically discussed in the academic literature and popular press. They repeatedly suggested about four hours or more constituting a binge. Binge watching was associated with watching the same television series in one sitting. It was incongruent to participants that one could binge watch different television shows – even in the same genre – and still consider the session a "binge."

Binge watching was found to sometimes be quite intentional, and planned out, while other times it just happened, a sort of "Netflix made me do it," refrain. It is something people love doing on their own, and with close others – if they kept their questions about the content to a minimum. We thought the motives were diverse, and the descriptions of how users felt while binge watching deserving of more attention. It also became apparent that a more theoretically rigorous approach would be needed to generate data that would be consistent, practically valuable, and produce as thorough and robust results as possible. A noted limitation of using this approach is the lack of theory building and predictive power. Predictive power, long discussed by others as being a primary criterion to which to hold social scientific theories to, is concerned with the ability for a theory to make valuable predictions moving forward (Chaffee & Berger, 1987; Shoemaker, Tankard, & Lasosa, 2003). Our focus group results reveal motivations to binge watch that appeared across other studies, most notably suspense/ anticipation, social, and relaxation/ escapism gratifications.

However, without applying a more rigorous combination of theories, studies using this line of research will continue to produce research findings which may produce a variety of different typologies *explaining* motives to binge watch, but will continue to struggle with results that can make *predictive* implications for binge watching, or other new viewing behaviors. The qualitative empirical research exploring what motivates binge watching does cast a wider net than the bulk of the quantitative research – we see here suspense, emotional connections, procrastination, along with concepts also found in the uses and gratifications framed studies, such as social motives. It would be a great applied benefit of theory building and demonstration of predictive power to better understand how to create viewing experiences and content to encourage binge watching. For instance, does the use of cliffhangers make viewers more likely to binge? Are there interface options, such as autoplay functions, that lead to a greater percentage of viewers watching more episodes in one sitting? These are empirical questions that could be answered in this framework: If we believe that individuals are making generally rational choices related to media use, and they're making those choices to meet certain goals, further study of the use (i.e., binge watching) could lead to building of predictive power and thus more applicable findings for industry.

Uses and Gratifications Criticisms

However, the assumptions of this approach are not immune to criticism, and some scholars may suggest that building predictive power into binge-watching research may require a different theoretical approach entirely. Uses and gratifications, like most long-standing theories in the communication discipline, has faced criticism.

Some concern is directed at the measures of constructs. The concept of "activity," and what exactly constitutes an active audience member has been a subject of debate, with nearly all in agreement that it is a hard-to-define, multidimensional concept. Biocca (1988) identified multiple dimensions of the concept, including *selectivity, utilitarianism, intentionality, involvement*, and *imperviousness to influence*. He argues that this breadth makes the concept unfalsifiable: "It is, by definition, nearly impossible for the audience to not be active," (p. 59). Biocca advocated for abandoning the term in favor of exploring its so-called sub-dimensions with more rigor.

The approach has also faced criticism at the operational level. Uses and gratifications inspired work most often takes a relatively simplistic approach to a relatively simplistic question: It asks media users why they use the media that they do. By virtue, this reliance on self-report creates a falsifiability issue. Regardless of *if* an individual has a motive in mind when engaging with the media use in question, when given a number of items to endorse as potential motives, a person is biased to answer that some of those motives apply. Given how these self-report questions are often posed to participants, this rationalizing may be occurring retroactively, especially when the role of habit is omitted from motive options, as it often is (LaRose, 2010). Thus, it can be argued that the bias in asking media users about *what* goals they have when selecting media is in assuming that they do indeed have goals. Certainly, there are methodological ways around this issue to some extent. The uses and gratifications approach inherently looks for the intentional, aware goals related to media use, while the habitual, automatic nature of media use is not addressed on an equal level. We explore the nature of habits, media habits, and discuss the ways in which binge-watching research could benefit from exploring motives *and* habits in the next section.

Binge Watching as Habit

Habit: Origins, Definition

Habit, or habituation, has a long-standing history within psychology; its earliest mention is found in the work of William James. James proposed that a habit was a fully automatic behavioral response to channels that deepened over time and with repetition (James, 1890; LaRose 2010). More recently, perspectives on habits view them as cognitive structures that can be triggered by environmental cues. Habits have been defined as "response dispositions that are activated automatically by the content cues that co-occurred with responses during past performance" (Neal,

Wood, & Quinn, 2006, p. 198). Habits "are a form of automaticity in responding that develops as people repeat actions in stable circumstances" (Verplanken & Wood, 2006, p. 91). Consistent to all definitions of habit is *automaticity*.

The capacity to develop habits originates in the human need to distinguish signals from noise. In a natural – and in a mediated – world, humans' cognitive systems rely on automaticity to get through basic, nonconscious decision-making, a necessity given the amount of stimuli in an individuals' environment. There is simply too much information available for individuals to process, and so semi and nonconscious modes of processing emerge as an efficient way of getting through the day. The conceptualization of individuals as limited capacity processors is widespread in the psychological tradition (Kahneman, 1973), and theoretical work in media psychology (Lang, 2000, 2009). With some distinctions related to pools of resources, it is generally accepted in both social psychology and media psychology traditions that humans have cognitive limits which affect processing, and automaticity and other tools such as relying on heuristic rules-of-thumb are employed unconsciously (and consciously) to deal with the onslaught of information we encounter daily. LaRose (2010) states that the neurological role of habits is, indeed, to protect individuals from being overwhelmed with information processing and daily activities. Neuroscience has documented the prominent role of the basal ganglia, part of the "old brain," in habit formation (Saling & Phillips, 2007).

The formation of a habit or repeated actions is often triggered by situational use such as people, places, or preceding actions (Morsella, Bargh, & Gollwitzer, 2008; Wood & Neal, 2007). Habits are more influential determinants of behavior when there is *frequent opportunity* to engage in them. McGuire (1974) stated

> People show clear and loyal preferences among equally accessible mass communications. Such characteristic persistence cannot be viewed as mere continuation of a change habit, if we remember learning theory's fundamental law of effect that repetition does not stamp in a response unless there is reinforcement; without reinforcement, repeated exposure would have the opposite effect of extinguishing the habit. (p. 168–169)

However, even events that happen relatively infrequently can spur habits under stable context cues. Indeed, Ouellette and Wood (1998) offer a context-dependent theory of habit in a meta-analysis. They demonstrate that the defining characteristic of habitual behaviors concerning media are context dependent. So, a media opportunity that comes along relatively infrequently, like mega-events (e.g., The Oscars, The Superbowl) can still activate habits which influence behavior. An alternative view presented by Aarts and Dijksterhuis (2000) place an emphasis not on context dependence, but on goal dependence. This can be seen with media habits that grow out of repeated gratifications satisfaction: If watching Netflix consistently entertains me, and I'm in the mood to be entertained, my default processing may lead me to choose Netflix whenever I have the goal of entertainment in mind.

Media Habits

Consistent environmental cues and goals may both play a major role in the development of many a habit. LaRose speaks of media habits as being acquired through repeating media use behaviors that are initially goal-directed. This line of research suggests that habits are not only efficient but rewarding for users. Interest in media habits and automaticity of media behaviors are often overlooked in communication research, only to be rediscovered periodically (LaRose, 2010). Media habits have been defined as "a form of automaticity that develops as people repeat media consumption behavior in stable circumstances" (LaRose 2010; LaRose & Eastin, 2004). It is estimated that over half of media behaviors are habitual (Wood, Quinn, & Kashy, 2002), and more recent theoretical advancements have noted that 50% is likely an *underestimate*, due to habit activation occurring across more inconsistent or low-frequency contexts, such as mega-events (LaRose, 2010).

Over time, activation of a media habit is thought to be influenced by goal dependence *and* context or environmental cues (Duhigg, 2012). When a media behavior becomes habitual and automatic, the habits can act either alone or together with conscious intentions. Those intentions are framed by expected outcomes (LaRose, 2010). LaRose distinguishes between habit *formation* and *activation*: a necessary distinction of two processes loosely separated by time. Here, habit formation is based on association between media behaviors and immediate expected outcomes of the external variety (including time, location, presence of others, etc.), and of the internal variety (such as moods, goals, thoughts). The strength of the stimuli (or media experience) and how an individual processes the initial connection have played a major role in habit formation research (Lally, Jaarsveld, Potts, & Wardle, 2010; Yerkes & Dodson, 1908).

One can imagine the number of scenarios in which binge watching is closely connected with outcome expectancies. Previous research has identified some overlaps in the most common outcome expectancies of binge watching, including immersion, anticipation, suspense, and qualities of the narrative and characters that identify involvement and identification. A combination of these outcome expectancies is likely to be met *every time* an individual binge watches a television show. If they are not met, individuals would be likely to select a different show or viewing platform. Every time a person binge watches content, they're likely meeting emotional-based outcome expectancies. Otherwise, it becomes a shorter viewing session. While binge watching is conceptualized as phenomenologically distinct, the length of time spent doing it is also part of a conceptual definition. This suggests that binge-watching habits may be even quicker to develop than appointment viewing or other types of television viewing.

Once a habit is formed, the strength of the habitual behavior can vary widely. Lally, Wardle, and Gardner (2011) found that external cues had the strongest impact on behavior maintenance of habit. Likewise, LaRose (2010) speaks of media habit *activation* depending on the ease in which the association between the behavior and the outcomes can be learned, where more easily made connections make for quicker or perhaps stronger habit acquisition. La Rose (2010) also contends that habit acquisition is dependent upon the number of repetitions, or opportunities to perform the behavior, as that once acquired, behavior is ultimately determined by both the habit and active goal directedness.

In the case of binge watching television, preliminary and exploratory reports – along with anecdotal evidence and reports from the popular press – find that people are most likely to binge watch at home, in the evening. This sounds like an ideal number of opportunities to frequently be presented with location and time cues: Most of us are at home at some point in the evening, *every evening*. Binge watching is not dependent upon being home at 9 p.m. on Thursdays to catch your favorite show that airs for 18 or 22 weeks of the year: Binge watching is largely an affordance of the wide variety and amount of available programming offered by most OTT services. Netflix and others make their libraries of content available for binging 24 hours a day, any time a person would like. Unwinding in the evening while watching television is a pastime shared by many – in fact, it is the most frequent leisure activity among Americans. Television viewing as a habit lends itself to binge watching being an extension of that habit.

Habitual behavior has often been explained in large part by deficient self-control, or self-regulation (LaRose, 2010; LaRose & Eastin, 2004; Tokunga, 2016). Deficient self-control allows automatic systems to determine behavior, and thus habits to form (LaRose, Lin, & Eastin, 2004). While media use habits may begin as goal-directed and beneficial, some media use habits may devolve into situations where self-control becomes ineffective, and behavior ceases to be goal-directed. This deficiency in self-regulation can lead to problem habit behaviors, such as working less effectively because one is always checking email, or not enjoying TV viewing because one is channel-surfing on a whim. Habit and deficient self-control have been linked in several studies of habits experimentally (Neal et al., 2006; Peters, 2009). Self-control is conceptualized as an outcome of self-regulation capabilities, of which, LaRose (2010) states are comprised of issues related to self-observation and self-reaction. Peters (2009) states that within social cognitive theory, "habit is a failure of the self-monitoring sub-function of self-regulation" (p. 78).

Some media habits, just as all media behaviors, may be efficient and help us reach our goals, or they may become ineffective over time. Binge watching presents an interesting behavior of interest to those studying habits. It begs the question, *is binge watching just a television habit gone bad?* Does watching an episode or two of a television series help an individual meet their goals, but is watching three, four, or more largely an effect of diminished self-regulation and self-control? Chapter 6 reviews research done in health sciences about the negative mental and physical health outcomes related to heavy television viewing. We contend that binge watching is a distinct mode of viewing, which seems to be the first step in acknowledging that all binge watching *is not* just a television viewing habit gone awry. Here, we can expound on the binging metaphor. Consuming one, maybe two alcoholic drinks in a social setting results in a qualitatively distinct experience as compared to consuming three, four, or more in the same setting.

Self-Regulation and Social Cognitive Theory, SCT. Habit-based behavior, and the relationship it shares with self-regulation, can be viewed as an extension of Bandura's Social Cognitive Theory, SCT (Bandura, 2001a, 2001b). SCT maintains that human behavior can be explained by a triadic reciprocal causation between personal determinants, behavioral determinants, and environmental determinants (Bandura, 2001a). A broad model of human behavior, Bandura has expounded how SCT best applies in communication contexts (Bandura, 2001b). The theory is largely applied to studies of how children model behavior (often problematic, violent, or aggressive behaviors) based on media representations, as well as in health contexts, where the theory offers models for studying how individuals process and adopt pro-social and/or unhealthy attitudes, behavioral intentions, and behaviors based on media content. SCT is *both complex and comprehensive*, making predictions about concepts at the macro and micro levels. It is common for other researchers to build on a singular concept or subset of concepts and relationships between them and another behavior or outcome (Peters, 2009). Indeed, SCT offers some groundwork essential to both observational learning and assumptions about humans in the media environment. Within this framework and the model of media attendance posed by LaRose, it is assumed that people with deficient self-control may also be expected to engage in habitual behavior – but also any other sort of impulsive behavior not related to habitual behavior. Further, when resource capacity is low, self-regulation suffers, resulting in a default to processing information in a more automatic state, which also leads to habits being more likely to determine behavior.

Research examining the role of habit in influencing media behaviors has largely been successful in demonstrating a positive significant impact of habit on media behaviors, while generally demonstrating weaker or non-existent effects of stated intentions or gratifications sought. LaRose, Lin, and Eastin (2004), for instance, tested four main effect determinants of Internet use: expected outcomes, self-efficacy, habit strength, and deficient self-regulation (as well as several mediating relationships). While all four contributed to explaining 37% of the variance in Internet use, outcome expectations contributed the smallest Beta weight, and habit strength contributed the largest. A test of the model of media attendance in the context of predicting mobile video phone calling found that while expected outcomes were a significant and large predictor of habit strength – they were *not* an independent predictor of actual usage. Peters (2009) found habit strength to be the only significant, and relatively large, predictor of technology adoption. In contrast, the media habit literature is smaller in size than the uses and gratifications approach, although there are more consistent trends in the studies employing this framework.

Media as Social Action. A related theoretical approach emphasizes the impact of routines on media behaviors. The Social Action perspective focuses on both audience and situational determinants of behavior. This approach has been applied to the study of media audiences and media use (Renckstorf & Wester, 2001). In this approach, "mass media and their messages are merely 'objects' in the actor's social environment, which provide the person with situations to be defined" (Renckstorf & Wester, 2004, p. 55). They argue that media users are not just recipients of media messages but create an interpretation of the message based on their own perceptions and experiences, and they act on this interpretation.

Westerik, Renckstorf, Wester, and Lammers (2005) suggest the media as social action, or MASA, can reconcile the tensions that exist between research focusing on audience duplication and Uses and Gratifications through the inclusion of routinization. Routinization refers to actions that are routine responses that recur regularly and are impacted by situations. One of the tenets of MASA is that intentionality guides human behavior through one of two possible pathways toward action (Westerik et al., 2005). The first pathway is utilized when an individual faces a new situation, one for which a routine response does not yet exist. In this pathway, an individual will be aware that the routine response does not exist, consider possible solutions, and make decisions about which solution to employ. This process may be extended and requires a considerable amount of effort from the individual. The second pathway is utilized when an individual faces a familiar situation. In this pathway, the individual will likely have a routine, and the process will be much shorter. Renckstorf (1996) indicates that the second pathway is more common than the first pathway and allows individuals to function in their everyday life.

Westerik et al. (2005) argue that television viewing is a routine which is impacted by situations. Within a household, television viewing is an activity that may be shared similar to meals and can create a sense of family unity. However, television viewing may also be a substitute for companionship when a real-world partner is not present. For example, Westerik et al. (2005) suggest both TV viewing and the experience of parasocial interactions are a substitute for companionship. MASA was also used to examine programming selection and viewing patterns by Adams (2000). Adams found that the two pathways identified above are also evident in the viewing selection process of television programming. The results demonstrated that individual television viewers displayed strong program loyalty and repeat viewing of some programs and that these types of viewing behaviors led to viewing habits or routine viewing patterns.

Finding a Middle Ground Between Motives and Habits

Thus far we've reviewed a uses and gratifications approach to understanding binge-watching motivations – an approach most popular in the academic literature when stated explicitly or implicitly, as well as the contributions from the theoretical developments in media habits. The first approach treats individuals as active users, making goal-directed choices: The logical hypothesis from this approach about binge watching would be that users binge watch in order to satisfy gratifications that they are aware of. Currently, the state of research in this field shows some overlaps between common motivations of binge watching, although not solid agreement, among a relevant small number of available research efforts. Research employing uses and gratifications is moderately successful at explaining why people may binge watch, but it largely fails to separate binge watching from other types of television watching, and it fails to make a priori hypotheses and thus offer any predictions on what encourages binge watching.

The second approach understands individuals to be goal-directed, and capable of making choices, but that ultimately media behaviors are co-determined by both conscious goals of the user *and* media habits. These media habits are formed when connections between media behaviors and positive outcomes are met clearly and frequently and activated by a number of external or internal context cues. This perspective promotes the inclusion of habit in determining media behaviors, but not, theoretically, at the exclusion of outcome expectations, or gratifications sought. However, this line of research typically finds media behaviors to be more habit driven than not. In this final section of the chapter, we examine where there are conceptual similarities and differences, as well as spend time reviewing two recent publications (of which, one is our own) that in our opinion employ the best of both worlds. Both research papers *include the role of habit in determining binge-watching behavior* (1) and they both *rely on theory or previous empirical work to make directional hypotheses about a specific outcome expectancy/ gratification posed* (2). Making these a priori hypotheses about gratifications and binge watching is an important distinction than the continued scale development and motives research that continues to grow in a somewhat repetitive nature.

Automaticity and the Active Audience

To further delve into why people binge watch, and how (or if!) they make conscious decisions to do so, an in-depth look at two related – and perhaps – corresponding concepts from each theoretical perspective previously reviewed are explored in this section: automaticity and activity. In Biocca's (1988) work examining the shortcomings of the active audience approach, he claims that early attempts to define the active audience were often explained simply by offering its contrast: the passive audience. While Biocca offers the most relevant and wide-ranging conceptualizations of audience "activity," he does not believe his five stated dimensions are orthogonal, nor should remain unstudied as some large "meta-construct" (p. 53). Table 5.1 shows the four components of automaticity, as articulated by LaRose (2010) and the five dimensions of the active audience, as identified by Biocca (1988). LaRose (2010) describes four dimensions of automaticity as related to media habits: *lack of awareness* (1), *attention* (2), *intentionality* (3), and *controllability* (4). These qualifications of automaticity read as opposite ends of a continuum for many, if not all the multi-dimensions Biocca (1988) claims create the concept of audience activity, as used across the literature.

Selectivity, a component of the active audience, is largely concerned with theories of selective exposure and selective attention. It is the process by which individuals select what information to devote further attentional resources to. It maps onto LaRose's characterization of audience *attention*. Both explicitly refer to *intentionality*, another sub-dimension of audience activity. The active audience acts with conscious intentions in mind, whereas automaticity is described as acting without conscious attention and *intent*. Also, of interest here is *controllability* as a foil to *imperviousness to influence*, which refers largely to the degree of influence audience members are viewed as exerting control over the intended effects that media creators and distributors may have. Both controllability and imperviousness to influence can be seen as opposite ends of a continuum of agency.

Table 5.1: Sub-dimensions of Automaticity and the Active Audience

LaRose's Automaticity	Biocca's Active Audience
Lack of awareness	Selectivity
Lack of attention	Involvement
Lack of intentionality	Intentionality
Lack of controllability	Utilitarianism
	Imperviousness to influence

It seems that the concept of an active audience is often conceptualized as at odds with explaining behaviors by automatic habits. However, habit has been studied in the realm of uses and gratifications – often as a gratification sought or obtained. Named "habit," or to "pass the time," these gratifications have often long been included in studies of television viewing and uses and gratifications (Greenberg, 1974). LaRose notes that early uses and gratifications models included habit, such as those seen in Palmgreen et al., 1985. Over time the traditional exploratory factor analyses used to determine gratifications of technology often showed habit-related items as appearing across several different factors (Rubin, 1983). This led to Rubin's distinction between a ritualistic orientation to viewing and a goal-directed, instrumental orientation to viewing. LaRose (2010) notes the similarities and differences between ritualistic viewing and otherwise conceptualized habit-based viewing. However, he notes that ritualistic viewing orientations confounds habit-based behavior and affinity for the behavior itself, that is, the viewer mindlessly watches TV because they like TV, not necessarily the programming it carries. This confounds the automaticity of habit-driven behaviors and attitudes toward a medium in the uses and gratifications approach.

Habit, Motives, and Binge Watching

While this chapter has documented the application of habit and motivation-based approaches to studying media choices, research that expertly applies one or both approaches to binge watching *and* another form of viewing are still recently emerging. Conlin, Billings, and Auverset (2016) paid attention to the role habit plays in appointment viewing and binge watching. Some individuals might make it a habit to tune in at a certain time to watch some form of television content, whether it be a daily exposure to the early morning news or catching their favorite show every Thursday night. Other viewers might create habits of binge watching television shows. In doing so, they are either catching up on the content missed or desire to view an uninterrupted narrative story. They explore habit as rational for *both types of television viewing.* Flayelle's (2017) and Rubenking et al.'s (2018) focus group explorations of associated gratifications of binge-watching touch on issues that suggest the influence of more habit-driven or automatic behaviors, such as "addiction" to viewing, self-control, and the unintended nature of binge watching. Our own work cites several direct quotes from participants describing the quick, nearly non-decision to keep watching when an episode finished on Netflix, only to begin a countdown in the bottom corner of the screen until the next episode starts. Indeed, both articles point to the structural characteristics of binge watching that may act as context cues to activate habitual binge-watching behavior.

On the contrary, Pittman and Sheehan (2015) argue that habit cannot be associated as a factor of binge watching. The researchers mention that motivation influenced by habit suggests an automatic decision to be exposed to the television content. Binge watching is then argued as occurring when an individual has engaged in a decision and seeks to be exposed to multiple episodes of a specific series. Additionally, Pena (2015) found that those who appointment view television did so out of habit more often than those that binge watched, in an experiment that treated the way of viewing as a between-subjects constant variable. Pena (2015) states that binge watching increases the frequency that one views television content and is, in return, considered a television habit, muddling the waters between the modes of viewing.

Two recent articles leaning on a combination of these habit-based approaches have examined binge watching. Set in the context of concern for the health issues that may accompany frequent, long binge viewing sessions, one recent piece applied several SCT constructs (including outcome expectations, and self-efficacy, along with automaticity, anticipated regret, goal conflict, and goal facilitation to predict binge-watching behavior (Walton-Pattison, Dombrowshi, & Presseau, 2018). The outcome expectations covered anticipated physical, affective, and social outcomes, and automaticity was measured via the self-report automaticity index (Gardner, de Bruijn, & Lally, 2011). A regression analysis with outcome expectations, intention, and self-efficacy entered in the first block, followed by automaticity in the second block, revealed that both outcome expectations and automaticity were significant predictors of binge watching in the final block, of near equal Beta weights. Automaticity explained an additional 5% of variance after the SCT variables in block one, to explain 30% of the variance in all. These results suggest that automaticity, as measured as habit and specific outcome expectancies, plays a role in binge-watching behavior.

The present authors' work (Rubenking & Bracken, 2018) also applied social cognitive theory concepts with other variables of theoretical and empirical relevance to a survey study examining the predictors of binge-watching and appointment viewing frequency across a student and adult sample (total $N = 797$). This study explored two major outcome expectancies of interest, based on previously gathered qualitative data. The first was *emotion regulation*. We hypothesized that binge watching television met one type of goal above all else, those that were emotional in nature. We also included an outcome expectancy measure based on empirical (largely qualitative) data of our own that suggested anticipation of content, suspenseful narratives, and desire to manage moods were driving forces behind binge watching. We labeled this *"Anticipation/Suspense,"* and argued that this and the habit-based measure had a theoretical linkage to binge watching, but not quite one with appointment viewing. This study also included measures of self-efficacy and binge-watching "addiction," as well as demographic controls in the first step. The final block predicting the frequency that one binge watches television explained 39% of the variance, and included age, sex, emotion regulation (outcome expectancy), self-control, viewing addiction, viewing efficacy, suspense/anticipation, and habit. Of these, four variables significantly contributed: The largest among them was habit (β = .37), followed by suspense/ anticipation (β = .15), emotion regulation (β =. 10), and age (β = -.09). This study as well as Walton-Pattison et al. (2018) demonstrate that SCT contrasts of outcome expectancies, similar in concept to gratifications, play no larger role than habit in determining binge-watching behavior. Rubenking and Bracken also found appointment viewing frequency to be determined by (older) age and viewing efficacy, suggesting that different phenomenon may, indeed, be predicted by different combinations of relevant concepts within this theoretical approach.

Conclusion

This chapter has discussed the largely academic literature on what motivates individuals to binge watch. Of the two theoretical approaches reviewed, uses and gratifications' conceptualization of an active audience has garnered the most empirical work that explores why individuals binge watch. We have made the case that focusing on empirical data and/ or other theory to *make a priori hypotheses about specific gratifications sought, or outcome expectancies, while also exploring the role of habit is the most comprehensive method of building knowledge in this growing area.* That is not to say that there are outcome expectancies that others and ourselves have not explored that may contribute in a meaningful way. Nor is to say that these are the only approaches to empirically studying binge watching: There are many other questions to ask and be answered beyond why someone performs a media behavior.

The state of research paints a picture of binge watching as entertaining, in large part because of the suspenseful narratives that the most-binged content offers. The emotional connections to characters, engagement with the story, and social-related outcomes are all a part of the typical binge-watching experience. While the research is still emerging and distinct qualities of binge watching as compared to other modes of viewing remain to be demonstrated across studies and populations, the research thus far overwhelmingly supports that binge watching is a generally positive experience. Those who binge watch are reporting the often positive outcomes associated with this media behavior. In the following chapter, we look at the dynamic nature of motives and outcomes – which may be the same thing.

References

Aarts, H., & Dijksterhuis, A. (2000). Habits as knowledge structures: Automaticity in goal-directed behavior. *Journal of Personality and Social Psychology*, *78*(1), 53–63. doi: 10.1037/0022-3514.78.1.53

Adams, J. (2000). How people watch television as investigated using focus group techniques. *Journal of Broadcasting & Electronic Media*, *44*(1), 78–93. doi: 10.1207/s15506878jobem4401_6

Bandura, A. (2001a). Social cognitive theory: An agentic perspective. *Annual Review of Psychology*, *52*(1), 1–26. doi: 10.1146/annurev.psych.52.1.1

Bandura, A. (2001b). Social cognitive theory of mass communication. *Media Psychology*, *3*(3), 265–299. doi: 10.1207/S1532785XMEP0303_03

Berelson, B. (1949). What's missing the newspapers means. In P. F. Lazarsfeld, & F. M. Stanton (Eds.), *Communications research 1948–1949* (pp. 111–129). New York: Duell, Sloan and Pearce.

Berger, C. R., Roloff, M. E., & Roskos-Ewoldsen, D. R. (2016). What is communication science? In C. R. Berger, M. E. Roloff, & D. R. Roskos-Ewoldsen (Eds.), *The handbook of communication science* (pp. 3–20). Thousand Oaks, CA: Sage.

Biocca, F. (1988). Opposing conceptions of the audience: The active and passive hemispheres of mass communication theory. *Annals of the International Communication Association*, *11*(1), 51–80.

Blumler, J. G., & Katz, E. (1974). *The uses of mass communications: Current perspectives on gratifications research. Sage Annual Reviews of Communication Research* (Vol. III). Beverly Hills, CA: Sage.

Chaffee, S. H., & Berger, C. R. (1987). What communication scientists do. In C. R. Berger, & S. H. Chaffee (Eds.), *Handbook of communication science* (pp. 99–122). Newbury Park, CA: Sage.

Conlin, L., Billings, A. C., & Auverset, L. (2016). Time-shifting vs. appointment viewing: The role of fear of missing out within TV consumption behaviors. *Communication and Society*, *29*(4), 151–164. doi:10.15581/003.29.4.151-164

Devasagayam, R. (2014, March). Media bingeing: A qualitative study of psychological influences. In D. DeLong, D. Edmiston, & R. Hightower Jr. (Eds.), *Once Retro Now Novel Again: 2014 Annual Spring Conference Proceedings of the Marketing Management Association* (pp. 40–44). Chicago, IL: Marketing Management Association.

Duhigg, C. (2012). *The power of habit: Why we do what we do in life and business.* New York: Random House.

Flayelle, M., Maurage, P., & Billieux, J. (2017). Toward a qualitative understanding of binge-watching behaviors: A focus group approach. *Journal of Behavioral Addictions, 6*(4), 457–471. doi: 10.1556/2006.6.2017.060

Gardner, B., de Bruijn, G. J., & Lally, P. (2011). A systematic review and meta-analysis of applications of the self-report habit index to nutrition and physical activity behaviours. *Annuals of Behavioral Medicine, 42,* 174–187. doi: 10.1007/s12160-011-9282-0

Greenberg, B. S. (1974). Gratifications of television viewing and their correlates for British children. In J. G. Blumler, & E. Katz (Eds.), *The uses of mass communications: Current perspectives on gratifications research* (pp. 71–92). Beverly Hills, CA: Sage.

James, W. (1890). *The principles of psychology.* New York: H. Holt & Company.

Kahneman, D. (1973). *Attention and effort.* Englewood Cliffs, NJ: Prentice-Hall

Katz, E., Blumler, J., & Gurevitch, M. (1974). Utilization of mass communication by the individual. In J. Blumler, & E. Katz (Eds.) *The uses of mass communications: Current perspectives on gratifications research* (pp. 19–32). Beverly Hills, CA: Sage.

Lally, P., Wardle, J., & Gardner, B. (2011). Experiences of habit formation: A qualitative study. *Psychology, Health & Medicine, 16*(4), 484–489. doi: 10.1080/13548506.2011.555774

Lally, P., Van Jaarsveld, C. H., Potts, H. W., & Wardle, J. (2010). How are habits formed: Modelling habit formation in the real world. *European Journal of Social Psychology, 40*(6), 998–1009. doi: 10.1002/ejsp.674

Lang, A. (2000). The limited capacity model of mediated message processing. *Journal of Communication, 50*(1), 46–70. doi: 10.1111/j.1460-2466.2000.tb02833.x

Lang, A. (2009). The limited capacity model of motivated mediated message processing. In R. Nabi, & M. B. Oliver (Eds.), *The SAGE handbook of media processes and effects* (pp. 193–204). Thousand Oaks, CA: Sage.

LaRose, R. (2010). The problem of media habits. *Communication Theory, 20*(2), 194–222. doi: 10.1111/j.1468-2885.2010.01360.x

LaRose, R., & Eastin, M. S. (2004). A social cognitive theory of Internet uses and gratifications: Toward a new model of media attendance. *Journal of Broadcasting & Electronic Media, 48*(3), 358–377. doi: 10.1207/s15506878jobem4803_2

McGuire, W. J. (1974). Psychological motives and communication gratification. In J. G. Blumler, & E. Katz (Eds.), *The use of mass communications: Current perspective on gratifications research* (pp. 167–196). Beverly Hills, CA: Sage.

Mendelsohn, H. (1964). Listening to the radio. In L. A. Dexter & D. M. White (Eds.), *People society and mass communication* (pp. 239–248). New York: Free Press.

Mikos, L. (2016). Digital media platforms and the use of TV content: Binge watching and video-on-demand in Germany. *Media and Communication, 4*(3). doi: 10.17645/mac.v4i3.542

Morsella, E., Bargh, J. A., & Gollwitzer, P. M. (2009). *Oxford handbook of human action* (Vol. 2). Oxford, England: Oxford University Press.

Neal, D. T., Wood, W., & Quinn, J. M. (2006). Habits—A repeat performance. *Current Directions in Psychological Science, 15*(4), 198–202. doi: 10.1111/j.1467-8721.2006.00435.x

Ouellette, J. A., & Wood, W. (1998). Habit and intention in everyday life: The multiple processes by which past behavior predicts future behavior. *Psychological Bulletin, 124*(1), 54–74. doi: 10.1037/0033-2909.124.1.54

Owen, W. F. (1984). Interpretive themes in relational communication. *Quarterly Journal of Speech, 70*(3), pp. 274–287. doi: 10.1080/10570318509374177

Palmgreen, P., Wenner, L. A., & Rosengren, K. E. (1985). Uses and gratifications research: The past ten years. In K. E. Rosengren, L. A. Wenner, & P. Palmgreen (Eds.), *Media gratifications research: Current perspectives* (pp. 11–37). Beverly Hills, CA: Sage.

Panda, S., & Pandey, S. C. (2017). Binge watching and college students: Motivations and outcomes. *Young Consumers, 18*(4), 425–438. doi: 10.1108/YC-07-2017-00707

Papacharissi, Z., & Mendelson, A. L. (2007). An exploratory study of reality appeal: Uses and gratifications of reality TV shows. *Journal of Broadcasting & Electronic Media, 51*(2), 355–370.

Papacharissi, Z., & Rubin, A. M. (2000). Predictors of internet use. *Journal of Broadcasting & Electronic Media, 44*, 175–196. doi: 10.1207/s15506878jobem4402_2

Pena, L. L. (2015). *Breaking binge: Exploring the effects of binge watching on television viewer reception* (Doctoral Dissertation). Syracuse University, Syracuse, NY, United States.

Peters, O. (2009). A social cognitive perspective on mobile communication technology use and adoption. *Social Science Computer Review, 27*(1), 76–95. doi: 10.1177/0894439308322594

Pittman, M., & Sheehan, K. (2015). Sprinting a media marathon: Uses and gratifications of binge-watching television through Netflix. *First Monday, 20*, doi: 10.1207/S15327825MCS0301_02

Renckstorf, K. (1996). Media use as social action: A theoretical perspective. In K. Renckstorf, D. McQuail, & N. Jankowski (Eds.), *Media Use as Social Action: A European approach to audience studies* (pp. 18–31). London: John Libbey.

Renckstorf, K., & Wester, F. (2001). The media use as social action approach: Theory, methodology, and research evidence so far. *Communications: The European Journal of Communication Research, 26*(4), 389–419.

Renckstorf, K., & Wester, F. (2004). The 'media use as social action approach': Theory, methodology, and research evidence so far. In K. Renckstorf, D. McQuail, J. E., Rosenbaum, & G. Schaap (Eds.), *Action Theory and Communication Research* (pp. 51–83). New York: Mount de Gruyter.

Rubenking, B., & Bracken, C. C. (2018). Binge-watching: A suspenseful, emotional, habit. *Communication Research Reports, 35*(5), 381–391. doi: 10.1080/08824096.2018.1525346

Rubenking, B., Bracken, C. C., Sandoval, J., & Rister, A. (2018). Defining new viewing behaviors: What makes and motivates TV binge watching. *International Journal of Digital Television, 9*, 69–85. doi: 10.1386/jdtv.9.1.69_1

Rubin, A. M. (1983). Television uses and gratifications: the interactions of viewing patterns and motivations. *Journal of Broadcasting & Electronic Media, 27*, 37–51. doi: 10.1080/08838158309386471

Ruggiero, T. E. (2000). Uses and gratifications theory in the 21st century. *Mass Communication and Society, 3*, 3–37. doi: 10.1207/S15327825MCS0301_02

Saling, L. L., & Phillips, J. G. (2007). Automatic behaviour: Efficient not mindless. *Brain Research Bulletin, 73*(1–3), 1–20. doi: 10.1016/j.brainresbull.2007.02.009

Shim, H.., & Kim, K. H. (2018). An exploration of the motivations for binge-watching and the role of individual differences. *Computers in Human Behavior, 82*, 94–100.

Shoemaker, P. J., Tankard Jr, J. W., & Lasorsa, D. L. (2003). *How to build social science theories*. Thousand Oaks, CA: Sage.

Sung, Y. H., Kang, E. Y., & Lee, W. N. (2015). *A bad habit for your health? An exploration of psychological factors for binge-watching behavior*. Paper presented at the Annual International Communication Association Conference, San Juan, Puerto Rico.

Tokunaga, R. S. (2016). An examination of functional difficulties from Internet use: Media habit and displacement theory explanations. *Human Communication Research, 42*(3), 339–370. doi: 10.1111/hcre.12081

Verplanken, B., & Wood, W. (2006). Interventions to break and create consumer habits. *Journal of Public Policy & Marketing, 25*(1), 90–103. doi: 10.1509/jppm.25.1.90

Walton-Pattison, E., Dombrowski, S. U., & Presseau, J. (2018). 'Just one more episode:' Frequency and theoretical correlates of television binge watching. *Journal of Health Psychology, 23*(1), 17–24. doi: 10.1177/1359105316643379

Webster, J. G., Phalen, J., & Lichty, L. W. (2000). *Rating analysis: The theory and practice of audience research* (2nd Edition). Mahwah, NJ: Lawrence Erlbaum.

Westerik, H., Renckstorf, K., Wester, F., et al. (2005). The situational and time-varying context of routines in television viewing: An event history analysis. *Communications, 30*(2), 155–182. doi:10.1515/comm.2005.30.2.155

Wood, W., & Neal, D. T. (2007). A new look at habits and the habit-goal interface. *Psychological Review, 114*(4), 843–863. doi: 10.1037/0033-295X.114.4.843

Wood, W., Quinn, J. M., & Kashy, D. A. (2002). Habits in everyday life: Thought, emotion, and action. *Journal of Personality and Social Psychology, 83*(6), 1281–1297. doi: 10.1037/0022-3514.83.6.1281

Yerkes, R. M., & Dodson, J. D. (1908). The relation of strength of stimulus to rapidity of habit-formation. *Journal of Comparative Neurology, 18*(5), 459–482. doi: 10.1002/cne.920180503

CHAPTER SIX

Implications of Binge Watching

The previous chapter discussed the largely academic and theoretical work that has gone into asking the obvious yet essential question, *what motivates people to binge watch?* It is, of course, a variation of a question that arises for academics and industry insiders alike whenever a new media technology or mode of media consumption becomes widely adopted or adopted by a desirable media audience. People are watching television in a fundamentally different way. It is logical to ask why, and to follow up with asking how this new way, or mode, of viewing effects downstream outcomes. People are binge watching. How does this way of viewing influence: Future viewing choices and preferences? Enjoyment? Entertainment? Advertising effectiveness? Attitude change? Cable subscription rates? Streaming options? Do extended viewing sessions impact well-being, health, and sleep patterns? Does this new mode of viewing favor some industry players over others? These are culturally – and industry – relevant questions that empirical work and theory can work toward answering.

At the individual level, the pre-binging and post-binging framing of these "motives" and "outcomes" is relatively arbitrary, as they reinforce one another over time. The same concepts are studied as both motive *and* outcome – involvement, discussed below for example, is both heightened by binge watching and a motive underlying binge-watching behavior. This makes conceptualization – and operationalization – murky. The communication literature can still often be reduced to

Lasswell's standard "Who says what to whom and to what effect?" model. Other scholars have eloquently synthesized the concerns and the critical fallacies of one-shot, media effects studies (Lang, 2013; Lang, Potter, & Bolls, 2009). We do not subscribe to a technological determinism model, where the media or technology is the primary agent of change and has linear, unidirectional effects on individuals. While the current dominant paradigm in social scientific media and communication research recognizes individuals as active agents in media and technology use, a smaller contingent of active media processing research takes the critical factor of *time* into account. Doing so makes the very term "media effect" somewhat arbitrary. A measurement of one's outcome variable is always at a relatively arbitrary point in time. It is impossible to control for all other influences in a dynamic system. Indeed, Lang (2014) introduced a communication theory that incorporates this attention to dynamic systems: The Dynamic Human-Centered Communication Systems Theory. Things are always changing. It is our understanding that any media "effect" is not purely a downstream, outcome variable; Viewing choices, knowledge learned, buying intentions, etc. *influence* media use, and *are influenced by* media use and a vast number of other variables. Looking at one outcome, at one time, is not going to be explained mostly or even moderately by any one viewing exposure. As other scholars have noted, the quite modest measurable "effects" of media are apparent across television exposure studies, such as the small correlational effects found across cultivation theory research (Lang, 2013).

The two theoretical perspectives discussed in large part in the previous chapter both exemplify how looking purely at outcome variables, at one point in time, fails to capture the whole process that is of interest. In uses and gratifications research, gratifications are conceptualized as those "sought" (i.e., pre media use) and those "obtained" (i.e., post media use). Theoretically, what serves as a motive prior to a media use is then an effect of that use; operationally, individuals are typically given the same measure before and then after use as a measure of both gratifications sought and obtained. In real life, this happens over and over: If television *never* meets our needs for social gratifications, for example, a sane person will stop seeking social gratifications from television – they'll use social media, make a phone call, or choose a non-media/ technology to meet that need. Likewise, if watching television regularly meets one's motivations for escapism/ relaxation, one is likely to continue choosing that medium when one wants to escape and relax. The problem is that there is a mismatch between media effects research which has stagnated using one shot in time methodological studies, while the television viewing world we live in is dynamic; everything happens over time. Indeed, the habit literature discussed in the previous chapter discusses patterns of learned behavior. But following the same logic, is "habit" a motive for viewing? Or is it an outcome? We would argue it isn't distinctly one or the other. It is just a part of the binge-watching cycle. While this chapter reviews the so-called effects of binge watching, we maintain this distinction of before and after is relatively arbitrary. It is, however, the way in which much of the current literature is divided up.

The discussion of the uses and gratifications literature in the previous chapter attempted to detail motivations for binge watching, for better or worse. In short, we have a long list of the possible motivations to binge watch, because previous researchers have explored phenomenon like binge watching before. As the simplicity of uses and gratifications becomes apparent after decades of application, we observe that studies about uses and gratifications and new media technologies and behaviors often employ multiple theoretical frameworks. A common theoretical approach used alongside uses and gratifications in the academic literature on binge watching has been the concepts and frameworks of involvement, transportation, and flow. While treated as conceptually distinct by many researchers, the common thread among these approaches focuses on a viewing experience which requires attention and engrossment in a narrative, "getting lost in the story." This is a mechanism proposed that *keeps* people watching a serialized drama. When one is engrossed and captivated by the narrative, watching one episode turns into two, three, four, etc. if the distribution style and platform allow for it. And so, involvement (or transportation, or flow – all are hypothesized as functioning the same in this context) is a fundamental part of the binge-watching experience, and may influence binging before, during, or after a binge-watching session. On its face, being heavily involved in the show one is watching is as good a reason as any to *keep* watching it. This is where the colloquial understanding of "binging" comes in. One *can*, typically, eat a regularly portioned meal, enjoy a responsible drink with said meal, and then proceed to watch *an* episode of a television series after dinner. Binging comes into play when one is receiving immediate rewards from continuing to eat, drink, or watch more episodes. Despite more positive descriptors such as "media marathoning," (Perks, 2018), or slightly more ambivalent ones such as "high dosage" (Conlin & Tefertiller, 2016), the term "binge" itself should elicit a bit of concern. This concern can range from guilty pleasure listicles of what to binge watch, to worry and concern for the children who may adopt unhealthy media habits (Matrix, 2014), to a growing number of empirical articles where binge watching is framed as a legitimate public health concern. The concerns about children's vulnerability to media messages places binge watching behind a long list of media platforms that worry the elders about potential effects on youth (see most early television research, violent media research, video game research, social media, and mobile phone research of today). The following chapter addresses the following topics in this order; it reviews research that explores the potential positives of binge watching: enjoyment and finding meaning; achieving need satisfaction and well-being, as an aid in meeting therapeutic or coping needs; encouraging the ability to feel close to mediated others via parasocial relationships; and managing one's cognitive load to meet one's current needs: either highly engaging and involved, or spending less cognitive energy on relaxing and comforting viewing experiences. Next, the potential negatives are reviewed: theories of addiction and media technology–related models of addiction and etiologies, followed by research on the potential health and emotional well-being costs associated with television viewing and binge watching specifically (where available).

In addition to looking at what happens post-binge, or what downstream effects this viewing mode can have on individuals, this chapter takes a multi-level approach to the scope of binge-watching "effects." To this end, the final section of this chapter explores what binge watching means for the television/ film/ advertising/ entertainment industries. Is binge watching driving cord-cutting and cord-shaving? How does binge watching influence the effectiveness of advertising – which was the basis of the economic structure of commercial television in the United States since its inception? A look at parallel developments in industry trends are examined, and the relationship between these trends and new viewing behaviors, such as binge watching, are discussed.

Binge-Watching Outcomes at the Individual Level: The Good

The common conception of binge watching is one of being sucked into compelling, dramatic narrative content, that, at least in the moment, is quite an enjoyable media experience for the viewer. This viewing experience likely contains emotional ups and downs, as a well-liked protagonist or antihero sees trials, tribulations, and some successes. The suspense of the plot and character development inherent to the shows we talk about as "binge-worthy" make for an engrossing, entertaining experience. Logically, if binge watching was a very negative experience, or even just a boring one, it seems likely that an individual would not feel compelled to continue viewing, and simply stop viewing. Binge watching is intended to be an involving, emotional experience that is entertaining. It is not, however, conceptualized here as a solely hedonistically positive experience throughout the whole binge.

Eudemonic Enjoyment: Watching for Entertainment

An engrossing dramatic narrative has obvious ebbs and flows – watching a beloved character struggle before coming out ahead, moral dilemmas playing out, etc. These examples are all part of a more complex view of media enjoyment or entertainment that has received much attention in the literature in the past decade. Entertainment is broadly conceptualized as an intrinsically rewarding experience or activity, and many studies in recent decades have moved to explore media entertainment as the multidimensional construct it is: comprised of hedonistic, pleasure-seeking fun, as well as more meaningful, appreciation-based experiences (Oliver & Bartsch, 2010). Indeed, Oliver and Bartsch (2010) review early studies employing more basic uses and gratifications perspective that find gratifications related to "meaningfulness" and "appreciation." For example, Katz, Haas, and Gurevitch (1973) found that beyond relaxation and entertainment, individuals reported using media to experience beauty and raise morale. A different study of movie gratifications revealed the typical positive entertainment motives, as well as a motivation labeled "self-development," which was concerned with viewing films so they could understand how others think and feel and experience strong emotions (Tesser, Millar, & Wu, 1988). Oliver and Bartsch (2010) argue for an expansion of what has been traditionally referred to as "entertainment gratifications." They proposed a multidimensional media entertainment construct with three sub-dimensions, which differentially predicted enjoyment across genres: fun, suspense, and meaningfulness (moving/thought-provoking). They talk about meaningful entertainment content being "appreciated," whereas hedonistic positive content is seen as fun and entertaining. Oliver and Bartsch (2010) note that fun and suspense motivations are explained by previously established and validated media entertainment theories and research in mood management theory and sensation-seeking. Additionally, they called for further investigations of the concept alongside theories of cognition and emotion.

More systematic approaches to the study of "serious" media entertainment emerged in earnest in the 2000s. One such clear distinction in media entertainment is offered by Oliver and Raney (2011). They outline a largely orthogonal view of media entertainment in which one dimension is hedonistic pleasure or positive experience, and the other is meaningfulness; based on eudaimonic goals of searching for and wrestling with life's meaning, truths, and purposes. The latter is concerned with introspection, personal expressiveness, self-realization, and personal development. Oliver and Raney (2011) advance eudaimonic needs as a logical rationale behind consistent findings (and film box office numbers and television ratings) that people consume and enjoy media narratives that is not pleasurable and happy, and indeed, can be quite sad and dark. One can see how much of the prestige content discussed in Chapter 3 would elicit eudaimonic enjoyment or entertainment.

Need Satisfaction: Watching for Well-Being

Other researchers have employed self-determination theory (Deci & Ryan, 2000) to a more complex understanding of how media entertainment may serve to meet three intrinsic needs from which psychological well-being is derived from: autonomy, competence, and relatedness (Ryan, Rigby, & Przybylski, 2006; Tamborini, Bowman, Eden, Grizzard, & Organ, 2010; Tamborini, Grizzard, Bowman, Reinecke, Lewis, & Eden, 2011). Originally applied in sport and game settings, SDT's early focus was on the inherent satisfaction derived from action (Ryan et al., 2006). SDT differs slightly from the motivation and goal-based theories which are applied to the same context in favor of exploring the *innate psychological needs* which underlie goal selection and goal pursuits, rather than goal selection and pursuit themselves (Deci & Ryan, 2000). Needs are conceptualized as "innate psychological nutriments that are essential for ongoing psychological growth, integrity, and well-being" (p. 228). *Autonomy* is concerned with a willingness or volition to complete a task, whereas the second psychological need, *competence*, is concerned with a need for challenge and feeling of effectiveness. *Relatedness* is experienced when one feels connected to others (Ryan et al., 2006). Ryan et al. (2006) applied SDT to video games, and across four studies found support for their hypotheses that game play enabled individuals meet these three psychological needs related to well-being. They note that many researchers are concerned with the negative impact of video games on individuals' well-being. While these studies look at play in the short-term, they found no real effects for game play on mood but did find mixed effects on state-level self-esteem. While game exposure was draining for participants, those who experienced autonomy and competence when playing displayed more positive outcomes (Ryan et al., 2006), suggesting a restorative effect for some.

In the media psychology literature, this functional approach positions entertainment and enjoyment as co-determined by both traditional hedonic needs, and these three non-hedonic intrinsic needs (Tamborini et al., 2012). Results from two studies reported in Tamborini et al. (2012) support their dual process of media enjoyment, such that hedonistic and non-hedonistic needs positively and independently contributed to unique variance in enjoyment. This multidimensional view of media enjoyment/ entertainment lends itself well to the binge-watching experience. While media applications of SDT have often been in a gaming context, the concept of non-hedonistic needs and goals being met by binge watching is an extremely relevant one. These advancements in our theoretical understanding of what media enjoyment and entertainment can look like – beyond simply pleasure-seeking could certainly help to shed light on binge watching as a distinct phenomenon. Tamborini et al. (2011) found that the three intrinsic needs and extrinsic needs differentially explained variance in game playing conditions which varied in interactivity. Exploring autonomy, competence, and relatedness in binge viewing may be a fruitful endeavor looking ahead. Examining the role of relatedness, or how connected to others a person feels, may be particularly salient given the small and growing binge-watching literature demonstrating the role of parasocial interaction and identification with characters. To the best of our knowledge this specific theory has not been applied in the binge-watching context.

"Media Marathoning" among the Temporarily Immobile: Watching as Therapy

Perks, who deliberately uses the term "media marathoning" instead of binge watching, has explored these related viewing behaviors as coping mechanisms among individuals who were suffering a health condition which kept them home or rendered them unable to complete their normal daily routines (Perks 2015, 2019). Media marathoning, as Perks describes it, is intentional in that it avoids stigmatized language inherent to "binging," encapsulates more than one medium (i.e., films, television, and books), and uses the longer timeframe of binge-watching definitions we've encountered in few other studies: viewing one season of a show in one week or less, watching three films in one week or less, or reading three books from the same series in one month. Media marathoning, according to Perks, "focuses on the holistic engagement with the narrative" (p. 314; Perks, 2019). In a series of qualitative, interview-based studies, Perks uses a grounded theory approach to document how restorative the experience of media marathoning can be for individuals who may be isolated and less mobile for some period of time (due to conditions such as pregnancy bed rest, surgery recovery, mental illness, injury, etc.). She found that marathoning narrative content offered the opposite of the disengaged, isolated couch potato stereotype. Three themes about coping which emerged in Perks (2019) were that of "parasocial encouragement," where characters' positive attitudes or perseverance encouraged those watching; second, participants often watched with others or discussed content with friends or family members; and lastly, interviewees who were struggling with depression or anxiety used what they learned about human relationships from narratives as a springboard for communication with others. Participants used media marathoning to both build social capital and facilitate social support, either with characters or real others. Interestingly, once interviewees were on the mend, they did taper their marathoning, suggesting that this coping mechanism may be better in acute settings rather than in the long term as a maintenance strategy. This last finding may cast doubt on the overall restorative benefits for all viewers who consistently binge watch, but it paints a convincing example of a context in which the benefits of marathoning or binging content decidedly outweigh the consequences. These findings may be reassuring to those who binge watched more frequently during various stay at home orders amidst the covid-19 pandemic.

Parasocial Relationships/ Interaction: Watching to Feel Involved with Characters

Several studies of binge watching have included measures of parasocial interaction (PSI) or of parasocial relationship (PSR) strength. PSI or PSR refers to the commonly occurring perceived closeness, friendship, or intimate bond with well-liked media characters that involvement with narratives often engender (Boon & Lomore, 2001). For instance, Erickson, Dal Cin, and Byl (2019) conducted a field experiment where participants were asked to watch three episodes of a narrative in one sitting or once weekly over the course of three weeks. In measures completed immediately after they finished viewing, those in the "binge" condition reported significantly greater transportation while viewing, along with a greater parasocial relationship with their favorite character. Subsequent analysis demonstrated that state transportation completely mediated the effect of being in the binge-watching condition on parasocial relationship strength (Erickson et al., 2019). They reason that increased speed of disclosure and reduction of uncertainty have been shown to increase the strength of interpersonal relationships (Perse & Rubin, 1989), and since binge watching can also speed up these perceptions, PSR should be greater in binge watching as compared to weekly viewing. A different study looked at transportation, enjoyment, parasocial relationship, and identification with characters across participants who either used a "marathon viewing" exemplar where viewing three episodes or more occurred in one sitting, or a "traditional viewing" exemplar where viewing occurred once weekly (Tukachinsky & Eyal, 2018). Those in the marathon viewing condition reported greater levels of parasocial relationship than those in the traditional viewing condition, and marginally greater transportation. There were no differences in character identification, hedonistic or eudaemonic enjoyment (Tukachinsky & Eyal, 2018). These few studies empirically and theoretically demonstrate that binging may elicit greater parasocial relationships with characters, while their results on similar concepts like transportation and involvement are more mixed.

Cognitive Involvement and Need for Cognition: Watching to Engage and Think

Other research has explored cognitive involvement with the narrative apart from parasocial relationships and identification with characters. One study adopted an information systems approach exploring increased behavioral and cognitive involvement's impact on user satisfaction of using streaming services to watch television (Merikivi, Salovaara, Mäntymäki, & Zhang, 2017). Their goal, ultimately, was to determine if streaming services building their business model on binge watching was a financially viable plan. The study draws on flow theory (Csikszentmihalyi, 1991; Sherry, 2004), which posits that an unflagging focus on a task, with the right balance of challenge and skill, leads to satisfaction. The researchers define cognitive involvement as one of focused absorption or immersion in viewing. Behavioral involvement is concerned with the extent that a user employs a system for a certain usage practice, that is, the degree to which one uses a streaming service to binge watch. They found no influence of cognitive involvement on satisfaction, and only a weak influence of behavioral involvement on satisfaction. They interpret their findings to conclude that the role of cognitive involvement in the content being binge watched may be overstated. Instead of binge watching all the time, users are more likely to watch two or three episodes in an evening. Merikivi et al. (2017) warn that viewing a few episodes per night instead of one could result in a higher relative production cost for streaming services as compared to networks since ultimately more content is being viewed by subscribers. However, the silver lining is that streaming service viewers are using a benefit-maximizing strategy, whereas, sometimes they binge watch, and sometimes they don't. The small variance in satisfaction explained by behavioral involvement suggests that the *option* to binge may be good enough to increase satisfaction with the service. Merikivi et al. (2017) employ the fabulous analogy of an "all you can eat buffet." Similar to restaurants offering all the food to customers, streaming services offer all the content to viewers. Meanwhile, only very few consume enough food or television content to cause a business to lose money. Users feel like they are getting more than they pay for, despite most users seldom making full use of the offer of non-stop binge-watching capabilities.

The concept of cognitive involvement, separate from identification with characters and transportation, is an interesting one. One group of researchers has found a positive relationship between greater need for cognition, NFC, among individuals, and extent of binge watching (Shim & Kim, 2018; Shim, Lim, Jung, & Shin, 2018). Need for cognition is generally understood to reflect the tendency an individual has to engage in elaborated thinking. Shim and Kim (2018) posit that those high in NFC are more likely to watch complex, serialized dramas, which require more cognitive resources to be devoted to processing. Cliffhangers may especially work to keep media users higher in NFC viewing, as the curiosity they inspire will be greater among those who are already likely to contemplate the plot and where it will go. Both studies by Shim and colleagues found a significant small-to-moderate positive influence for this individual difference variable on the extent of binge watching they reported. In a somewhat similar vein, Pittman and Steiner (2019) conceptualize narrative completion – the degree to which an individual believes it important to learn what happens next in a show – as a motivation to binge watch, not as an individual difference variable. However, they found no effect of narrative completion on binge-watching frequency.

Passive Audiences and Slow TV: Watching for Relaxation and Comfort

As discussed briefly in the previous chapter, uses and gratifications theory was among the foundational theories introduced during a paradigmatic, or at least general theoretical understanding of "active audiences." Indeed, "active" uses were described in the paradigm to describe conscious, content-dependent choices as opposed to habit-based, "ritualistic" medium-centric uses. Several persuasion theories introduced shortly after uses and gratifications such as the Elaboration Likelihood Model (ELM) (Petty & Cacioppo, 1986) and the Heuristic Systems Model (HSM) (Chaiken, 1999) posit two different processing routes to persuasion. ELM identifies a "central" route characterized by active, conscious engagement and cognitive involvement, and a "peripheral" route characterized by expending less cognitive effort and instead paying more attention to simple heuristic cues. Central processing results in more long-lasting attitude change and knowledge gained as compared to the more superficial processing of the peripheral route, both theoretically and empirically. While viewing television does not fall into the broader purview of persuasion communication literature; this distinction is incredibly important to currently defining and discussing the implications of binge watching.

These two modes of viewing, or the continuum between active and more passive consumption is not new to those in the industry either. Palmer (2007) talks about "casual" or "directed" viewers, the former of which is willing to let television take them wherever it takes them, while the latter "takes a proactive role in their television experience" (p. 113). Palmer notes that viewers can shift from one type of viewer to another, and it remains up to the "networks" of the future to provide a desirable path of content for casual viewers *and* adequate search functions for directed viewers who know what they wants to watch. Strangelove (2015) argues that both binge watching and distracted, multiscreen viewing is on the rise: seven out of 10 American television viewers describe themselves as binge watchers. However, the majority of viewers also split a large portion of their viewing time between TVs, smartphones, laptops, and tablets (Strangelove, 2015). As he notes, "With so many other, smarter screens in our lives we no longer give the 'idiot box' our undivided attention" (p. 130). Are we actively engaging in engrossing dramas and "binge watching" in that sense of the term, or does multitasking and the data showing "binging" and OTT streaming of shows like *The Office* and *Friends* really just show that televisions or screens are showing content, with or without someone paying rapt attention? These are million-dollar questions! Empirical ways to move forward surrounding this issue, including clearly defining what "binge watching" is and how it can be observed are discussed more thoroughly in the following chapter.

A fascinatingly dull television genre provides an interesting antidote to the compelling dramas discussed as "bingeworthy:" "Slow TV." This iteration of "Slow TV" began with a Norwegian broadcast of a seven-hour train ride. The series *Slow TV* (and the so-titled genre that has spurred other shows) offers extremely long-form episodes of mundane events such as knitting, salmon spawning, or long train rides (Heritage, 2013; Horeck, Jenner, & Kendall, 2018). The train ride first broadcast on public television in Norway in 2009 was quite literally uninterrupted footage from a camera at the front of a train for seven hours without any camera motion or edits. About one-quarter of all Norwegians tuned in for part of the broadcast. Unsurprisingly, Netflix acquired episodes of *Slow TV* in 2016. Horeck et al. (2018) state that streaming TV platforms may have emphasized high-intensity forms of viewer engagement but have also seen the development of "low-intensity" formats that allow viewers to zone out. Interestingly, this content is marathon-like: slow and steady and very, very long. Popular press on the phenomenon report viewers are not only surprised by the appeal of the content: It's creators and media professionals are also surprised (*CBS News*, 2017). The idea of television as comforting and habitual rather than exciting and captivating is creating a different viewer experience – an extremely passive one, or perhaps inwardly contemplative. It is reminiscent of the famous Andy Warhol film *Sleep*, which features a man, well, sleeping. This type of content is an alternative to the fast-paced, catchy, meme-worthy online video content, and television that can seem exhausting (Heritage, 2013). The extended running times of Slow TV is particularly interesting, as it invites a type of extended or heavy dosage viewing experience. However, with being one continuous episode, it certainly doesn't fit into definitions of binge watching which are (problematically) dependent upon the number of episodes of an individual watch, or the serialized, narrative format previously discussed. It is clear, however, that this niche content promotes a relaxing and perhaps comforting mediated entertainment experience.

Binge-Watching Outcomes at the Individual Level: The Bad?

The Addiction Debate

While many studies have found relationships between binge watching and involvement, entertainment, parasocial interaction, and enjoyment, others have studied the addictive potential of this mode of viewing. Researchers have been studying the potential negative impacts of television, including addiction to it, practically since in-home television use became the norm. In today's multiscreen viewing universe, screen time and, specifically, television viewing are still studied alongside health and well-being outcomes. Media addiction, or problematic media use, has been studied in relation to a variety of media technologies (Tukachinsky & Eyal, 2018). There is considerable debate whether the term "addiction" should apply to behaviors other than substance use. In the interest of conceptual clarity and of exploring relevant theoretical frameworks' applicability to the binge-watching phenomenon, an examination of whether binge watching should be called an "addiction" is necessary. In the past two chapters, we've discussed how both media content and media delivery platforms are being created and implemented to encourage binge watching. The "just one more episode" refrain is a common one. And, it is one that Netflix seems to gleefully play up in marketing campaigns and social media posts. We know the rhetoric surrounding binging – it is addicting, unhealthy, depends on a lack of self-control, and is often applied to problematic drinking, eating, or gambling. The metaphor is one of excess and extreme consumption (McCormick, 2016). An "addiction" to binge watching Netflix has been treated as a joke in commercials released by both Netflix and other companies. Indeed, scholars have noted how the relatively positive cultural attitudes that surround binge watching complicate the negative connotations that "binge" elicits. Viewers engage in self-aware, even ironic discourse regarding a lack of self-control and binging (McCormick, 2016). Public discourse on binge watching ranges from treating binge watching as a guilty pleasure or weekend treat to a serious health threat, especially for younger audiences.

Television viewing "addiction" has been explored prior to the rise of binge watching. Measures of well-being and concerns about health have been explored due to the sedentary nature of television viewing. And, general societal concern has sought to identify problem use as compared to "normal" use. Terms such as reliance, heavy exposure, excessive, pathological, and dependence have all been used in the study of what differentiates problem or "addictive" viewing (Horvath, 2004; Riddle, Peebles, Davis, & Xu, 2018). Although we've discussed the colloquialisms associated with binging – is there empirical evidence that over-indulging in television can become an addiction? The answer, as is so often the case when studying humans, is: It depends. Many factors play a role in findings related to television addiction: The theoretical models of addiction applied, the measures employed, the competing explanations for outcomes explored, the samples utilized, and the interpretations of the data by the researchers are some of the critical ones. Findings are mixed. While television has certainly received its fair share of research attention, deficient Internet usage, video games usage, and more recently social media and overall screen usage have been explored via similar approaches.

Models of Addiction. Models of media addiction often hypothesize that impulsivity or a lack of self-regulation are key mechanisms in this behavioral type of addiction, which could be categorized alongside other addiction or dependence types free of substances, such as compulsive buying or gambling. LaRose, Lin, and Eastin (2003) review the literature on what they term, "unregulated media usage," (p. 227) as well as introduce their own model based on Bandura's theory of self-regulation. Two views of addiction development have previously dominated the work on media addictions: those based on personality models of addiction, and those rooted in an operant conditioning model of addiction (LaRose et al., 2003). Commonalities or co-morbidity among media and substance addictions have been used by some to theorize underlying personality traits related to an "addictive personality" (McIlwraith, 1998) or "defective ego autonomy" (Smith, 1986). Indeed, television, video game, and Internet addictions have been shown to be moderately to highly correlated (Greenberg, Lewis, & Dodd, 1999). However, only smaller correlations have been shown between media addictions, substance addictions, and personality traits (Finn, 1992; McIlwrath, 1998). In contrast, some research has found inverse relationships between substance addictions and television addiction (Finn, 1992), thus making the same underlying cause behind both impossible. LaRose et al. (2003) maintain that simple learning theories can also oversimplify models of media addiction. Further, they cite evidence that correlations between addiction-related variables such as depression and low self-esteem can be as much a *consequence* of addiction as a *cause*.

In terms of qualifying addiction, LaRose et al. (2003) are quick to point out that addictive or problematic media usage may be excessive *relative* to the individual's own prior consumption, rather than to absolute terms. Experiencing other addictive symptoms is a critical part of problem use, despite overall levels of use. Those with much higher consumption levels may not do so in a negatively patterned way. Horvath (2004) also laments the inconsistencies in defining addiction based on overall viewing levels. Horvath notes that what may be average in some studies (Kubey & Csikzentmihalyi, 1990) can be light, medium, or heavy viewing, according to median or level splits in other television studies (Morgan & Signorelli, 1990). Greater use of a media (or a substance) is one symptom of addiction, although it is neither necessary nor sufficient (Horvath, 2004). Interestingly, there are parallels here between the operational terms of viewing addiction, just as there are in measuring binge watching. Several scholars – ourselves included – have defined binge watching for study participants in part by naming a number of episodes viewed. Horeck et al. (2018) argues that binge watching should *not* be defined as the number of episodes viewed. They maintain that there are more universal criteria to binge watching than the number of episodes, which different demographic, psychological, or situational factors could influence. For example, a college student on an academic break may have more free time to binge watch than parents of young children with full-time jobs, thus believing there may be a higher litmus to reach a "binge" than those who view less or in shorter durations. Horeck et al. (2018) state that self-determined viewing situations and viewing of serialized formats are better, constant, characteristics of binge viewing. Conceptually, identifying one magical number of episodes to define binge watching seems overly simplistic; however, we are not of the opinion that *time spent* is an irrelevant factor in the binge-watching experience. Thus, conceptually treating binge watching as a longer, or extended viewing session (of the same, serialized content) is critical to the concept. As Horeck notes, any number of individual differences can influence how many episodes an individual considers to constitute a binge. From a methodological standpoint, researchers put a number on time spent or episodes viewed in order to get everyone on the same page.

Somewhat in contrast with personality-based models, operant conditioning models of media addiction have also been quite popularly applied. Here, behavior progresses through four stages: initiation, transition to ongoing use, addiction, and behavior change (LaRose et al., 2003; Marlatt et al., 1998). In the initiation stage, social and personal outcomes play a crucial role, and in the transition to ongoing use, the behavior becomes habitualized. The transition to addiction occurs when the problem media behavior becomes the most important or only tool to relieve stress, loneliness, depression, or anxiety. The final stages are those that represent downward spirals and can only result in major life crisis. LaRose et al. (2003) raise questions about several aspects of this account. Primarily, if media is so widely available and viewed as acceptable, why are there so relatively few media addicts? And, if classical conditioning is being applied in a strict sense, therapies involving abstinence and habituation to cues that trigger a response (i.e., seeing the media device) should be the only successful treatment, while these seem improbable and certainly not reflective of a reality in which a very, very small portion of media users seek out professional intervention for help with their addiction.

Media "Addiction" Research. Citing the lack of crisis surrounding media addictions, LaRose et al. place deficient self-regulation as the cause of normal media behaviors slipping along a continuum to occasional lapses of self-control (watching an extra hour or two of television in an evening than originally planned) to problematic excessive usage (e.g., continually getting less sleep than is recommended because one is staying up watching television *every* night). These authors propose that many individuals in previous media addiction studies have not been "addicted" at all: There needs to be a distinction between merely impulsive or habitual behaviors and those that cause severe negative life consequences, such as divorce, loss of a job, or social isolation. LaRose et al. (2003) tested their model of self-regulation deficiency driving Internet addiction with a normal (non-addicted) college student sample. They found support for their hypothesis that self-regulation worked on a continuum with greater ability related to less Internet usage. They conclude that "lapses in effective self-regulation lead to the formation of media consumption habits, but not necessarily to harmful consumption patterns that might be termed addictive" (p. 243). They are not alone in their objection to overuse of the term "addiction" when applied to media behaviors. Blaszczynski (2008), for example, states that in the realm of video game research, there has not been enough evidence presented of true dependency and lack of control inherent to the definition of addiction and argues that the term should be relegated only in the context of substance abuse. While plenty of media scholars continue to use the term "addiction," others employ terms such as pathological or excessive regarding problematic media use (Riddle et al., 2018).

Recent moves to pathologize "Internet gaming," have led to disagreement among scholars that have played out in at times biting exchanges in academic articles (Aarseth et al., 2017; Ferguson & Colwell, 2019; Griffiths, Kuss, Lopez-Fernandez, & Pontes, 2017). Controversies and issues with diagnostic criteria plague recent moves by the American Psychiatric Association (APA) and the World Health Organization (WHO). Internet Gaming Disorder (IGD) was included as a provisional diagnosis disorder in the APA's 2013 Diagnostic and Statistical Manual for Mental Disorders (DSM-5). IGD is not yet a formal diagnosis, but as a provisional diagnosis, it is classified as a condition for future study. It lists nine symptoms analogous to symptom abuse, five of which must be met to meet the threshold for diagnosis. The inclusion of the word "Internet," to denote the online aspect of games, has been criticized, as a focus on gaming addiction in its entirety would be helpful in moving the research field forward (Kuss, Griffiths, & Pontes, 2017). The criteria has also been heavily criticized as logical for substance issues, but likely to produce many false positives in the context of gaming (Ferguson & Colwell, 2019). For instance, a preoccupation with heroin is obviously an important dimension of heroin addiction. However, spending considerable time thinking and talking about gaming is more similar to thinking and talking about any other, non-pathologized pastime activity.

In 2018, the World Health Organization (WHO) announced that it would be including "gaming disorder" as an official diagnosis in their International Classification of Diseases. In perhaps a move to avoid the criteria criticism, the WHO's official diagnosis includes no clear criteria beyond the interfering nature of gaming (Ferguson & Colwell, 2019). It has, of course, been criticized for giving clinicians considerable flexibility when diagnosing patients in the field. An attitude survey of video game scholars found significant disagreement on support for each of these diagnoses, as well as whether pathological gaming even is a mental health problem. While 60% agreed that pathological gaming could be a mental health problem, 49.7% supported the DSM-V Internet Gaming Disorder criteria, and 56.5% support WHO's gaming disorder diagnosis. Scholars disagree on any number of relevant issues: the comparison of pathological gaming to substance use, pathological gaming as a stand-alone disorder, and whether gaming should be singled out for a mental health disorder. Ferguson and Colwell (2019) note there are several areas researchers agree: While some people overdo it with gaming, pathological gaming is *quite rare*, and it typically occurs alongside other disorders.

Though the APA and WHO have not created diagnoses of television addiction specifically, researchers have certainly explored the addictive potential of television viewing. Similar to the research surrounding gaming addiction, questions on the etiology and diagnosis of television addiction persist, along with calls for additional research (Sussman & Moran, 2013). Horvath's (2004) piece on television addiction provides a symptoms-based approach to media addiction that provides a measure of addiction and conceptualization of the term often cited in the media effects literature. Noting the difficulty in defining addiction throughout health contexts because it can be defined by its contributing factors, symptoms, and consequences, Horvath provides a seven-item list of symptoms that the American Psychiatric Association's (1994) DSM-IV identifies as criteria for dependence. They are:

1. *Tolerance.* A need for more of the substance to achieve the same effect, or a diminished effect with the same amount of the substance.
2. *Withdrawal.* A substance-specific syndrome that results if the substance use is reduced or stopped that is unrelated to other physical illness, or use of the substance or related one to reduce withdrawal symptoms.
3. The substance is taken in *larger amounts over longer time than is intended.*
4. Persistent desire and/or *unsuccessful efforts to cut down* are experienced.
5. A *great deal of time* is present in obtaining, using, and recovering from the substance.
6. *Important activities* such as school, work, or time with friends are given up or reduced.
7. The individual *continues use* of the substance despite physical or psychological problems (p. 279).

To qualify as substance dependent, an individual need only to reply affirmatively to three of the criteria in the past 12-month period. A two-study validation of

Horvath's (2004) TV Addiction Scale reveals a four-factor solution, explaining moderate levels of variance in viewing on a continuum. Those dimensions are heavy viewing, problem viewing, craving for viewing, and withdrawal, with the first two explaining the largest parts of variance (Horvath, 2004). Sussman and Moran (2013) devote significant space in their selective review article about television addiction explaining how television may meet all seven of these criteria, though they do note that previous DSM versions included criteria about legal consequences and immediate physical danger that did not apply to television addiction.

Sussman and Moran (2013) argue that television addiction, defined as "out-of-control behavior pertaining to the medium of television, as opposed to a particular show on television" (p. 125) can be also be characterized as an accompanying craving to view, a preoccupation with viewing, a loss of control surrounding viewing, and negative life consequences due to excessive viewing. They trace back the first clinical case studies of television addiction to Meerloo (1954) and cite the first survey study of television addiction to Smith (1986). Sussman and Moran (2013) also comment multiple times that research subjects perceive television addiction to be a reality. They also cite studies (Kubey & Csikszenttmihalyi, 2002; McIlwraith, 1998) that use measures of self-identified television addiction – which find the "prevalence of self-identified television addiction is approximately 10% in the United States" (p. 126).

This is a bit of odd logic. If television addiction is as widespread as effecting up to 10% of the population, and researchers have been studying it since 1954, why isn't there more confirmatory empirical research on television addiction's prevalence, etiology, prevention, and treatment applications? Sussman and Moran (2013) point to several aspects of television that could encourage overuse, but surely connected gaming must also be able to encourage these behaviors, and the presence of others and interactivity feedback loops must be more addictive – but literature from the health sciences puts the "gaming disorder" prevalence at 1% or less. And, as with binge watching, defining a number of hours of viewing per day that qualifies television addiction is problematic. Different studies employ different numbers of hours viewing per day that lead to harmful outcomes, and self-identified "television addicts" themselves watch less the U.S. Bureau of Labor Statistics reported was average in 2012 (Sussman & Moran, 2013). The details of defining and measuring television addiction seem as confusing as gaming addiction and others, at the very least.

Addiction or Entertainment? Two Binge-Watching Studies. Several recent studies shed light on what these different approaches can contribute to our understanding of binge watching as simply a new way of entertaining oneself with television content or whether the excess indicative in a "binge" should be of concern. Two such studies specifically explore entertainment/ enjoyment theoretical approaches *and* addiction-based models (Riddle, et al., 2018; Tukachinsky & Eyal, 2018). Tukachinsky and Eyal (2018) examine three negative mental health issues (i.e., loneliness, social anxiety, and depression) that have been explored under a cognitive model of addiction to binge watching as well as psychological concepts related to media engagement (i.e., transportation, enjoyment, and parasocial relationships and identification with characters). The two studies reported by Tukachinsky and Eyal (2018) explored "marathon viewing," or consumption of multiple episodes of the same series in a condensed manner over several days. While they found that those with a less secure attachment style and greater depressive symptoms engaged in greater marathon viewing, the effect of depression was completely mediated by deficient self-regulation, following the theoretical model of LaRose et al.'s media addiction model. The extent of marathon viewing was then used as a predictor variable of transportation into the narrative, identification with characters, parasocial relationships with characters, and hedonic and eudemonic enjoyment. Greater marathon viewing was associated with greater character identification and parasocial relationships. A second study comparing marathon viewing to traditional television viewing found that of all the entertainment theory concepts, only parasocial relationships differed across viewing types, such that greater parasocial relationships were predicted by marathon viewing condition (Tukachinsky & Eyal, 2018). Tukachinsky and Eyal (2018) found support for some variables related to the addiction model and some variables related to the entertainment theoretical model – and neither set explained large percentages of the variance, suggesting that personality antecedents as well as the psychological experience of marathon viewing both play a role in this particular viewing behavior.

In a somewhat similar vein, Riddle et al. (2018) draw distinctions between two types of binge watching: unintentional binge viewing sessions, which theoretically may be more greatly associated with addiction symptoms and variables, as well as intentional, planned binge viewing sessions, which can, in part, be explained through a combination of media effects theoretical approaches. Impulsivity is used as the explanatory mechanism here that may drive unintentional binge watching, however not all binge watching is driven by this. Indeed, Riddle et al. (2018) did find that impulsivity was positively related to unintentional binging, though not to *intentional* binge watching. For those with greater impulsivity, there was also a significant positive relationship with addiction symptoms, as measured via select items from Horvath's (2004) TV Addiction Scale. Riddle et al. (2018) argue that binge watching should not be treated as a monolithic behavior – intentionality may play a large role in outcome variables related to binge watching.

Television, Screen Time, and Health Outcomes

Beyond scholarship using the somewhat contentious lens of "addiction," there is a long history of research on the ill effects of television on audiences. Broadly, different theoretical approaches have been used to investigate television's perceived negative impact on physical and mental health, as well as antisocial outcomes. Early empirical communication scholars were concerned with effects of specific content – for example, news topics, violent content, and persuasive messages – while critical cultural scholars have been interested in perhaps less tangible, and certainly less measurable effects of time spent with the medium itself (think cultural studies, McLuhan's "the medium is the message"). More recently, empirical scholars from across disciplines, as well as in communication and media, have taken an interest in the effects of time spent on media use and several well-being outcomes for individuals. There is considerable overlap with the variables explored in media addictions here: Depression, self-esteem, loneliness, sleep issues, physical well-being, and general mental health are believed to be outcomes of addiction in general and have been studied in relation to problematic media use. Here, we review some literature across new media and television use, since we've established the multiple ways that today's television viewing norms are quite different from those in the past and are certainly influenced by new media, Internet use and platforms. After this, we explore some of the recent literature that looks at these same variables, particularly in the realm of binge watching.

Negative Health Outcomes and Media Use. Some scholars in health-related fields examine behaviors associated with a more sedentary lifestyle, which has serious negative impacts on health. A sedentary lifestyle and physical inactivity have been cited as the greatest public health problem of this century (Trost, Blair, & Khan, 2014). A number of widely cited studies in prestigious journals with solid methodological considerations have found increased television viewing to be associated with a host of grave health outcomes: including major chronic disease and cardio health (Thorp, Healy, & Owen, 2010; Winjndaele, Healy, & Dunstan, 2010); cardiovascular mortality (Grontved & Hu, 2011); and decreased life expectancy (Veerman, Healy, & Cobiac, 2011). While this pattern of a relationship between greater time spent viewing television and more negative health outcomes is persistent across studies, countries, and ages of samples; articulating a causal, directional relationship is more complicated. Certainly, one can imagine that in an older population, being in poor health limits the physical activity one can perform. Thus, there is more time to watch television or engage with media screens. Even among normal healthy populations, too many factors to account for could be driving both poor health and increased television viewing time.

Negative effects of too much time spent viewing are associated with mental health as well. Increased time with television and screens has been demonstrated to be negatively associated with mental health and depression in youth and adolescents (Biddle & Asare, 2011; Primack, Swanier, & Georgiopoulus, 2009) as well as older adults (Hamer, Poole, Messerli-Burgy, 2011). Dempsey, Howard, Lynch, Owen, and Dunstan (2014) explored health-related quality of life and television viewing, such that perceptions of physical, mental, and social well-being, as well as vitality were considered along with a host of control and moderating variables. Each additional one hour of viewing per day increment was associated with lower physical health, mental health, and vitality, *after* controlling for demographics, behavioral attributes such as leisure time and diet quality, and known co-morbidities including waist circumference, diabetes, and cardiovascular disease (Dempsey et al., 2014). Several of these studies have found stronger relationships or effects of time spent viewing and depression and vitality in men, as compared to women (Dempsey et al., 2014; Primack et al., 2009). A study of U.S. adults found that television watching and computer use can predict greater depression symptoms after controlling for many well-known factors. Adults who viewed 4–6 hours per day or greater than 6 hours per day exhibited higher depression levels (Madhav, Sherchand, & Sherchan, 2017). Similar results have been found in a longitudinal study of adolescents (Babic et al., 2017). Over time, increases in recreational screen use and mobile use were negatively associated with physical self-concept and psychological well-being. However, non-recreational screen use (i.e., schoolwork) had no such negative relationship. The research on the influence of increased screen time and television viewing is relatively straight-forward: More of it leads to more negative physical and mental health outcomes, despite controlling for related confounding variables.

Screens and Sleep. While the relationship between increased television and screen use and negative health outcomes may have some issues of causality, the consensus of data supports a significant relationship between the two across populations and study methodologies. There is also considerable scholarship examining the relationship between screen use and sleep habits and problems. The more time spent watching television – which is most popular in the evening hours before most people go to bed – means less time for other things. Television viewing largely keeps viewers physically inactive and could function to delay sleep. We have all heard of the "one more episode" refrain; binge watching is clearly implicated here. Horeck et al. (2018) claim that the "endeavour to colonize sleep is at the heart of Netflix's business model" (p. 501). Indeed, Netflix CEO Reed Hastings has been quoted as saying, "… when you watch a show from Netflix and you get addicted to it, you stay up late at night. We're competing with sleep, on the margin"

(Sulleyman, 2017). Sleep as the competitor is definitely a different business model than other channels, OTT services, or social media and online browsing.

Professionals in the health sciences have treated television and sleep a bit more seriously than Hastings. One survey of Chinese university students found a significant relationship between greater screen use and poorer sleep quality (as well as a host of mental health problems, Wu, Tao, Zhang, Zhang, & Tao, 2015). While the relationship was purely correlational, Wu et al. (2015) also found a significant interaction effect, wherein those with less physical activity and greater screen use were more likely to have poorer sleep quality than those with greater physical activity and less screen time. A different study employed a quasi-experimental design by exploring populations in India that were rural who had no electricity and no television (*a*), electricity but not television access (*b*) electricity and TV access (*c*), and an urban population with electricity and television access. Those with television access reported the shortest sleep durations and more daytime sleepiness (Nag & Pradhan, 2012).

While these studies suggest too much television viewing may be related to sleep disorders, one well-constructed three-year longitudinal study of college students suggests – and finds support – for the assertion that sleep problems *predict* longer television viewing time and more time spent on social media. The cross-lag design allowed researchers to employ a causal, time-ordered test, and found no support for a relationship in the opposite direction, nor was there a significant relationship between media use and overall sleep duration (Tavernier & Willoughby, 2013). The authors suggest that emerging adults may be turning to television and social media to help cope with sleep issues. Other studies have failed to replicate the relationships between increased screen use and sleep issues in adult samples. Custers and Van den Bulck (2012), for example, explored sleep duration and tiredness as related to overall television and Internet use, as well as the influence of Internet and television devices in the bedroom, as removing such technologies is often recommended to improve sleep functions. In their study of adults in Belgium, they found some evidence of timeshifting sleep – of later bedtimes and rise times associated with greater use and availability, but they found no relationships between the volume of media use and reduced sleep lengths or reported tiredness (Custers & Van den Bulck, 2012).

Binge-Watching and Health and Emotional Outcomes

Thus far, we've reviewed research on overall media use or television viewing and its relationship with various health outcomes, including sleep. It is essential here to keep in mind that binge watching is phenomenologically distinct from simply watching 4–6 hours or 6 hours or more of television per day. Qualitatively, we talk about binge watching as an engaging experience in which viewers are paying attention to serialized, narrative content over some period. However, if the sedentary lifestyle that purely heavy television viewing is implicated in may function to deteriorate health, how can binge watching *not* share these same negative health effects? In the earliest days of academic investigations of binge watching, several conference papers, proceedings, and theses explored the relationship between increased depression and binge watching and found just that (e.g., Karmaker, Kruger, Elhai, & Kramer, 2015; Sung, Kang, & Lee, 2015). Both Wheeler (2015) and Sung et al. (2015) found a positive, small, non-directional relationship between depression and binge watching. Kruger et al. (2015) reported results wherein greater self-reported anxiety and stress predicted more frequent binge watching.

Depression or Self-Regulation and "Showholes." However, the full research articles (as compared to conference proceedings or thesis work) with more rigorously peer-reviewed methodologies and clear conceptualizations that followed these initial studies show a different pattern or mixed results. They also explore issues of self-regulation and self-control as moderators of the relationships between typically negative health states and binge-watching behavior. Tukachinsky and Eyal (2018) predicted that deficient self-regulation was the underlying mechanism explaining any link between the two. They found support for their hypothesis: The influence of depression on binge-watching behavior was completely mediated by self-regulation deficiency, which helped to explain further variance in the model. Merrill and Rubenking (2019) found no effect of self-control on the frequency nor the duration that people spent binge watching; however, they did find a small effect for greater self-regulation being related to more frequent binge-watching sessions.

Tefertiller and Maxwell (2018) explored depression and self-control as predictors of intent to binge watch, as well as anxiety and loneliness. In contrast to Tukachinsky and Eyal (2018), they found no effect of self-control on binge-watching intention. Tefertiller and Maxwell (2018) make the important distinction between an individual trait (i.e., depression) and a regular, commonplace and often sought out affective response to television content: sadness. They make the case that sadness and depression are two qualitatively distinct experiences beyond a trait/ state difference as well. For instance, depression includes a larger range of emotions besides purely sadness. It is not typically in response to some specific loss, as sadness is understood to be (Tefertiller & Maxwell, 2018). They discuss an Amazon Fire TV commercial that created term, *showhole*, and define it as implied in the commercial as a "combination of feelings of loss and melancholy associated with the end of binge watching a show" (p. 278). The authors examined these mixed feelings in the context of emotion and entertainment theory that examines the role of both eudaemonic and hedonistic enjoyment as media effect outcomes worthy of exploring when examining future viewing behavioral choices (Oliver & Bartsch, 2010). They found *no* effect of depression, anxiety, or loneliness as predictive of binge-watching intention. And, although the overall model was not significant, depression was *negatively* associated with binge-watching intent and anxiety was positively associated with it. As evidence of their distinction between the individual trait of depression and experiencing an affective response to television content that is not entirely hedonistically positive, Tefertiller & Maxwell (2018) found evidence for their "showhole" effect.

Negative Emotional Effects. There are also several research studies exploring negative affect related to binge watching that stop short of using addiction language or trait diagnosis terms such as depression. For instance, Panda and Pandey (2017) found that negative gratifications (such as guilt, tired "felt bad," "could not concentrate") were associated with greater time spent binge watching, despite positive gratifications (such as relaxing, "enjoyed it") not being related to time spent binging. Regret experienced after binge watching was explored by Pittman and Steiner (2019). They found that more attentive viewing was related to less regret after binge watching, while multitasking during viewing was related to more regret. One study found that participants who reported experiencing more guilt from binge watching did so more frequently (Merrill & Rubenking, 2018). Other researchers have explored the paradox of binge watching enabling both more self-determination *and* less self-control. Granow, Reinecke, and Ziegle (2018) state that binge watching gives viewers more control of television viewing, and this autonomy can lead to feelings of greater self-determination. However, binge watching can also demonstrate a lack of self-control and can result in feelings of guilt. Granow et al. (2018) did find evidence of this double-edged sword: When binge watching results in greater perceived autonomy, it resulted in greater recovery experience and greater enjoyment; however, when binge watching resulted in guilt, it diminished the recovery experience and vitality (although, not enjoyment). The authors posit that self-control and goal conflict are important underlying mechanisms behind positive and negative media effects.

Binging Outcomes and Implications at the Industry Level

The bulk of this chapter has discussed outcomes of binge watching at the individual level. The published research presents a mixed view of the outcomes of binge watching – it *can* be involving and entertaining, but the research also suggests that more television viewing has some negative health outcomes, which overuse can exacerbate. Other outcomes and related phenomenon on a more macro, social level are discussed in Chapter 4. The rest of this chapter focuses on the possible macro-level downstream effects of binge watching on the television industry. Surprisingly, academic research in this area is anemic, but several starting data points offer support for what common sense would suggest: The winners within the media industry are different when binge watching is the new norm than when appointment viewing was the norm. Viewing television content in different ways than tuning in weekly is now definitely the norm among viewers. Binge watching is one of these new modes of viewing that capitalizes on changes in content providers, distribution strategies, and the ever-increasing ability to view television "anytime, anywhere." Binge watching has been a norm for some time, and a return to appointment-only viewing seems highly unlikely.

Traditional TV Networks vs. Over-the-Top, OTT Services

The most recent decade of television in the United States tells the same, basic story. Cable subscription rates are falling as OTT streaming service subscriptions are growing.

While we currently may be in the "streaming wars" among competing streaming services, a sizeable number of individuals and an enviable amount of time are still being spent with regular old broadcast and cable television: which used to be the dominant and singular option for television content. However, it is clear at this point that "cord-cutting" is not a trend to be taken lightly. According to a Convergence Research Group study reported in *Variety*, 2019 represents a tipping point where the number of streaming subscriptions has surpassed the number of traditional pay cable subscriptions in the United States (Roettgers, 2019). A full 34% of U.S. households no longer have a traditional cable TV subscription after a 5% decline in 2019, and a 4% decline in 2018. Over 10 million subscribers dropped cable subscriptions between 2012 and 2018: And the number of cord cutters doubled from 2017 to 2018 (Fitzgerald, 2019a). Satellite companies have been particularly hard hit, with Dish Network and DirecTV losing 2.36 subscribers (Fitzgerald, 2019a). This comes at a time when Netflix, Hulu, and Amazon have topped 110 million subscribers.

Despite this shift in total number of subscribers, traditional cable TV makes approximately three times more money per subscriber than OTT services do (Roettgers, 2019; Spangler, 2018). The silver lining for MSOs, who are losing cable subscriptions, is that with OTT subscription growth, residential broadband subscription rates grow as well. Since most households get cable and Internet from the same provider, MSOs benefit from more households paying for Internet services, and perhaps at faster speeds to support streaming and gaming. Household broadband subscription rates surpassed household cable subscription rates for the first time in 2017 (Roettgers, 2019). The heavily consolidated industry continues to benefit from the vertical integration that mergers throughout the 1980s, 1990s, and 2000s have allowed.

This increase in money made from cable subscribers is precisely the top reason viewers are shying away from cable television: high costs. Throughout the recent, rapid falling cable subscription rates, cost has remained a top reason for cutting the cord reported by consumers. A multi-country study in 2015 found that cord cutters reported that a want or need to save money and not watching enough TV to justify the cost as the two most common reasons to eliminate household cable package (Ericsson Consumer Labs, 2015). Other reports support that while cable costs are a large factor, cord cutters may be value-minded. A 2019 study found that the average cord cutter has 3.2 streaming service subscriptions, and a majority say they provide a better value for the content they want to watch. Not all cord cutters are averse to paying for entertainment (Fitzgerald, 2019b).

Networks are still highly valued assets in major media conglomerate acquisitions. Television industry executives have notoriously played both sides of the field and offered any number of bold statements about the death of networks or television. Strangelove (2015) makes a compelling case that while the future of networks appears shaky if one is examining data on cord-cutting/ shaving/ nevers, one would have no reason for concern if they just listened to network executives on the matter. He maintains network executives' primary audience whenever speaking publicly about their brand is stockholders. When early doomsayers talked about cord-cutting at the birth of widespread household Internet access, networks unfailingly spoke about it as a myth. By the early to mid-2000s, some executives began taking a different tone, one of changing times (Lotz, 2007).

Indeed, even Nielsen, who for years underplayed the cord-cutting phenomenon (Steinberg, 2015), has recently begun reporting data on it, albeit with a highlight on those turning to broadcast television after cutting the cable cord. Nielsen finds the positive news for broadcast television amid a changing viewing landscape. Indeed, an August 2019 Nielsen online article states,

> Given today's digitally charged, on-demand media environment, it's easy to get caught up in the excitement around the growing array of video streaming options, especially amid the proliferation of internet-connected devices and smart TVs. And there's good reason for the buzz: 56% of U.S. adults stream non-linear content to their TVs. *That*

fact notwithstanding, our actual TV streaming habits have yet to truly live up to the buzz. (emphasis is ours)

The article goes on to highlight that the typical U.S. adult who accesses a streaming service via device or smart TV spends two hours and 42 minutes with linear TV and just 57 minutes with non-linear content in a regular day (Nielsen, 2019). Another Nielsen headline touts, "Choose it or lose it: Media choice abounds but many Americans stay with what they know" (Nielsen, 2019). The article reports Q1 findings from 2019 that find 22% of streaming service subscribers typically don't know what they want to watch at all prior to viewing, and among all streaming service subscribers, 58% say that when they don't know what they want to view, tuning into their favorite channels is their most likely choice. Perhaps unsurprisingly, Nielsen has explored two groups of cord cutters. The smaller of these groups, totaling 6.6 million homes in 2018, are watching television via digital antenna (Perez, 2019). They skew older and have a smaller median income, so their decision is largely seen as a cost-saving one. The larger group of cord cutters, totaling 9.4 million homes in 2018, have at least one OTT subscription and skew younger and more affluent. It is of course in Nielsen's best interest to show that some viewers, who are saying no thanks to cable, are still watching broadcast TV (Perez, 2019).

In addition to characterizing cord cutters into different audience segments, the television and OTT industries have long been fascinated with a group that they've termed "cord nevers," or those individuals who are typically young and have never subscribed to cable TV. Nearly 31 million adults in the United States – 12% of the adult population – have never paid for traditional cable television access (Balderston, 2019). In 2017, just 9% were categorized that way. While the story has traditionally been that young people would say they were waiting until they got their first well-paying job to subscribe to cable television services, the median age for a cord-never is now 33, and their household income has increased 27% from 2017 to 2019, now sitting at $52,800. However, about 27% of cord-nevers still say they'll likely sign up for a pay-tv service in the next six months (Balderston, 2019). There is some evidence of cord cutters and cord-nevers being a younger audience segment (Fitzgerald, 2019b; Spangler, 2016). Consumers ages 14–25 have spent more time watching streaming services than live TV as early as 2015 (Spangler, 2016).

Effects for Television Advertising

While cable companies are an obvious loser if trends toward cord-cutting and cord-nevers continue in the direction and at the pace that they currently are headed, traditional television advertising is posed to take a direct hit as well. With few notable exceptions, OTT services operate on an entirely subscription-based business model, and all of them, by definition, incorporate at least some of their revenue from subscriptions. Hulu is the notable exception, and currently incorporates both advertising (which users cannot skip without paying a premium monthly rate) and a subscription model. Interestingly, one study found that cord cutters and cord shavers were not averse to advertising, and actually welcomed advertising messages that were relevant to them (Fitzgerald, 2019b).

Few studies have explored binge watching and advertising, with the notable exception of researchers who worked with Hulu and used their viewing records as data (Schweidel & Moe, 2016). They report several interesting findings. Click-through rates were highest during animation/ cartoons, food and leisure, and reality/ game shows; and lowest during horror/ suspense, music, and drama (click-through rates were .87% of all impressions). They found that advertising responsiveness declines for everyone over time and declines more sharply when people are watching a variety of programs as compared to a single program. In terms of user-specific traits, Schweidel and Moe (2016) found that binge watchers made up less than one-fifth of all users, but consume 50% of all content. Further, those who were binge watchers were less likely as a group to click on ads than non-bingers. These results seriously call into question how effective a lot of these ad placements were. Other research has demonstrated that dramas are the most commonly binged genre of content: 53% of individuals say they most often binge watch drama, followed by 17% reporting comedies, and 7% reality television.

Binge Watching's Industry Impact

Given the lack of data on advertising and binge watching, as well as more academic- or theory-driven research on decision-making processes regarding paying for television and film content, it is difficult to make blanket statements on the specific role that binge watching is having on a number of industry trends. The perceived value of viewing options – the desirability of access to specific content and the price of access to that content should play a major role in decisions to subscribe. Certainly, the distribution strategies, along with the new ways in which streaming services manage audience flow from one show to another, as discussed in Chapter 3, are also relevant here. Besides content and distribution strategies, the ease with which viewers can view content at any time, and on any connected device (or not connected – downloadable content is certainly an option to look for in the upcoming streaming wars) is a critical plus in the pros column of OTT subscriptions as compared to cable subscriptions.

While new modes of viewing are relevant to trends in subscription rates, it is important to not overstate cause and effect. From empirical data, we know that viewers find cable to be too expensive, and that no major cable companies can boast excellent customer satisfaction (Bode, 2018). We also know that viewers appreciate the variety and quality of OTT service content, the cost-value of OTTs, and the ability to timeshift and watch across multiple devices. We also know binge watchers are not ashamed of binging, and they see the ability to do so as another checkmark in the "pro" list for OTT services.

Beyond the seemingly endless news of Comcast's abysmal customer service, the 2018 American Consumer Satisfaction Index study of over 45,000 U.S.-based customers revealed that public perception of cable companies is at an 11-year low (Bode, 2018). Indeed, a *Vice* article notes:

> To be clear: Scoring as poorly as cable and broadband providers routinely do takes some serious effort. Comcast and Charter [Spectrum] rate worse than some of the most disliked companies and organizations in America, consistently beating the airline industry, banks, insurance companies, and even the IRS in terms of consumer dissatisfaction. (Bode, 2018)

Streaming services are consistently rated higher, with even the lowest rated OTT provider (Crackle) rated more satisfactory than nearly all the major cable providers. While it may make sense for cable companies to be attempting to provide better customer service and support in the wake of stiff competitors, it seems the biggest players do not see that as an investment worth making. While cable and Internet providers are not positioned to disappear anytime soon, OTT services can look forward to continuing to offer subscribers more aspects of the viewing experience they say that they currently value.

References

Aarseth, E., Bean, A. M., Boonen, H., Colder Carras, M., Coulson, M., Das, D., ... & Haagsma, M. C. (2017). Scholars' open debate paper on the World Health Organization ICD-11 Gaming Disorder proposal. *Journal of Behavioral Addictions, 6*(3), 267–270. doi: 10.1556/2006.5.2016.088

Babic, M. J., Smith, J. J., Morgan, P. J., Eather, N., Plotnikoff, R. C., & Lubans, D. R. (2017). Longitudinal associations between changes in screen-time and mental health outcomes in adolescents. *Mental Health and Physical Activity, 12,* 124–131. doi: 10.1016/j.mhpa.2017.04.001

Balderston, M. (2019, April 17). Nearly 31 million Americans have never paid for traditional TV. Retrieved from: https://www.tvtechnology.com/news/nearly-31-million-americans-have-never-paid-for-traditional-tv

Biddle, S. J., & Asare, M. (2011). Physical activity and mental health in children and adolescents: A review of reviews. *British Journal of Sports Medicine, 45*(11), 886–895. doi: 10.1136/bjsports-2011-090185

Blaszczynski, A. (2008). Commentary: A response to "Problems with the concept of video game "addiction": Some case study examples". *International Journal of Mental Health and Addiction, 6*(2), 179–181. doi: 10.1007/s11469-007-9132-2

Bode, K. (2018, March). America hates Comcast more than ever: A new survey indicates Americans' dislike of giant cable companies is only growing, and the rising flood of streaming alternatives like Netflix are beating the industry at its own game. *Vice.* Retrieved from: https://www.vice.com/en_us/article/7xmxza/america-hates-comcast-more-than-ever

Boon, S. D., & Lomore, C. D. (2001). Admirer-celebrity relationships among young adults: Explaining perceptions of celebrity influence on identity. *Human Communication Research, 27*(3), 432–465. doi: 10.1111/j.1468-2958.2001.tb00788.x

CBS News (2017). Norway's slow TV: Fascinating viewers for hours or days at a time. Retrieved from https://www.cbsnews.com/news/norways-slow-tv-fascinating-viewers-for-hours-or-days-at-a-time/

Chaiken, S. (1999). The heuristic—systematic. In S. Chaiken, & Y. Trope (Eds.), *Dual-process theories in social psychology* (pp. 73–95). New York: Guilford Press.

Conlin, L., & Tefertiller, A. C. (2016). Binge-watching is the new reading: Comparing the entertainment and transportation outcomes of reading, playing video games, and watching TV. In *annual conference of the National Communication Association*, Philadelphia, PA.

Csikszentmihalyi, M. (1991). *Flow: The psychology of optimal experience*. New York: Harper Perennial.

Custers, K., & Van den Bulck, J. (2012). Television viewing, internet use, and self-reported bedtime and rise time in adults: Implications for sleep hygiene recommendations from an exploratory cross-sectional study. *Behavioral Sleep Medicine, 10*(2), 96–105. doi: 10.1080/15402002.2011.596599

Deci, E. L., & Ryan, R. M. (2000). The "what" and "why" of goal pursuits: Human needs and the self-determination of behavior. *Psychological Inquiry, 11*(4), 227–268. doi: 10.1207/S15327965PLI1104_01

Dempsey, P. C., Howard, B. J., Lynch, B. M., Owen, N., & Dunstan, D. W. (2014). Associations of television viewing time with adults' well-being and vitality. *Preventive Medicine, 69*, 69–74. doi: 10.1016/j.ypmed.2014.09.007

Ericsson Consumer Labs (2015). TV and the media 2015: The empowered TV and media's consumers influence. Retrieved from https://www.ericsson.com/assets/local/news/2015/9/ericsson-consumerlab-tv-media-2015.pdf

Erickson, S. E., Dal Cin, S., & Byl, H. (2019). An experimental examination of binge watching and narrative engagement. *Social Sciences, 8*(1), 19–28. doi: 10.3390/socsci8010019

Ferguson, C. J., & Colwell, J. (2019). Lack of consensus among scholars on the issue of video game "addiction." *Psychology of Popular Media Culture.* doi: 10.1037/ppm0000243

Finn, S. (1992). Television "addiction?" An evaluation of four competing media-use models. *Journalism Quarterly, 69*(2), 422–435. doi: 10.1177/107769909206900216

Fitzgerald, T. (2019a, March 6). Why cord cutting doubled in 2018 and 10 million have left since 2010. *Forbes*. Retrieved from: https://www.forbes.com/sites/tonifitzgerald/2019/03/06/why-cord-cutting-doubled-in-2018-and-10-million-have-left-since-2012/#33cfc79e409f

Fitzgerald, T. (2019b, June 29). Portrait of a cord cutter: Who's doing it and why. *Forbes*. Retrieved from: https://www.forbes.com/sites/tonifitzgerald/2019/06/29/portrait-of-a-cord-cutter-whos-doing-it-and-why/#11dc6b4e163f

Granow, V. C., Reinecke, L., & Ziegele, M. (2018). Binge-watching and psychological well being: Media use between lack of control and perceived autonomy. *Communication Research Reports*, *35*(5), 392–401. Doi: 10.1080/08824096.2018.1525347

Greenberg, J. L., Lewis, S. E., & Dodd, D. K. (1999). Overlapping addictions and self-esteem among college men and women. *Addictive Behaviors*, *24*(4), 565–571. doi: 10.1016/S0306-4603(98)00080-X

Griffiths, M. D., Kuss, D. J., Lopez-Fernandez, O., & Pontes, H. M. (2017). Problematic gaming exists and is an example of disordered gaming: Commentary on: Scholars' open debate paper on the World Health Organization ICD-11 Gaming Disorder proposal (Aarseth et al.). *Journal of Behavioral Addictions*, *6*(3), 296–301. doi: 10.1556/2006.6.2017.037

Grøntved, A., & Hu, F. B. (2011). Television viewing and risk of type 2 diabetes, cardiovascular disease, and all-cause mortality: A meta-analysis. *JAMA*, *305*(23), 2448–2455. doi: 10.1001/jama.2011.812

Hamer, M., Poole, L., & Messerli-Bürgy, N. (2013). Television viewing, C-reactive protein, and depressive symptoms in older adults. *Brain, Behavior, and Immunity*, *33*, 29–32. doi: 10.1016/j.bbi.2013.05.001

Heritage, S. (2013, October). Slow TV: The Norwegian movement with universal appeal. *The Guardian*. Retrieved from: https://www.theguardian.com/tv-and-radio/tvandradioblog/2013/oct/04/slow-tv-norwegian-movement-nrk

Horeck, T., Jenner, M., & Kendall, T. (2018). On binge-watching: Nine critical propositions. *Critical Studies in Television*, *13*(4), 499–504. doi: 10.1177/1527476419848578

Horvath, C. W. (2004). Measuring television addiction. *Journal of Broadcasting & Electronic Media*, *48*(3), 378–398. doi: 10.1207/s15506878jobem4803_3

Katz, E., Haas, H., & Gurevitch, M. (1973). On the use of the mass media for important things. *American Sociological Review*, *38*, 164–181.

Karmakar, M., Kruger, J. S., Elhai, J., & Kramer, E. (2015, November). Viewing patterns and addiction to television among adults who self-identify as binge-watchers. In *2015 APHA Annual Meeting & Expo*. American Public Health Association.

Kruger, J. S., Karmakar, M., Elhai, J., & Kramer, A. (2015). Screening for sleep problems: Binge watching in the Internet Era and its relationship to sleep habits. 143rd APHA Annual Meeting and Exposition, Chicago, Illinois.

Kubey, R., & Csikszentmihalyi, M. (2002). Television addiction is no mere metaphor. *Scientific American*, *286*(2), 74–80.

Kuss, D. J., Griffiths, M. D., & Pontes, H. M. (2017). Chaos and confusion in DSM-5 diagnosis of Internet Gaming Disorder: Issues, concerns, and recommendations for clarity in the field. *Journal of Behavioral Addictions*, *6*(2), 103–109. doi: 10.1556/2006.5.2016.062

Lang, A. (2013). Discipline in crisis? The shifting paradigm of mass communication research. *Communication Theory, 23*(1), 10–24. doi: 10.1111/comt.12000

Lang, A. (2014). Dynamic human-centered communication systems theory. *The Information Society, 30*(1), 60–70. doi: 10.1080/01972243.2013.856364

Lang, A., Potter, R. F., & Bolls, P. (2009). Where psychophysiology meets the media: Taking the effects out of mass media research. In J. Bryant, & M.B. Oliver (Eds.), *Media effects: Advances in theory and research* (pp. 201–222). New York: Routledge.

LaRose, R., Lin, C. A., & Eastin, M. S. (2003). Unregulated Internet usage: Addiction, habit, or deficient self-regulation? *Media Psychology, 5*(3), 225–253. doi: 10.1207/S1532785XMEP0503_01

Lotz, A. D. (2007). *The television will be revolutionized*. New York: New York University Press.

Madhav, K. C., Sherchand, S. P., & Sherchan, S. (2017). Association between screen time and depression among US adults. *Preventive Medicine Reports, 8*, 67–71. doi: 10.1016/j.pmedr.2017.08.005

Marlatt, G. A., Baer, J. S., Kivlahan, D. R., Dimeff, L. A., Larimer, M. E., Quigley, L. A., Somers, L. A., & Williams, E. (1998). Screening and brief intervention for high-risk college student drinkers: results from a 2-year follow-up assessment. *Journal of Consulting and Clinical Psychology, 66*(4), 604–615. doi: 10.1037/0022-006X.66.4.604

Matrix, S. (2014). The Netflix effect: Teens, binge watching, and on-demand digital media trends. *Jeunesse: Young People, Texts, Cultures, 6*(1), 119–138. doi: 10.1353/jeu.2014.0002

McCormick, C. J. (2016). "Forward is the battle cry:" Binge-viewing Netflix's House of Cards. In K. McDonald, & D. Smith-Rovey's (Eds.), *The Netflix effect: Technology and entertainment in the 21st century*. New York, NY: Bloomsbury.

McIlwraith, R. D. (1998). "I'm addicted to television": The personality, imagination, and TV watching patterns of self-identified TV addicts. *Journal of Broadcasting & Electronic Media, 42*(3), 371–386. doi: 10.1080/08838159809364456

Meerloo, J. A. (1954). Television addiction and reactive apathy. *The Journal of Nervous and Mental Disease, 120*(3), 290–291.

Merikivi, J., Salovaara, A., Mäntymäki, M., & Zhang, L. (2018). On the way to understanding binge watching behavior: The over-estimated role of involvement. *Electronic Markets, 28*(1), 111–122. doi: 10.1007/s12525-017-0271-4

Merrill Jr., K., & Rubenking, B. (2019). Go long or go often: Influences on binge watching frequency and duration among college students. *Social Sciences, 8*(1), 10–22, doi: 10.3390/socsci8010010

Morgan, M., & Signorelli, N. (1990). Cultivation analysis: Conceptual issues and methodology. In *Cultivation analysis: New directions in media effects research* (pp. 8–32). Newbury Park: Sage.

Nag, C., & Pradhan, R. K. (2012). Impact of television on sleep habits. *Biological Rhythm Research, 43*(4), 423–430. doi: 10.1080/09291016.2011.599630

(No Author). Streaming: friend or foe to local markets? (2019, September 5). *Nielsen*. Retrieved from: https://www.nielsen.com/us/en/insights/article/2019/streaming-friend-or-foe-to-local-markets/

(No Author). Norway's slow TV: Fascinating viewers for hours or days at a time. (2017, May). CBS News. Retrieved from: https://www.cbsnews.com/news/norways-slow-tv-fascinating-viewers-for-hours-or-days-at-a-time/

(No Author). TV and Media: 2015. Ericsson ConsumerLab. Retrieved from: https://www.ericsson.com/assets/local/news/2015/9/ericsson-consumerlab-tv-media-2015.pdf

Oliver, M. B., & Bartsch, A. (2010). Appreciation as audience response: Exploring entertainment gratifications beyond hedonism. *Human Communication Research*, *36*(1), 53–81. doi: 10.1111/j.1468-2958.2009.01368.x

Oliver, M. B., & Raney, A. A. (2011). Entertainment as pleasurable and meaningful: Identifying hedonic and eudaimonic motivations for entertainment consumption. *Journal of Communication*, *61*(5), 984–1004. doi: 10.1111/j.1460-2466.2011.01585.x

Palmer, S. (2006). *Television disrupted: The transition from network to networked TV*. Oxford, England: Elsevier.

Panda, S., & Pandey, S. C. (2017). Binge watching and college students: Motivations and outcomes. *Young Consumers*, *18*(4), 425–438. doi: 10.1108/YC-07-2017-00707

Perez, S. (2019, January 15). Nielsen: 16M U.S. homes now get TV over-the-air, a 48% increase over past 8 years. *Techcrunch*. Retrieved from: https://techcrunch.com/2019/01/15/nielsen-16m-u-s-homes-now-get-tv-over-the-air-a-48-increase-over-past-8-years/

Perks, L. G. (2015). *Media Marathoning: Immersions in Morality*. Lanham, MD: Lexington Books.

Perks, L. G. (2018). Media marathoning through health struggles: Filling a social reservoir. *Journal of Communication Inquiry*, *43*(3), 313–332. doi: 10.1177/0196859918814826

Perse, E. M., & Rubin, R. B. (1989). Attribution in social and parasocial relationships. *Communication Research*, *16*(1), 59–77. doi: 10.1177/009365089016001003

Petty, R. E., & Cacioppo, J. T. (1986). The elaboration likelihood model of persuasion. In *Communication and persuasion* (pp. 1–24). New York: Springer.

Pittman, M., & Steiner, E. (2019). Transportation or Narrative Completion? Attentiveness during binge-watching moderates regret. *Social Sciences*, *8*(3), 99–113. doi: 10.3390/socsci8030099

Primack, B. A., Swanier, B., Georgiopoulos, A. M., Land, S. R., & Fine, M. J. (2009). Association between media use in adolescence and depression in young adulthood: a longitudinal study. *Archives of general psychiatry*, *66*(2), 181–188. doi: 10.1001/archgenpsychiatry.2008.532

Riddle, K., Peebles, A., Davis, C., Xu, F., & Schroeder, E. (2018). The addictive potential of television binge watching: Comparing intentional and unintentional binges. *Psychology of Popular Media Culture*, *7*(4), 589–604. doi: 10.1037/ppm0000167

Roettgers, J. (2019, April 22). Cord cutting will accelerate in 2019, skinny bundles poised to fail (report). *Variety*, Retrieved from: https://variety.com/2019/digital/news/2019-cord-cutting-data-1203194387/

Ryan, R. M., Rigby, C. S., & Przybylski, A. (2006). The motivational pull of video games: A self-determination theory approach. *Motivation and Emotion*, *30*(4), 344–360. doi: 10.1007/s11031-006-9051-8

Schweidel, D. A., & Moe, W. W. (2016). Binge watching and advertising. *Journal of Marketing*, *80*(5), 1–19. doi: 10.1509/jm.15.0258

Sherry, J. L. (2004). Flow and media enjoyment. *Communication Theory*, *14*(4), 328–347. doi: 10.1111/j.1468-2885.2004.tb00318.x

Shim, H., & Kim, K. J. (2018). An exploration of the motivations for binge-watching and the role of individual differences. *Computers in Human Behavior*, *82*, 94–100. doi: 10.1016/j.chb.2017.12.032

Shim, H., Lim, S., Jung, E. E., & Shin, E. (2018). I hate binge-watching but I can't help doing it: The moderating effect of immediate gratification and need for cognition on binge-watching attitude-behavior relation. *Telematics and Informatics*, *35*(7), 1971–1979. doi: 10.1016/j.tele.2018.07.001

Smith, R. (1986). Television addiction. In J. Bryant & D. Zillman (Eds.), *Perspectives on media effects* (pp. 109–128). Hillsdale, NJ: Lawrence Erlbaum.

Spangler, T. (2016, March 23). Binge nation: 70% of Americans engage in marathon TV viewing. *Variety*. Retrieved from: https://variety.com/2016/digital/news/binge-watching-us-study-deloitte-1201737245/

Spangler, Y. (2018, July 24). Cord-cutting keeps churning: U.S. pay-TV cancelers to hit 33 million in 2018 (Study). *Variety*. Retrieved from: https://variety.com/2018/digital/news/cord-cutting-2018-estimates-33-million-us-study-1202881488/

Steinberg, B. (2015, April 23). Nielsen casts doubt on "cord cutting" trend. *Variety*. Retrieved from: https://variety.com/2015/tv/news/cord-cutting-nielsen-1201478391/

Strangelove, M. (2015). *Post-TV: Piracy, cord-cutting, and the future of television*. Toronto, CA: University of Toronto Press.

Sulleyman, A. (April 19, 2017). Netflix's biggest competition is sleep, says CEO Reed Hastings. *The Independent*. Retrieved from: https://www.independent.co.uk/life-style/gadgets-and-tech/news/netflix-downloads-sleep-biggest-competition-video-streaming-ceo-reed-hastings-amazon-prime-sky-go-a7690561.html

Sung, Y. H., Kang, E. Y., & Lee, W. N. (2015, May). A bad habit for your health? An exploration of psychological factors for binge-watching behavior. In *65th Annual International Communication Association Conference*, San Juan, Puerto Rico.

Sussman, S., & Moran, M. B. (2013). Hidden addiction: Television. *Journal of Behavioral Addictions*, *2*(3), 125–132. doi: 10.1556/JBA.2.2013.008

Tamborini, R., Bowman, N. D., Eden, A., Grizzard, M., & Organ, A. (2010). Defining media enjoyment as the satisfaction of intrinsic needs. *Journal of Communication*, *60*(4), 758–777. doi: 10.1111/j.1460-2466.2010.01513.x

Tamborini, R., Grizzard, M., Bowman, N. D., Reinecke, L., Lewis, R. J., & Eden, A. (2011). Media enjoyment as need satisfaction: The contribution of hedonic and nonhedonic needs. *Journal of Communication*, *61*(6), 1025–1042. doi: 10.1111/j.1460-2466.2011.01593.x

Tavernier, R., & Willoughby, T. (2014). Sleep problems: Predictor or outcome of media use among emerging adults at university? *Journal of Sleep Research*, *23*(4), 389–396. doi: 10.1111/jsr.12132

Tefertiller, A. C., & Maxwell, L. C. (2018). Depression, emotional states, and the experience of binge-watching narrative television. *Atlantic Journal of Communication, 26*(5), 278–290. doi: 10.1080/15456870.2018.1517765

Tesser, A., Millar, K., & Wu, C. H. (1988). On the perceived functions of movies. *The Journal of Psychology, 122*(5), 441–449.

Thorp, A. A., Healy, G. N., Owen, N., Salmon, J., Ball, K., Shaw, J. E., Zimmet, P. Z., & Dunstan, D. W. (2010). Deleterious associations of sitting time and television viewing time with cardiometabolic risk biomarkers: Australian Diabetes, Obesity and Lifestyle (AusDiab) study 2004–2005. *Diabetes Care, 33*(2), 327–334. doi: 10.2337/dc09-0493

Trost, S. G., Blair, S. N., & Khan, K. M. (2014). Physical inactivity remains the greatest public health problem of the 21st century: Evidence, improved methods and solutions using the "7 investments that work" as a framework. *British Journal of Sports Medicine, 48,* doi: 10.1136/bjsports-2013-093372

Tukachinsky, R., & Eyal, K. (2018). The psychology of marathon television viewing: Antecedents and viewer involvement. *Mass Communication and Society, 21*(3), 275–295. doi: 10.1080/15205436.2017.1422765

Veerman, J. L., Healy, G. N., Cobiac, L. J., Vos, T., Winkler, E. A., Owen, N., & Dunstan, D. W. (2012). Television viewing time and reduced life expectancy: a life table analysis. *British Journal of Sports Medicine, 46*(13), 927–930. doi: 10.1136/bjsports-2011-085662

Wheeler, K. S. (2015). The relationships between television viewing behaviors, attachment, loneliness, depression, and psychological well-being. An Honors Thesis from Georgia Southern University.

Wijndaele, K., Healy, G. N., Dunstan, D. W., Barnett, A. G., Salmon, J., Shaw, J. E., Zimmet, P. Z., & Owen, N. (2010). Increased cardio-metabolic risk is associated with increased TV viewing time. *Medicine & Science in Sports & Exercise, 42*(8), 1511–1518. doi: 10.1249/MSSt5r5t.0b013e3181d322ac

Wu, X., Tao, S., Zhang, Y., Zhang, S., & Tao, F. (2015). Low physical activity and high screen time can increase the risks of mental health problems and poor sleep quality among Chinese college students. *PloS One, 10*(3), 1–10. doi: 10.1371/journal.pone.0119607

CHAPTER SEVEN

Conclusion: Where Do We Go From Here?

This text has attempted to situate binge watching in the larger context of today's media landscape. It began with an introduction to the concept, including defining the often-debated term as long periods of focused, deliberate viewing of sequential television content that is generally narrative, suspenseful, and dramatic in nature. We introduced three central arguments we hoped the following chapters would illustrate as accurate (or, at least reasonable). The second chapter starts at the early television days in the United States and reviews how television fundamentally shifted individuals' leisure time and time spent with family. It explored early audience research, and the introduction of the VCR, which afforded timeshifting, a crucial first step moving toward increased viewer choice and agency. Next, Chapter 3 reviewed the industry competitors related to television viewing and binge watching today, the content we are binge watching, and how those industry players are replacing traditional television programming strategies with data-driven algorithms and using technology to their advantage in managing audience flow. Chapter 4 explored situational determinants of television viewing, media multitasking and second screening, and the many iterations of social television viewing. It revealed how the technologies used, the physical locations where we watch, and with whom we view has evolved, but the social nature of television viewing is a long-standing practice. Chapters 5 and 6 tackle the recent academic investigations of binge watching and the theoretical approaches which guided them. Discussions of audience activity, habituation, and uses and gratifications in Chapter 5 reveals mixed findings on motives, although entertainment, enjoyment, and habit are consistently found to motivate binge watching. Discussions of entertainment, need satisfaction, addiction typologies and approaches, and cord-cutting are discussed in Chapter 6. We weigh in on the entertainment vs. addiction debate in this chapter.

This final chapter is divided into three sections. The first section returns to the central arguments of the text introduced in Chapter 1. We work to elaborate on these ideas and synthesize the literature which supports them. The following section details key findings from this book: What knowledge can this text offer? The final section looks forward, knowing what we now know, what are the critical issues to address moving forward when researching binge watching, and other new ways of viewing television?

Central Arguments: A Recap

Argument 1: Binge watching, a new norm in television viewing, presents a critical and consequential difference in viewing from the currently accepted assumptions under the existing methodological and theoretical framework employed in the academic study of media effects.

The epistemological, theoretical, and methodological problems in "media effects" research has been eloquently articulated elsewhere (Lang, 2013; Lang & Ewoldsen, 2010; Livingstone, 1996; Weber, 2015). We concur with the major points made by the above-cited authors, even up to the point that the notion of effects is a bit "ridiculous" (Lang, 2013, p. 19), if an effect is assumed to have a stable starting point and end point, or the change we expect to see. As we've discussed in Chapter 6, the motives and outcomes of binge watching are often one and the same: The drawing of a line between motive and outcome is arbitrary because individuals interact with media – and binge watch – over time. This should not be understated.

We do, however, maintain that binge watching is a qualitatively distinct form of consuming television narratives, and how that has come to be, and what that changes for individuals, content providers, and content itself is interesting and worthy of study for academics and industry alike. At a macro, systems level and a micro, individual level, binge watching can influence downstream variables.

At the individual media effects level, media effects research continues to mostly use surveys and experimental designs to look for relationships between variables of interest and exposure to media, often television messages. The research field abounds in "effects" experiments, wherein a pre-test measure is given to participants in a within-subjects design, or participants are randomly assigned to two or more treatment or control groups, prior to watching the media message(s) of interest. Afterwards, a post-test measure is given to gauge the "effects" of interest. These one-shot studies have been (rightfully) criticized by others. However, longitudinal surveys are also employed by media researchers, and while they offer only correlational evidence, they can more easily follow up with participants over time (Livingstone, 1996). The artificiality and the lack of external validity or ability to generalize results to a larger population are the drawbacks of experimental designs, while the ability to establish "causal" relationships is generally seen as an advantage. However, a classic meta-analysis of television effects studies found an inverse relationship between ecological validity and effect size, such that the more ecologically valid a study was deemed, the smaller effect size it reported (Hearold, 1986). This is still troublesome.

The argument made here is that television "effects" studies have never been *less* ecologically valid than they are today. We *fundamentally watch television differently* than the ways in which "television viewing" or media exposure are manipulated in experimental designs. Further, the same differences are also ignored in survey designs, where there is typically no measurement of how viewing occurred which would allow for controlling for them in data analysis as confounding variables. Just a few of those fundamental differences and their demonstrated empirical "effects" are:

- We watch television with others (either physically co-located, or via communication technology). This has long been ignored. But we know that watching with others increases a feel of belonging and connectedness to a group (Cohen & Lancaster 2014; Han & Lee, 2014; Kramer et al. 2015; Chen, Gao, & Rau 2017) and heightens emotional experiences (Cohen & Lancaster 2014; Wenner & Gantz, 1998).
- We watch television and media multitask. Research rather unequivocally demonstrates that multitasking hinders cognitive outcomes such as attention, memory, and learning related to the primary task (i.e., television viewing; Jeong & Hwang, 2012; Ophir, Nass, & Wagner, 2009; Wang & Tchernev, 2012). It further has differential effects on entertainment and emotional outcomes, based on cognitive load and enjoyment of the primary task (Oviedo, Tornquist, Cameron, & Chaippe, 2015; Wang & Tchernev, 2012). Recent research suggests the assumption of television viewing as the primary task and computer or mobile device as a secondary task is likely outdated, especially when studying younger individuals (Wiradhany & Baumgartner, 2019).

- We binge watch. And that increases enjoyment, engagement, and immersion (Flayelle, Maurage, & Billieux, 2017; Shim & Kim, 2018) and parasocial relationships with characters (Erickson, Dal Cin, & Byl, 2019; Tukachinsky & Eyal, 2018).

Together these behaviors present major hurdles for those who are interested in studying how exposure to a specific message affects other variables that could be even marginally influenced by: feeling connected to others, emotion, attention, memory, learning, entertainment, immersion, engagement and/ or parasocial relationships. That is quite a list. While our focus in this text has been on exploring binge watching as an intriguing and relevant new viewing behavior, we do not maintain it as the only one which contributes to a changed media landscape, where past assumptions about viewing can simply no longer remain the same.

We certainly do not have all the solutions to the methodological murkiness that is studying humans and media. However, we would argue further research articulating how the television viewing experience – and all that it entails – is a step in the right direction toward a better understanding of how individuals process and may later be influenced by television messages. We also believe that more indirect measures of variables are advantageous as research moves beyond descriptive. An example from the media multitasking literature of indirect measures and a shift in results is found in Yeykelis, Cummings, and Reeves (2014). Screen capture software revealed the frequency with which individuals were switching tabs on their computers. Their results showed that users were switching between tabs, on average, every 19 seconds, whereas previous data had found switching between content on the same device to occur every 1–2 minutes. It is clearly unlikely that individuals are capable of reporting this behavior with such reliable, fine-grained accuracy. This is just one way in which a new reality of television viewing (and media use in general) can benefit from studies that go beyond asking people why they behave in the ways that they do. Indirect measures of binge watching would need to include more data points than screen capture alone, but combinations of indirect data points may be one avenue of research down the line. Eye tracking hardware together with screen capture could provide a clearer picture of viewers behaviors. Developing new ways to measure, and perhaps experimentally manipulate, binge watching should be of primary importance moving forward.

Argument 2: Binge watching is a human-centered phenomenon.

The second premise introduced in this text is that binge watching is a human-centered phenomenon. Binge watching is not merely more television viewing, or a direct effect of Netflix and new distribution strategies. A number of industry changes have, together, allowed for binge watching with greater ease than in the past. Indeed, the new viewing suggestion algorithms, personalized content, auto play features, and increased flexibility in what you view, when, and where squarely place control of the television viewing experience with the viewer. It is critical to understand these movements in industry and technology as *responding to audience demand*.

We like stories. Humans have long turned to "marathoning" narrative entertainment content. Every person who has stayed up later than intended reading a novel or a comic book knows this to be true. We maintain that these changes toward giving the viewer more control and agency began with the introduction of the VCR, which users soon started using to timeshift. In the 1980s, the explosion of cable options that became available also took advantage of viewers' desire to watch serialized content in one sitting and began scheduling marathons of comedies and dramas. Cable and broadcast networks alike often schedule off-network syndicated shows back-to-back. Humans like stories – and if they're good stories, we like to keep reading/ listening to/ watching them. Sometimes, we do this long enough to qualify as a "binge." OTT providers have just been better positioned to capitalize on this than traditional television networks have been.

We are social beings. The social nature of television viewing – which has changed in interesting ways over time – can also be considered as evidence of binge watching enabling one of the most basic, inherently human needs: To connect with others. Throughout this text, we see evidence of the social nature of television viewing. One study of early television users revealed that "entertainment" was a second reason why they most liked having television. The top reason – which 50% of households reported – was that they liked having a television the most because it kept their family at home. Chapter 4 chronicles the changes in watching television together: from in the living room as a traditional nuclear family, to connecting with known and unknown others via messaging apps and social media while one views alone. In studies across social viewing, the most common "effect" of social viewing is a feeling of connectedness or belonging.

Most binge watching is *not* done with an entire family gathered in the living room. However, when we watch content that better lends itself to paying careful attention and following a story, we fulfill these social needs in other ways. One of the most consistent findings in the motives and "effects" research literatures on binge watching (beyond entertainment/ engagement) is that – as contrasted with appointment viewing – (Erickson, Dal Cin, & Byl, 2019) it accelerates our parasocial relationships/ interactions with characters. This indicates that social connection is critical across multiple ways of viewing content, and multiple types of content. In certain viewing modes, connecting with other *characters*, rather than other *audience members* satisfies a seemingly ever-present social need. As discussed in Chapter 6, differences were found in the time it takes to develop strong parasocial relationships with liked characters when people binge watch as compared to watching the same program in appointment viewing style (one episode per week). Additionally, Perks (2019) reported that when people are incapacitated, they tend to engage in "parasocial encouragement" where the viewer is inspired by a character's positive attitude or perseverance.

Binge watching to discuss content with others – either in real-time, online, face-to-face, or at work the next day, or watching for social gratifications, also comes up frequently in the literature. Individuals may watch alone, and then connect with others and form or maintain bonds over shared viewing experiences.

Social media and other social viewing opportunities did not create a social species. Humans are social beings, and binge watching and a number of other features of television viewing today allow and encourage fulfillment of social needs. These social needs may be met via a number of avenues, including identifying with characters, as well as interacting with others who view the content who are co-located or geographically distant, in real-time, or after viewing.

Engaging with stories and fulfilling social needs are inherently human. In the incredibly short period of human history that television has existed, it should be no wonder that those creating and distributing content are improving the viewing experience by appealing to basic human drives. Television has been in the majority of U.S. homes since the 1950s/1960s: It only follows that some general user improvements which better enable viewer choice and flexibility have been rolled out slowly over time.

Argument 3: Binge watching can and should move beyond exploratory, descriptive studies and into more theoretically and operationally rigorous areas.

As Dobrow's (1990) generations of research characterizations demonstrate, typical research on new communication/ media technologies follows a predictable order. A first generation of research characterizes uses and users, a second generation explores patterns of use and gratifications observed, and a third generation takes a step back and is able to situate the new technology in the larger social and cultural context. We have documented that early television (and television technology) research followed this pattern. While broad characterizations, these patterns of research were observed *prior* to *exactly* this happening with every Internet and social media related technology, app, and behavior. Binge watching has been no exception to this pattern of research. We are safely in the second-generation research phase, though some research is beginning to resemble third-generation research. The current research, of which we have only contributed a small part to, contains any number of well-designed and measured studies which employ a range of relevant theoretical approaches. The current state of first and second generations of research on binge watching have yielded generalizable descriptive results.

We, as a field, can stop doing exploratory research, with no a priori hypotheses on what motivates individuals to binge watch, and what gratifications it helps them obtain.

Those in industry will continue to benefit from up-to-date descriptive data on who is binge watching, on what platforms, etc. Just as overall television viewing per day has passed its peak (Madrigal, 2018), and Peak TV has passed its peak (Garber, Sims, Cruz, & Gilbert, 2015), binge watching may also peak and then diminish over time. However, the larger part of viewer-centered changes in viewing – Timeshifting, on-demand, personalized viewing interfaces, and curated viewing sessions, and all of this available across multiple devices with a click of a button – guarantees that television viewing is not headed backward, toward a rigid schedule of appointment viewing. Similarly, and with few exceptions, gone are the days where the majority of the population is watching the same episode of the same show at the same time based on the available viewing options. Indeed, the increased personalization that today's television viewing and binge-watching norms encourage is unprecedented.

The social scientific literature on enjoyment has identified two media-based prerequisites for enjoyment. The first prerequisite is adequate technology and aesthetics (e.g., media content and form) and the second is personal relevance or meaning for users (Vorderer, Klimmt, & Ritterfeld, 2004). The current state of media technology is providing programming choices for viewers at a highly individualized level. This level of personalized program selection allows viewers to select programming that has personal relevance for them.

But if part of being human is participating in shared meaning-making, where is the threshold when we no longer have the same stories? We already see the polarizing effect of selective attention of political communication. But what if entertainment technology allows audiences to customize not only which content to view, but also to customize the story content? Might we find ourselves not watching a TV series with the ending being selected for us individually by a media content algorithm based on what we would most enjoy? Billard (2019) argues that

> Binge-watching provides new opportunities for self-determined forms of entertainment consumption and can positively influence media enjoyment and well-being through perceived autonomy. At the same time, the new freedom granted by video-on-demand services is a double-edged sword, as the new possibilities of continuous watching increase the risks of goal conflicts between entertainment consumption and other goals and obligations, resulting in feelings of guilt and diminishing the potential positive effects of entertaining media use on well-being. (p. 397–398)

This potential goal conflict and fragmentation of shared meaning is but one of several areas we offer as fruitful concepts to research in the future. A more thorough discussion of potential research topics is presented at the end of this chapter.

What We Learned (and We Hope You Did Too).

Binge Watching Is Entertaining and Enjoyable.

As mentioned several places in this text, people watch television and engage in binge watching because they find it both entertaining and enjoyable. Researchers have consistently reported entertainment/enjoyment as a primary motivation for television viewing (Bartsch, 2012; Schramm, Lyle, & Parker, 1961; Zillman & Bryant, 1994). The reasons television viewing is identified as enjoyable are numerous. One reason is that we use binge watching to spend time with characters who we feel connected to or have a parasocial relationship with (Erickson et al., 2019; Tukachinsky & Eyal, 2018).

We know that binge watching can be entertaining, enjoyable, and elicit greater feelings of identification or parasocial interaction. We also know that binge watching can be habit-based, and binge watchers can feel that they're sucked into watching content much later into the night or longer than they intended. But binge watching can also be planned in advance, have no relation to self-control, and be done with others or by oneself (but more often by oneself). While some studies have found mixed results on specific other gratifications, and some studies have not compared these gratifications with any type of control condition or contrasting mode of viewing, we have basic knowledge about the entertaining nature of binge watching. Several studies have failed to find differences in motives and goals between binge watching and variations of more traditional, appointment-style viewing. However, we are wholly unaware of any research that has found appointment viewing to be *more* entertaining, immersing, engaging, or to encourage greater identification with characters and parasocial interaction, as compared to binge watching.

While media enjoyment is typically investigated as solely an emotional response (Bartsch & Oliver, 2011), some scholars have suggested that media has the potential to serve as "intellectual entertainment," allowing media users to fulfill their intrinsic needs of autonomy, competence, and relatedness while also enhancing their relationships with others while providing challenges (Latorre & Soto-Sanfiel, 2014). However, it appears that the most complex narratives drive our desire to binge watch. People report enjoying binge watching or watching TV programming in a sequential fashion (Rubenking et al., 2018). In Chapter 3, we discussed how narrative structures and story arcs might be highly involving and draw viewers into the story, encouraging them to view subsequent episodes back-to-back. There is strong evidence that numerous shows have been able to capitalize on this format – though not all (i.e., Netflix's *Love*, which has been criticized for its sloppy editing, perhaps based on assumptions that viewers would give the show several episodes to get somewhere good). We may also enjoy this newer viewing style because it helps us follow complex narratives and keeps storylines together.

Binge Watching Should Not Be Characterized as an "Addiction"

We maintain that although the term "binge watching" certainly suggests a negative connotation, like nearly all media habits and behaviors, binge watching may function as either efficient and helpful, or deficient and unhelpful. Currently high-quality programming (and good marketing) has been successful at creating a social norm of binge watching TV programs. Highly personalized, curated content provides viewers with the ability to meet our needs and wants (Green & Jenkings, 2014). The sum of the uses and gratifications research – although not uniform in identifying the consistent gratifications of binge watching which make it distinct from other experiences of viewing – does suggest one general theme. *Users are binge watching because it is enjoyable and entertaining, not because they are dependent upon this activity.* If users are reporting general satisfaction with binge watching, as large-scale surveys reveal (Ericsson Consumer Lab, 2015), it cannot simply be a media habit gone bad for all viewers. Indeed, a review of the gratifications typical of TV watching and binge watching in Chapter 5 doesn't include motives that suggest harmful or dangerous undertones. It is our position that even if well-done research studies exploring binge watching through an addiction lens finds some support, that finding is more indicative of some potential drawbacks of the behavior, but not of actual widespread addiction to binge watching in light of the dozens of other well-done research publications which find it to be an enjoyable, entertaining experience. We concur with others that there is no need to over-pathologize this typical media entertainment behavior.

At best, applying the theoretical frameworks rooted in the addiction literature is helpful in establishing qualities of content or individuals that may contribute to overdoing it. There can be too much of a good thing, and Netflix has outright said that their main competitor is sleep. It is helpful, as others have done (Riddle, Peebles, Davis, Xu, & Schroeder, 2018; Tukachinsky & Eyal, 2018), to compare diverging theoretical models to the same media behavior to isolate patterns and strengths of relationships between variables. At worst, applying addiction frameworks to binge watching is fear-mongering. The adjacent field of game studies is at odds with one another on whether gaming addiction is a legitimate concern. Gaming has many features which could make it more "addicting" than television viewing. And yet, researchers are mostly in agreement that if it is a concern, that Internet gaming addiction affects less than one percent of the game playing population. Before binge watching was a widespread viewing norm, those studying television addiction estimated that 10% of audiences were "addicted" (Sussman & Morgan, 2013). We clearly have a discrepancy in what constitutes an addiction. As others have pointed out, where are all the television addicts? This is an addiction that yields no addicts seeking recovery.

This approach is rooted in a long-standing wariness of technology and concern over younger audiences' perceived susceptibility to influence. There is certainly a subset of those who are vocal critics of the "kids always on their phones these days," and this can be seen as an extension of that. While "addiction" to viewing is explored in Chapter 6, the data summarized are not describing the negative consequences that would encompass an actual "binging" disorder, nor even mostly negative affect toward binge watching. Researchers are beginning to investigate the nuances of binge watching and have argued (like us) for further investigation (Flayelle, Maurage, Karila, Vögele, & Billieux, 2019). Self-diagnosed binge-watching "addicts," as some studies report, is a play on the colloquial use of the term. To the best of our knowledge, no one has studied heavy consumers of news content, or "news junkies" as addicts. This demonstrates the bias toward entertainment technologies and content. We do not believe that the empirical data on binge watching indicates a valid health concern at this time.

Netflix Has Been Great for Binge Watching. But It Isn't Synonymous with It.

According to our definition of binge watching, viewers must be attending to the content over an extended period of time and not just have it on in the background. This is important as 5% of viewing time on Netflix is comprised of watching *Friends* and *The Office* reruns (Flint & Sharma, 2019). We have also discussed how high-quality narrative dramas are attracting viewers to OTT services. Disney+ is counting on well-known titles to draw viewers to their service. But it is not a guarantee. Silvia (2006) states "familiar things tend to be enjoyable, whereas new things tend to be interesting" (Silvia, 2006, p. 25). Other researchers have linked the emotion of interest or curiosity as a viewing motive for entertainment media (Silvia, 2006; Vorderer & Hartman, 2009). However, our motivation to re-watch programs may be because humans are always balancing sensory stimulation with exhausted physiological resources (Vorderer & Hartman, 2009). Re-watching content appears "to foster pleasure that adds to the overall feeling of being entertained" (Vorderer & Hartman, 2009, p. 539). Re-watching programs such as *Friends* allows us to feel less alone and renew our parasocial relationships when our physiological resources are fatigued. If this is as pervasive at it seems, this type of content should be studied alongside highly complex, visually compelling content. This does not mean we think people will stop binge watching, but we may feel less compelled to view newer content as the quality of new programs decreases. Additionally, companionship viewing may continue to dominate our viewing habits.

Avenues for Future Research

This concluding section offers some broad thoughts on avenues of research, related to binge watching, that may be fruitful looking ahead. Throughout the text, we have attempted to highlight gaps in the current state of research. As Raney and Oliver (2014) suggest, media scholars should strive in their research "to keep pace with our ability to customize characters, narratives, interfaces, and media – reception environments" (p. 567). The emergence of the COVID-19 pandemic, and ensuing stay-at-home orders much of the world faced in 2020, is a large-scale example of a radically different "reception environment." The implications of the pandemic could have quite an interesting impact on binge watching, and we are excited to see what empirical research about it reveals. Here, we elaborate on some of the concepts which we believe could spur numerous areas of inquiry.

Binge Watching's Relationship to Content and Industry Players

Thus far, the empirical research on binge watching has excelled in establishing why viewers binge watch, and what possible effects it could exert on them. If one wanted to take a systems-level approach, while being cognizant of the overtime dynamics, there are many more players in this phenomenon with varying directions of influence. Content is an appealing place to start. Content creators, and those responsible for acquiring content for various platforms, are responding to changes in distribution. As discussed in Chapter 3, content producers are changing their content to fit distribution patterns that make all episodes of a season available at once (Lynch, 2015). Changes in the popularity of content when new distribution opportunities become available is not a new phenomenon in the film industry. As global audience size for American films has increased in recent decades, film content that emphasizes visceral responses (e.g., action films) have become more popular and financially successful overseas as nuanced language subtleties present less of an issue to non-English speaking audiences in these types of films. Similarly, casting of actors also changes when an international market is kept in mind by producers: We've started to see more Chinese, Korean, and Australian actors as these markets are financially desirable (Brook, 2014). It would be naive to think that content creators and producers were *not* attempting to leverage the advantages that OTT service dissemination could offer certain types of content and storytelling.

At a more macro-level than individual-level effects, there are many relevant industry players as binge watching has emerged as a new norm in television viewing. There are, of course, audience members, and the traditional broadcast and cable networks, for whom much "binge-worthy" content was originally produced. There are MSOs, who could stand to benefit from *either* cable subscriptions or broadband Internet subscriptions. Content creators are an essential piece of the puzzle as well, as they now have more options for distribution than previously. And lastly, there are traditional advertisers, who have seen television ratings decrease over time as more households cut (or shave) the cord (Fitzgerald, 2019). All of these players: content, audiences, OTT services, cable and broadcast networks, MSOs, content creators, and advertisers are part of multiple flows of influence between them. We've just discussed how content and content creators are responding to influences in distribution strategies employed by OTT services. Content can certainly influence the success of OTT services, networks, and advertisers. Binge watching has relationships with each of these major players and competitors.

There are many directions of influence to study here. While binge-watching research has focused on the influence of binge watching on audiences, the prevalence of audiences that are binge watching also influences other industry players. How have networks adapted programming strategies to counter losing audiences to OTT – are they trying to attract binge watchers or those who are not interested in binge watching? Are MSOs changing bundles to encourage cable subscriptions? Most of these relationships remain unstudied, as critical as they are.

Binge Watching and Downstream Outcomes

While we have argued here that the time has come to move beyond the descriptive data studies about *why* people binge watch, at the individual level, there is still a remarkably small body of research about *how binge watching influences later behaviors of binge watchers*. In Chapter 6, we discuss the potential impact of enjoying this new mode of viewing so much, that it, along with the other perceived advantages of OTT services, motivates individuals to switch from cable television to several OTT providers for their entertainment television content. We could not find one academic study linking binge watching – or timeshifting, or other ways of viewing now enabled by OTT providers to cord-cutting or any other decision-making surrounding paying for television content. While Nielsen and others have examined the role of cost and value in cord-cutting decisions, the advantages of one type of service should also be considered. It may not be that individuals are unsatisfied with cable television – it may just be that they can get what they want from OTT providers instead, at a lower cost. This should certainly be explored.

There is also sparse research literature on binge watching and advertising effectiveness, or any persuasion-based outcomes for that matter. The one study completed with access to Hulu viewing records did not paint a great picture of binge watching for advertising. The longer viewers watched, the less likely they were to click through on an ad, and binge watchers, in addition to consuming 50% of all content despite constituting only one-fifth of all viewers, were less likely than others to click on advertisements to begin with (Schweidel & Moe, 2016). Hulu is a rarity in comparison to other OTT providers in their hybrid subscription and advertisement based model. Hulu's content catalog has marked differences from Netflix, for example. Hulu has a wider variety of current television shows, including sitcoms and dramas. Netflix, as we've documented elsewhere in this text, has a fast-growing, huge catalog of originals and many more film and documentary offerings as compared to Hulu. Does a content catalog contribute to success or failure of Hulu's unique monetization model? Is there something different about Hulu binge watchers as compared to Netflix binge watchers? Does the content being viewed, or binged, influence click-through rates, looking up at a brand advertised at the time, or later in time? Are ads effective in more downstream outcomes, such as attitude change or strengthening, or purchase decisions and actual purchase behaviors?

Likewise, if we believe binge watching may influence advertising effectiveness in different ways than watching television in other ways, are other attitude change–based outcomes also variable? Are pro-social, education-entertainment storylines, for example, more readily adopted by viewers who are binge watching as compared to appointment viewing? Are product integration strategies more effective, or becoming more common because advertisers are losing opportunities for their messages to be seen on television platforms which contain traditional advertising messages?

Is Binge Watching Good for Business in the Long Run?

As examined in Chapter 2, much of the early research on television viewing was concerned with what leisure time activities television viewing was displacing. As we've discussed elsewhere, average television viewing per day has peaked, yet remains as high as it does due to the prevalence of media multitasking while viewing television. Is binge watching keeping television a stable entertainment option? If overall television viewing is slowly dropping, but the length of time spent and the frequency of binge watching has only been increasing since the term was popularized in 2013, then binge watching seems like a promising mode of viewing if one is professionally invested in time spent with television content. There are many arguments on whether new media complement older media, or displace older media (Dimmick & Rothenbuhler, 1984; Lin, Zhang, Jung, & Kim, 2013).

A question posed by other entertainment researchers is, why? Why are people willing to spend so much of their time binge watching? There is also the question of how binge watching shapes future viewing choices related to content. At an individual level, is binge watching attractive enough to viewers to lure them away from time that would otherwise be spent with non-narrative television content, or other mediated entertainment?

Schweidel and Moe (2016) questioned the economic feasibility of offering more and more content – which obviously has higher costs associated with it – to satisfy viewers. In a subscription-based service model, those who watch one hour of content per week pay as much as someone who watches 70 hours per week (which actually averages out to less total time than an average American watches television per day, Madrigal, 2018). Meanwhile Merikivi et al. (2017) likened the relationship between subscribers, OTT providers, and content to an "all you can eat buffet." The model stays profitable for the restaurant (and the OTT provider) because very few customers *actually* consume enough food (content) to hurt the bottom line of the restaurant (OTT provider). Customers think they're getting a great value, and sometimes the mere option of eating (viewing) more is worth paying for, even if you're always full after two plates (episodes). Will this model continue to be true as cable subscriptions continue to drop, and the number of OTT services one can access continues to increase? There are many empirical unknowns in this area.

Content Selection

How do viewers make real-time viewing choices amid an increasing quantity of titles that range in quality and that are presented in an optimal, personalized fashion? How do these viewing choices relate to binge watching vs. other modes of viewing? With highly personalized interfaces of options available to us (see Chapter 3 for a review on Netflix's pioneering data analysis and implementation), are they offering the greatest breadth of content that may be of interest to any one individual? In a previous television viewing era, researchers discussed limited channel repertoires and the "paradox of choice," which suggests that most viewers enjoy a limited amount of options when selecting content. This assumes we watch a very narrow set of programming genres. However, as the data algorithms get only more precise, and the growing number of niche content offerings increase, it is possible that viewers could miss out on content deemed not especially of interest to them. Viewer content choices, when the choices are seemingly limitless yet incredibly targeted based on previous viewing selections, are interesting areas of research to pursue.

Binge Watching and the Family

What role does binge watching play in family dynamics? The history of television research reviewed in Chapter 2 and the coviewing, social viewing, and second screening literature reviewed in Chapter 4 emphasize that we have always underestimated the impact of viewing with others who are physically or virtually present (or to talk about it with others later). As the lines between "mass communication" and "human" or "interpersonal" communication continue to blur (Lang, 2013), employing theoretical approaches from the scholarship in computer-mediated communication and human communication may be helpful here.

Intercultural Differences

Binge watching is an international phenomenon with audiences worldwide engaging in this new viewing behavior (Ahmed, 2017; Mikos, 2016) with content from their own and other countries. Are their cultural differences in the duration and types of programming audiences are binge watching? To what extent are international audiences engaged in social viewing? The presence of international streaming service options, such as Netflix and Amazon Prime, as well as country-specific OTT providers, may provide interesting comparisons.

Viewing Location and Devices

The choice of media devices has exploded over the past decade. Large screen TVs continue to get larger and mobile devices make accessing OTT services possible in places not imaginable even in the 1990s. Large screen televisions as well as mobile communication devices are being used to binge watch. Does the location and/or the device we are using impact our content selections? Or even the level of enjoyment we experience? We are binge watching in various locations not only within our homes (e.g., or living room, bedroom, or dorm room) but also outside of our personal spaces (e.g., while traveling, between classes). The situational determinants of binge watching may also be evolving over time – a consideration of viewing settings and technological features of devices should not go unstudied.

Closing Thoughts

Critical scholars have suggested that media choice has contributed to further cultural divergences in the United States. In particular, Gans (1979) suggested that the introduction of the VCR led to a diversification of tastes and that newer media technologies have led to additional cultural niches. Currently, the high-quality programming provided by OTT services appeals to paying viewers who are primarily attracted to how the experience is "not TV" (Feuer, 2007). "It boasts of not being TV, thus creating a new segment of viewers who treat the traditional TV with contempt or as a form of guilty pleasure" (Filiciak, 2018, p. 8). However, while some predict that OTT will eventually dissolve into offering lower quality, mediocre programming that, according to our research, leads to lower levels of binge watching, TV will not be easy to kill off. Salmon (2018) describes TV as a "lean-back, experiential medium where people like to waste time. It's not an information-delivery mechanism; it's an entertainment format that has been perfected and optimized over many decades." So, while our viewing habits and content preferences evolve, audiences will continue to consume professionally produced, narrative, audio-visual content.

In conclusion, we started this project with three assumptions that we were able to support with empirical evidence. We have traced the history of related viewing behaviors, technological changes, and industry competitors and their content strategies. We have highlighted the social aspects of television viewing both in physical groups and via new communication technologies to engage in social viewing. We have documented that timeshifting and entertainment/enjoyment are primarily reasons for engaging in binge watching.

Additionally, we have suggested future avenues of research that extend our knowledge of binge-watching behaviors beyond first- and second-generation research questions. We have also addressed how binge watching has interrupted the traditional broadcast model. But most of all, we have demonstrated that binge watching is new viewing behavior that viewers across the world are engaging in to meet a number of entertainment and social goals.

References

Ahmed, A. (2017). New era of TV-watching behavior: Binge-watching and its psychological effects. *Media Watch, 8*, 192–207. doi:10.15655/mw/2017/v8i2/49006

Bartsch, A. (2012). Emotional gratification in entertainment experience: Why viewers of movies and television series find it rewarding to experience emotions. *Media Psychology, 15*(3), 267–302. doi: 10.1080/15213269.2012.693811

Billard, T. J. (2019). Experimental evidence for differences in the prosocial effects of binge-watched versus appointment-viewed television programs. *Journalism & Mass Communication Quarterly, 96*(4), 1025–1051. doi:10.1177/1077699019843856

Brook, T. (2014, October). How the global box office is changing Hollywood. *BBC.* Retrieved from: http://www.bbc.com/culture/story/20130620-is-china-hollywoods-future

Chen, Y., Gao, Q., & Rau, P.-L. P. (2017). Watching a movie alone yet together: Understanding reasons for watching Danmaku videos. *International Journal of Human–Computer Interaction, 33*(9), 731–743. doi: 10.1080/10447318.2017.1282187

Cohen, E. L., & Lancaster, A. L. (2014). Individual differences in in-person and social media television coviewing: the role of emotional contagion, need to belong, and coviewing orientation. *Cyberpsychology, Behavior, and Social Networking, 17*(8), 512–518. doi: 10.1089/cyber.2013.0484

Dimmick, J., & Rothenbuhler, E. (1984). The theory of the niche: Quantifying Competition among media industries. *Journal of Communication, 34*(1), 103–119. doi: 10.1111/j.1460-2466.1984.tb02988.x

Dobrow, J. R. (1990). *Social and cultural aspects of VCR use.* Hillsdale, NJ: Lawrence Erlbaum.

Erickson, S. E., Dal Cin, S., & Byl, H. (2019). An experimental examination of binge watching and narrative engagement. *Social Sciences, 8*(1), 19–28. doi: 10.3390/socsci8010019

Ericsson ConsumerLab (2015). TV and Media: 2015. Retrieved from: https://www.ericsson.com/assets/local/news/2015/9/ericsson-consumerlab-tv-media-2015.pdf

Feuer, J. (2007). HBO and the concept of quality TV. In J. McCabe, & K. Akass (Eds.), *Quality TV: Contemporary American television and beyond* (pp. 145–158). London: IB Tauris.

Flayelle, M., Maurage, P., & Billieux, J. (2017). Toward a qualitative understanding of binge-watching behaviors: A focus group approach. *Journal of Behavioral Addictions, 6*(4), 457–471. doi: 10.1556/2006.6.2017.060

Flint, J., & Sharma, A. (2019, April 24). Netflix Fights to Keep Its Most Watched Shows: 'Friends' and 'The Office.' *The Wall Street Journal.* Retrieved from https://www.wsj.com/articles/netflix-battles-rivals-for-its-most-watched-shows-friends-and-the-office-11556120136

Filiciak, M. (2018). Will you awaken when your *Netflix* no longer works? American films, television productions and social transformations in Poland. *European Journal of American Studies, 13*(3). doi : 10.4000/ejas.13568

Fitzgerald, T. (2019, June 29). Portrait of a cord cutter: Who's doing it and why. *Forbes.* Retrieved from: https://www.forbes.com/sites/tonifitzgerald/2019/06/29/portrait-of-a-cord-cutter-whos-doing-it-and-why/#11dc6b4e163f

Flayelle, M., Maurage, P., & Billieux, J. (2017). Toward a qualitative understanding of binge-watching behaviors: A focus group approach. *Journal of Behavioral Addictions, 6*(4), 457–471. doi: 10.1556/2006.6.2017.060

Flayelle, M., Maurage, P. Karila, L., Vögele, C., & Billieux, J. (2019). Overcoming the unitary exploration of binge-watching: A cluster analytical approach. *Journal of Behavioral Addictions, 8*(3), 586–602. doi: 10.1556/2006.8.2019.53

Ganz, H. (1979). *Popular culture and high culture: An analysis and evaluation of taste.* New York: Basic Books.

Garber, M., Sims, D., Cruz, L., & Gilbert, S. (2015, August 12). Have We Reached 'Peak TV'? *The Atlantic*. Retrieved from: https://www.theatlantic.com/entertainment/archive/2015/08/have-we-reached-peak-tv/401009/

Green, M. C., & Jenkins, K. M. (2014). Interactive narratives: Processes and outcomes in user-directed stories. *Journal of Communication, 64*, 479–500. doi:10.1111/jcom.12093

Han, E., & Lee, S-W. (2014). Motivations for the complementary use of text-based media during linear TV viewing: An exploratory study. *Computers in Human Behavior, 32*, 235–243. doi: 10.1016/j.chb.2013.12.015

Hearold, S. (1986). A synthesis of 1043 effects of television on social behavior. In G. Comstock (Ed.), *Public communications and behavior: Volume 1* (pp. 65–133). New York: Academic Press.

Jeong, S. H., & Hwang, Y. (2016). Media multitasking effects on cognitive vs. attitudinal outcomes: A meta-analysis. *Human Communication Research, 42*(4), 599–618. doi: doi.org/10.1111/hcre.12089

Krämer, N. C., Winter, S., Benninghoff, B., & Gallus, C. (2015). How "social" is social TV? The influence of social motives and expected outcomes on the usage of Social TV applications. *Computers in Human Behavior, 51*, 255–262. doi 10.1016/j.chb.2015.05.005

Lang, A. (2013). Discipline in crisis? The shifting paradigm of mass communication research. *Communication Theory, 23*(1), 10–24. doi: 10.1111/comt.12000

Lang, A., & Ewoldsen, D. (2010). Beyond effects: Conceptualizing communication as dynamic, complex, nonlinear, and fundamental. In S. Allan (Ed.), *Rethinking communication: Keywords in communication research* (pp. 111–122). Cresskill, NJ: Hampton Press.

Latorre, J. I., & Soto-Sanfiel, M. T. (2011). Toward a theory of intellectual entertainment. *Journal of Media Psychology: Theories, Methods, and Applications, 23*(1), 52–59. doi:10.1027/1864-1105/A000033

Lin, W.-Y., Zhang, X., Jung, J.-Y., & Kim, Y.-C. (2013). From the wired to wireless generation? Investigating teens' Internet use through the mobile phone. *Telecommunications Policy, 37*(8), 651–661. doi: 10.1016/j.telpol.2012.09.008

Livingstone, S. (1996). On the continuing problems of media effects research. In J. Curran, & M. Gurevitch (Eds.), *Mass media and society* (2nd Edition, pp. 305–324). London, UK: Edward Arnold.

Lynch, J. (2015, March 20). Here's the recipe Netflix uses to make binge-worthy TV. *Quartz*. Retrieved from: https://qz.com/367117/heres-the-recipe-netflix-uses-to-make-binge-worthy-tv/

Madrigal, A. C. (May, 2018). When did TV watching peak? *The Atlantic*. Retrieved from: https://www.theatlantic.com/technology/archive/2018/05/when-did-tv-watching-peak/561464/

Merikivi, J., Salovaara, A., Mäntymäki, M., & Zhang, L. (2018). On the way to understanding binge watching behavior: The over-estimated role of involvement. *Electronic Markets, 28*(1), 111–122. doi: 10.1007/s12525-017-0271-4

Mikos, L. (2016). Digital media platforms and the use of TV content: Binge watching and video-on-demand in Germany. *Media and Communication, 4*(3), 154–161. doi:10.17645/mac.v4i3.542

Ophir, E., Nass, C., & Wagner, A. D. (2009). Cognitive control in media multitaskers. *Proceedings of the National Academy of Sciences of the United States of America, 106*(37), 15583–15587. doi:10.1073/pnas.0903620106

Oviedo, V., Tornquist, M., Cameron, T., & Chiappe, D. (2015). Effects of media multi-tasking with Facebook on the enjoyment and encoding of TV episodes. *Computers in Human Behavior, 51*, 407–417. doi: 10.1016/j.chb.2015.05.022

Perks, L. G. (2019). *Media marathoning: Immersions through morality*. Lanham, MD: Lexington Books.

Raney, A. A., & Oliver, M. B. (2014). Expanding the boundaries of entertainment research: An epilogue. *Communication Theory, 64*, 566–568.

Riddle, K., Peebles, A., Davis, C., Xu, F., & Schroeder, E. (2018). The addictive potential of television binge watching: Comparing intentional and unintentional binges. *Psychology of Popular Media Culture, 7*(4), 589–604. doi: 10.1037/ppm0000167

Rubenking, B., Bracken, C. C., Sandoval, J., & Rister, A. (2018). Defining new viewing behaviors: What makes and motivates TV binge watching. *International Journal of Digital Television, 9*, 69–85. doi: 10.1386/jdtv.9.1.69_1

Silvia, P. (2006). *Exploring the psychology of interest*. New York: Oxford University Press.

Salmon, F. (August 14, 2018). The future of television is … more television. Retrieved from https://www.wired.com/story/netflix-new-tv-television-future-jeffrey-katzenberg/

Schramm, W., Lyle, J., & Parker, E. (1961). *Television in the lives of our children*. Palo Alto, CA: Stanford University Press.

Schweidel, D. A., & Moe, W. W. (2016). Binge watching and advertising. *Journal of Marketing, 80*(5), 1–19. doi: 10.1509/jm.15.0258

Shim, H.., & Kim, K. H. (2018). An exploration of the motivations for binge-watching and the role of individual differences. *Computers in Human Behavior, 82*, 94–100. doi: 10.1016/j.chb.2017.12.032

Sussman, S., & Moran, M. B. (2013). Hidden addiction: Television. *Journal of Behavioral Addictions, 2*(3), 125–132. doi:10.1556/jba.2.2013.008

Tukachinsky, R., & Eyal, K. (2018). The psychology of marathon television viewing: Antecedents and viewer involvement. *Mass Communication and Society, 21*(3), 275–295. doi: 10.1080/15205436.2017.1422765

Vorderer, P. A., & Hartmann, T. (2009). Entertainment and enjoyment as media effects. In J. Bryant, & M. B. Oliver (Eds.), *Media effects* (pp. 532–550). New York: Routledge.

Vorderer, P.A., Klimmt, C., & Ritterfeld, U. (2004). Enjoyment: At the heart of media entertainment. *Communication Theory, 14*, 388–408. doi:10.1111/j.1468-2885.2004.tb00321.x

Wang, Z., & Tchernev, J. M. (2012). The "myth" of media multitasking: Reciprocal dynamics of media multitasking, personal needs, and gratifications. *Journal of Communication, 62*(3), 493–513. doi:10.1111/j.1460-2466.2012.01641.x

Weber, R. (2015). Biology and brains—Methodological innovations in communication science: Introduction to the Special Issue. *Communication Methods and Measures, 9*(2). 1–4. doi: 10.1080/19312458.2014.999755

Wenner, L. A., & Gantz, W. (1998). Watching sports on television: Audience experience, gender, fanship, and marriage. In L.A. Wenner & W. Gantz (Eds.). *MediaSport* (pp. 233–251). New York: Routledge.

Wiradhany, W., & Baumgartner, S. E. (2019). Exploring the variability of media multitasking choice behaviour using a network approach. *Behaviour & Information Technology*, 1–14. doi: 10.1080/014429X.2019.1589575

Yeykelis, L., Cummings, J. J., & Reeves, B. (2014). Multitasking on a single device: Arousal and the frequency, anticipation, and prediction of switching between media content on a computer. *Journal of Communication*, *64*(1), 167–192. doi: 10.1111/jcom.12070

Zillmann, D., & Bryant, J. (1994). Entertainment as media effect. In J. Bryant & D. Zillmann (Eds.), *Media effects: Advances in theory and research* (pp. 437–461). Hillsdale, NJ: Erlbaum

Index

Active Audience 129
Addiction Models 149
Antihereos 53, 57–59
Attitude Formation 28
Audiences
   Profile 22
Audience Availability 83, 84, 85, 86
Audience Duplication 85, 127
Automaticity 129

Bandura, A. 114, 126, 149
Bedroom Culture 81, 95
Binge Watching 6
   Downstream Outcomes 147
   Gratifications and Motives 117
   Habit 122, 130
   Industry Impact 163
   Qualitative Examinations 119
Binge-watching Engagement and
   Symptoms Scale 118
Biocca, F. 94, 121, 129
BETAMAX 31

Chaffee, S. 81, 121
"Channel Repertoire" 63
Cognitive Involvement 144, 145
"Concept-Oriented" 79
Content Characteristics 52
Content Curation 64, 67, 68
Coviewing 80, 81, 82, 88, 89, 90, 94

Designated Market Areas (DMAs) 45
Diagnostic and Statistical Manual for
   Mental Disorders (DSM) 152
Digital Video Recorder (DVR) 35
   Advertising 36
Dobrow, J. R. 13, 21, 176

Early Adopters 23
Effects of Communication on the
   Individual 27
Elaboration Likelihood Model
   (ELM) 146
Emery, F. E. 28
Emotional Contagion 94

Emotional Outcomes 157
   Depression 158
   Negative Effects 159
Engagement 94
"Episode Hook" 60
Eudemonic Enjoyment 140

Family Hour 78
Flayelle, M. 9, 118, 120, 174
Future Research 171

Golden Age of Television 55–56
Generations of Research 176
Group Viewing 83, 84, 86–89, 94

Habitual Viewing 85
Health Outcomes 155
   Negative outcomes 155
Heuristic Systems Model 146
Human-Centered Phenomenon 174

Intercultural Difference 185

Ji, Q. 89, 91, 93
Journal of Communication 22

Katz, E. 114, 140

Lang, A. 12, 100, 101, 123
LaRose, R. 84, 114, 122, 124, 125, 126, 129, 137, 149, 150, 172
Leisure Time 24

Matrix TV 44
Media Addiction 9
   Debate 147
   Research 150
Media Effects
   Early Research 146
Media Marathoning 143
Media as Social Action (MASA) 127
Media Habits 119, 121

Media Multitasking 25, 52, 96, 98
   Binge Watching 102
   Media Multitasking Index 98
   Theoretical Approaches 100
Mood Management 28
Multiple Systems Operator (MSO) 45

Need for Cognition 144
Network TV 44
Networked TV 44

Oliver, M. B. 140–141, 158, 178, 181
Over-the-top (OTT) 44, 47

Parasocial Relationships 144
Passive Audience 146
Peak TV 55, 62, 67
Perks, L.G. 143, 175
"Post-Network Era" 44
"Post TV" 44

Renckstorf, K. 127
Riddle, K. 150, 154, 179
Rubenking, B. 6
Rubin, A. 59, 94, 114–116, 130

Schram, W. 26–27
Second Screening 99
Situational Determinants 77, 83, 84, 102, 127, 185
Social Cognitive Theory (SCT) 126
Social viewing 72, 78, 88, 90–95, 100
   Effects of Social Viewing 93
Social Trust 95
Social TV 12, 88–91
"Socio-Oriented" 79
Syndication 52, 87

Tamborini, R. 141–142
Telepresence 22

Television
    Early Growth 22
Television Advertising
    Effects 162
Television Network 22
Timeshifting 33
    Digital 35
"Traditional Network Model" 49
Tukachinsky, R. 3, 5, 8, 144, 147, 153, 158, 174, 178–179
TV Addiction Scale 152

U.S. Surgeon General's Scientific Advisory Committee on Television and Social Behavior 29
Uses and Gratifications 13, 15, 33, 83, 114, 116–121, 126–128, 130, 138, 139, 140, 146, 179
    Criticism 121

Van den Bulck, J. 34
V Chip 79
Video Cassette Recorder (VCR) 31
Viewing Habits 25
VOD 47

Watching TV Series Motives
    Scale 118
Westerik, H. 127–128

Zapping 37

www.ingramcontent.com/pod-product-compliance
Lightning Source LLC
Chambersburg PA
CBHW071410300426
44114CB00016B/2251